Time Out Guides Ltd
Universal House
251 Tottenham Court Road
London W1T 7AB
United Kingdom
Tel: +44 (0)20 7813 3000
Fax: +44 (0)20 7813 6001
Email: guides@timeout.com
www.timeout.com

Published by Time Out Guides Ltd, a wholly owned subsidiary of Time Out Group Ltd.
Time Out and the Time Out logo are trademarks of Time Out Group Ltd.

This edition first published in Great Britain in 2011 by Ebury Publishing.
A Random House Group Company
20 Vauxhall Bridge Road, London SW1V 2SA

Random House Australia Pty Ltd 20 Alfred Street, Milsons Point, Sydney, New South Wales 2061, Australia

Random House New Zealand Ltd 18 Poland Road, Glenfield, Auckland 10, New Zealand

Random House South Africa (Pty) Ltd Isle of Houghton, Corner Boundary Road & Carse O'Gowrie, Houghton
2198, South Africa

Random House UK Limited Reg. No. 954009

Distributed in the US and Latin America by Publishers Group West (1-510-809-3700)
Distributed in Canada by Publishers Group Canada (1-800-747-8147)

For further distribution details, see www.timeout.com.

ISBN: 978-1-84670-232-7

A CIP catalogue record for this book is available from the British Library.

Printed and bound by Firmengruppe APPL, aprinta druck, Wemding, Germany.

The Random House Group Limited supports The Forest Stewardship Council (FSC®), the leading international forest
certification organisation. Our books carrying the FSC label are printed on FSC® certified paper. FSC is the only
forest certification scheme endorsed by the leading environmental organisations, including Greenpeace. Our paper
procurement policy can be found at www.randomhouse.co.uk/environment

Time Out carbon-offsets its flights with Trees for Cities (www.treesforcities.org).

MIX
Paper from
responsible sources
FSC
www.fsc.org   FSC™ C004592

Contents

Published by
Time Out Guides Limited
Universal House
251 Tottenham Court Road
London W1T 7AB
Tel +44 (0)20 7813 3000
Fax +44 (0)20 7813 6001
email guides@timeout.com
www.timeout.com

Editorial
Consultant Editor Nigel Kendall
Editor Kate Kaegler
Listings Editors William Crow, Jamie Warburton
Proofreader John Pym
Indexer William Crow

Managing Director Peter Fiennes
Editorial Director Sarah Guy
Editorial Manager Holly Pick
Management Accountants Margaret Wright, Clare Turner

Design
Art Director Scott Moore
Art Editor Pinelope Kourmouzoglou
Senior Designer Kei Ishimaru
Group Commercial Designer Jodi Sher

Picture Desk
Picture Editor Jael Marschner
Picture Desk Assistant/Researcher Ben Rowe

Advertising
New Business & Commercial Director Mark Phillips

Marketing
Senior Publishing Brand Manager Luthfa Begum
Guides Marketing Manager Colette Whitehouse
Group Commercial Art Director Anthony Huggins

Production
Group Production Manager Brendan McKeown
Production Controller Katie Mulhern

Time Out Group
Director & Founder Tony Elliott
Chief Executive Officer David King
Chief Operating Officer Aksel Van der Wal
Group Financial Director Paul Rakkar
Group General Manager/Director Nichola Coulthard
Time Out Communications Ltd MD David Pepper
Time Out International Ltd MD Cathy Runciman
Group Commercial Director Graeme Tottle
Group IT Director Simon Chappell
Group Marketing Director Andrew Booth

Key Contributors
This guide could not have been completed without the collaboration of Tourism for All (www.tourismforall.org.uk), a charity that aims to to improve accessible facilities and services across the UK. It also provides information and advice for disabled travellers, with the assistance of data provided by VisitEngland (www.visitengland.org) and DisabledGo (www.disabledgo.com). Tourism for All provides access information across Britain at www.openbritain.org.

Thanks
Nigel Kendall would like to thank Dave Faulkner, Kate Kaegler and Yuka Sonobé for their help in producing this guidebook. Thanks, too, to all at the London Organising Committee of the Olympic and Paralympic Games (LOCOG).

Maps john@jsgraphics.co.uk, except London Tube map.

Front cover photography ImageSelect/Alamy
Retouching by Pinelope Kourmouzoglou
Back cover photography Abigail Lelliott, TfL, Ming Tang-Evans, LOCOG

Photography pages 3, 210/211, 213 www.simonleigh.com; 5 (top left), 80 (bottom) Abigail Lelliott; 5 (top middle and bottom right), 97 (top right), 152, 153 (top and bottom right), 161, 183, 194 (bottom left), 197 (right and bottom right) Ming Tang-Evans; 5 (top right), 143 (top right and bottom left), 189 Anthony Webb; 5 (middle), 111 (top left and bottom) Visit Britain Images; 5 (bottom left), 69, 106, 120 (bottom left), 125, 134, 137, 140, 158, 202 (bottom), 204 (top left and bottom right) Ben Rowe; 5 (bottom middle), 83 Elena Elisseeva/Shutterstock; 9, 16 Copyright TfL; 10 Shutterstock; 31 Heike Bohnstengel; 45 (bottom) 77 (top), 89, 92 (top) Andrew Brackenbury; 49, 54, 56/57, 58, 65, 66 ODA; 50, 51, 59 LOCOG; 67, 104 (top), 157, 176, 192 (bottom), 197 (left), 200 (top), 201, 207 (bottom) Rob Greig; 72, 192 (top) r.nagy/Shutterstock; 74, 97 (bottom left), 98, 120 (top left), 139 (bottom), 147, 169, 199, 207 (top), 212, 214 Jonathan Perugia; 77 (bottom) Susannah Stone; 80 (top) EDF Energy London Eye; 92 (bottom), 126 (top left), 139 (top), 147, 166, 200 (bottom) Britta Jaschinski; 97 (top left and bottom right) Emma Wood; 103, 111 (top right), 114, 143 (top left and bottom left), 165, 190, 204 (top right and bottom left), 209, 217 Michelle Grant; 119, 120 (bottom right) Heloise Bergman; 120 (top right) Christina Theisen; 126 (top left) Oliver Knight; 126 (bottom) Wellcome Library; 129 (top) Danny Evans; 129 (bottom left) Jack Boothby; 129 (bottom right) Ross Paxton; 151 John Samsom; 153 (bottom left) Tricia de Courcy Ling; 154, 173 Michael Franke; 162 Jitka Hynkova; 179 Haris Artemis; 108 Rob Wilson/Shutterstock; 188 richardrowland.co.uk; 193 (top), 194 (right), 237 Olivia Rutherford; 193 (bottom) Belinda Lawley; 194 (top) Scott Wishart; 199 (bottom), Ed Marshall; 202 (top) Elisabeth Blanchet; 202, 217 (middle right) Alys Tomlinson.

The following images were supplied by the featured establishments/artists: 30, 32, 35, 36, 37, 38, 40, 42, 44, 45 (top), 47, 104 (bottom).

Open London

About the guide

Time Out Open London Guide

This is the first edition of the *Time Out Open London Guide*, produced by the people behind the listings magazines and travel guide series, in conjunction with Tourism for All. The guide mixes *Time Out*'s expert reviews with accessibility information from a variety of sources (*see right for details*). Our thanks to Tourism for All, VisitEngland and DisabledGo for their kind assistance and advice with accessibility information.

The lowdown on the listings

Addresses, phone numbers, websites, transport information, opening times, and price guides are included in the listings. All venues accept credit cards, except where explicitly noted in the text. Details of facilities, services and events were all checked and correct as we went to press.

Before you go out of your way, however, we advise you to phone and check opening times, ticket prices and other details. This is particularly important for wheelchair users, since ramps, lifts and other facilities may occasionally be unavailable.

While every effort has been made to ensure the accuracy of the information contained in this guide, the publishers cannot accept any responsibility for any errors that it may contain.

Information for everyone

London is a great city, and this book is designed to help everyone make the most of it. Attractions of special interest to children and families are highlighted throughout, though for a more family-focused guide, we recommend the latest edition of our companion guidebook, *London for Children*.

For older visitors with special mobility requirements or for disabled visitors, this book contains access information for all venues reviewed, plus details on the availability of accessible toilet facilities and car parking. Do check before setting out, as listed facilities may not always be available.

The lie of the land

Maps of Greater London, central London and the London Underground are provided on pages 244-256. In addition, the chapter devoted to the London 2012 Olympic Games and Paralympic Games contains detailed maps of London's brand new Olympic village. For more detailed maps of London, a standard A-Z map of the city is still unbeatable.

Phone numbers

The area code for London is 020. All phone numbers given in this guide take this code unless otherwise stated, so add 020 if you're calling from outside London; otherwise, simply dial the number as written. The international dialling code for the UK is 44.

Let us know what you think

We hope that you enjoy this book and we'd like to know what you think of it. Email us at guides@timeout.com.

Access symbols

⠿ **Accessible to wheelchair users**

⠿ **Accessible to wheelchair users with assistance**

⠿ **Accessible to mobility-impaired walkers**

⠿ **Seating available**

⠿ **Wheelchair accessible toilet**

⠿ **Accessible changing rooms**

⠿ **Changing places**

P★★★ **On-site parking**

P★★ **Blue Badge parking**

P★ **Public car park**

⠿ **Accessible accommodation**

⠿ **Sign language used**

⠿ **Disability awareness trained staff**

☺ **Access trained staff**

⠿ **Facilities for visually impaired people**

⠿ **Induction loops**

⠿ **Other hearing facilities**

L **Large print information**

⠿ **Braille information**

⠿ **Assistance dogs welcome**

INFORMATION SOURCES

Access information in this book has been compiled from a variety of sources. To help readers identify these sources, and the best avenues for further information, we have colour-coded the symbols used throughout this book.

☺ **Blue symbols** Information supplied by **Open Britain**, a joint project between the disability rights organisation **RADAR** and **Tourism for All** (see p224). Consult the online database at: www.openbritain.net. For more about RADAR, see www.radar.org.uk. For further information about Tourism for All, see www.tourismforall.org.uk.

☺ **Burgundy symbols** Information based on access guides available at **www.disabledgo.com**. All venues have been assessed in person by trained surveyors. For independently assessed information to over 15,000 venues in London and more than 75,000 across the UK visit www.disabledgo.com..

☺ **Black symbols** Information collated by *Time Out*, based on details held in our database, combined with information supplied by the venue itself. *Time Out* is London's best guide to the week ahead. For the latest news, views and must-sees, see www.timeout.com.

Channel 4 are proud to be the official broadcaster of the London 2012 Paralympic Games

official broadcaster of the London 2012 Paralympic Games

Sponsored by
Sainsbury's
and

BT

Planning your trip

Welcome to London

The 2012 Games are huge, but they're not the only show in town.

In the year to the end of 2011, London will have played host to some 20.1 million international tourists, more than any other city in the world. Tourism accounts for 13 per cent of employment in the city, and 10 per cent of the wealth it generates.

To understand this seemingly magnetic attraction, all you need to do is look around. Stand on any London street, and you stand on a palimpsest of history, layer after layer of development over thousands of years, punctuated and defined by invasion, immigration and constant building and rebuilding (*see right*). The city's influences are as diverse as the people who visit. That is why almost everyone can find something here that seems tailor-made for them.

As the city prepares to host the London 2012 Olympic Games and Paralympic Games, there's fresh determination to welcome visitors of all ages and all physical abilities to the capital.

In the United Kingdom alone, there are 10 million people with a disability, and across Europe the number is around 85 million. London is determined to make itself accessible to as many people as possible, and the information in this book reflects that determination.

It's certainly true that historic London, with its cobbled streets, rickety staircases and narrow alleyways can sometimes seem to conspire against visitors with physical impairments, or against families with young children in tow.

But look closer, and London will surprise you. Many of its most historic sights and attractions have in recent years made alterations and upgrades to accommodate visitors with special requirements, from extra ramps and seating, to visual and hearing assistance. London's hotels, shops and restaurants, meanwhile, can claim not only to be among the best in the world, but among the most accessible to everyone.

The 2012 Games will surely boost London's visitor numbers, but they are just one of thousands of events taking place across the capital in 2012. The greatest city in the world is waiting. It's up to you to make the most of it.

Key events
London's history in brief

43 The Romans invade; the settlement of Londinium is founded.
61 Boudicca burns Londinium; the city is rebuilt and made provincial capital.
200 A city wall is built.
410 Roman troops evacuate Britain.
c600 Saxon London is built to the west.
841 The Norse raid for the first time.
c871 The Danes occupy London.
886 Alfred the Great takes London.
1013 The Danes take back London.
1042 Edward the Confessor builds a palace and 'West Minster' upstream.
1066 William I is crowned in Westminster Abbey.
1078 The Tower of London is begun.
1123 St Bart's Hospital is founded.
1197 Henry Fitzalwin is the first mayor.
1215 The mayor signs the Magna Carta.
1240 First Parliament at Westminster.
1290 Jews are expelled from London.
1348 The Black Death arrives.
1381 The Peasants' Revolt.
1397 Richard Whittington is Lord Mayor.
1476 William Caxton sets up the first printing press at Westminster.
1534 Henry VIII cuts Britain off from the Catholic Church.
1555 Martyrs burned at Smithfield.
1565 Sir Thomas Gresham proposes the Royal Exchange.
1572 First known map of London.
1599 The Globe Theatre opens.
1605 Guy Fawkes's plot to blow up James I fails.
1642 The start of the Civil War.
1649 Charles I is executed; Cromwell establishes the Commonwealth.
1664 Beginning of the Great Plague.
1666 The Great Fire.
1675 Building starts on the new St Paul's Cathedral.
1694 The Bank of England is set up.
1710 St Paul's is completed.
1766 The city wall is demolished.
1773 The Stock Exchange is founded.
1824 The National Gallery is founded.
1833 The London Fire Brigade is set up.

1836 The first passenger railway opens; Charles Dickens' *The Pickwick Papers*, his first novel, begins serialisation.
1843 Trafalgar Square is laid out.
1851 The Great Exhibition takes place.
1858 The Great Stink: pollution in the Thames reaches hideous levels.
1863 The Metropolitan line opens as the world's first underground railway.
1866 London's last major cholera outbreak; the Sanitation Bill is passed.
1868 The last public execution is held at Newgate prison (now the Old Bailey).
1884 Greenwich Mean Time is established as a global standard.
1888 Jack the Ripper prowls the East End; London County Council is created.
1890 The Housing Act enables the LCC to clear the slums; the first electric underground railway opens.
1897 Motorised buses are introduced.
1908 London hosts the Olympic Games for the first time.
1915 Zeppelins begin three years of bombing raids on London.
1940 The Blitz begins.
1948 London again hosts the Olympic Games; forerunner of the Paralympics, the Stoke Mandeville Games are organised in Buckinghamshire by neurologist Sir Ludwig Guttman.
1951 The Festival of Britain is held.
1952 The last 'pea-souper' smog.
1953 Queen Elizabeth II is crowned.
1981 Riots in Brixton.
1982 The last London docks close.
1986 The GLC is abolished.
1992 One Canada Square tower opens on Canary Wharf.
2000 Ken Livingstone becomes London's first directly elected mayor; Tate Modern and the London Eye open.
2005 The city wins its bid to host the 2012 Games; suicide bombers kill 52 on public transport.
2008 Boris Johnson becomes mayor.
2010 Hung parliament leads to new Conservative–Liberal coalition.

What's on in London in 2012

January 2012

Grayson Perry: The Tomb of the Unknown Craftsman Artist uses archive objects in new show (until 19 Feb). *British Museum, see p93 (www.britishmuseum.org).*

Leonardo da Vinci: Painter at the Court of Milan The biggest display of da Vinci's paintings yet (until 5 Feb). *National Gallery, see p105 (www.nationalgallery.org.uk).*

2 New Year's Day Holiday

10-18 Test Event: Gymnastics *North Greenwich Arena, see p65 (www.londonpreparesseries.com).*

29 Chinese New Year Festival *(www.londonchinatown.org).*

14-29 London International Mime Festival *(www.mimefest.co.uk).*

February 2012

Ongoing Grayson Perry, Leonardo da Vinci *(see January).*

9 Feb-27 May Lucian Freud Portraits *National Portrait Gallery, see p107 (www.npg.org.uk).*

17-19 Test Event: Cycling – Track *Velodrome, Olympic Park, see p56 (www.londonpreparesseries.com).*

20-26 Test Event: Aquatics – Diving *Aquatics Centre, Olympic Park, see p56 (www.londonpreparesseries.com).*

21 Poulters Pancake Day Race Livery companies race while tossing pancakes *(www.poulters.org.uk).*

March 2012

Ongoing Lucian Freud *(see February).*

6 Maslenitsa Russian Festival The festival of the sun takes over Trafalgar Square for the first time *(www.maslenitsa.co.uk).*

Mar-Aug British Design 1948-2012 *Victoria & Albert Museum, see p116 (www.vam.ac.uk).*

31 Mar-6 Apr London Lesbian & Gay Film Festival *BFI Southbank, see p198 (www.llgff.org.uk).*

April 2012

Ongoing Lucian Freud *(see February)*; British Design, Lesbian & Gay Film Festival *(see March).*

5 Apr-9 Sept Damien Hirst The generation-defining multi-millionaire bad boy of British art. *Tate Modern, see p115 (www.tate.org.uk).*

6 Good Friday

7 Oxford & Cambridge Boat Race The 158th outing for Varsity rowers starts on the Thames at Putney *(www.theboatrace.org).*

9 Easter Monday

Early April-early May London Word Festival A month of hip literature events. *(www.londonwordfestival.com).*

Early Apr-mid May Spring Loaded London's premier contemporary dance festival *(www.theplace.org.uk).*

**18-22 Test Event: Aquatics –
Synchronised Swimming**
*Aquatics Centre, Olympic Park, see
p56 (www.londonpreparesseries.com).*

22 London Marathon
*Greenwich Park to the Mall
(www.virginlondonmarathon.com).*

**23 Apr-9 Sept World
Shakespeare Festival**
Global season of plays *(www.rsc.org.uk).*

26-29 Sundance London
London branch of Robert Redford's
independent film fest. *O2 Arena, see
p193 (www.sundance-london.com).*

Late Apr Camden Crawl
Fun multi-pub music 'microfestival' hits
Camden *(www.thecamdencrawl.com).*

Late Apr Breakin' Convention
Jonzi D's terrific street dance festival.
*Sadler's Wells, see p206
(www.breakinconvention.com).*

May 2012

Ongoing Lucian Freud (*see February*);
British Design (*see March*); Damien
Hirst, World Shakespeare Festival, Word
Festival, Spring Loaded (*see April*).

2-6 Test Event: Hockey
*Hockey Centre, Olympic Park, see p59
(www.londonpreparesseries.com).*

2-6 Test Event: Wheelchair Tennis
*Eton Manor, Olympic Park, see p58
(www.londonpreparesseries.com).*

3-6 Test Event: Aquatics – Water Polo
*Aquatics Centre, Olympic Park, see
p56 (www.londonpreparesseries.com).*

4-7 Test Event: Athletics
*Olympic Stadium, see p54
(www.londonpreparesseries.com).*

7 Early May Bank Holiday

8 Test Event: Paralympic Athletics
*Olympic Stadium, see p54
(www.londonpreparesseries.com).*

Late May Chelsea Flower Show
*Royal Hospital Chelsea, see p146
(www.rhs.org.uk).*

June 2012

Ongoing British Design (*see March*);
Damien Hirst, World Shakespeare
Festival (*see April*).

2-5 Diamond Jubilee
A huge flotilla (3 June) is planned for the
60th anniversary of the Queen's
accession to the throne (*www.thames
diamondjubileepageant.org*).

**4-5 Spring & Queen's Diamond
Jubilee Bank Holidays**

**6 June-9 July Tanztheater Wuppertal
Pina Bausch: World Cities 2012**
Superb troupe of the late German
choreographer explores ten global cities.
*Barbican, see p192; Sadler's Wells,
see p206 (www.pina-bausch.de/en).*

Early June-mid Aug Opera Holland Park
(www.operahollandpark.com).

Mid June Open Garden Squares
London's private gardens open to the
public *(www.opensquares.org).*

Mid June Meltdown
Music and culture festival, curated by a
different artiste every year.
*Southbank Centre, see p216
(www.southbank.co.uk).*

Mid June Trooping the Colour
The Queen's official birthday parade.
*Horse Guards Parade, St James's
(www.trooping-the-colour.co.uk).*

21 June-9 Sept London 2012 Festival
City-wide music festivals to celebrate the 2012 Games
(www.london2012.com/festival).

25 June-8 July Wimbledon Lawn Tennis Championships
All England Lawn Tennis and Croquet Club, see p201 (www.wimbledon.org).

28 June-14 Oct Edvard Munch: The Modern Eye
Painter of *The Scream* reassessed.
*Tate Modern, see p115
(www.tate.org.uk).*

Late June-mid Aug LIFT (London International Festival of Theatre)
(www.liftfest.org.uk).

**Late June-mid Aug
City of London Festival**
Mostly free music and art, often in historic City venues *(www.colf.org).*

Late June-early July Greenwich & Docklands International Festival
Outdoor theatricals, usually on an impressive scale *(www.festival.org).*

July 2012

Ongoing British Design (*see March*); Damien Hirst, World Shakespeare Festival (*see April*); World Cities 2012, Opera Holland Park, London 2012 Festival, Wimbledon, Edvard Munch, LIFT, City of London Festival, Greenwich & Docklands International Festival (*see June*).

Early July Wireless Festival
Three nights of rock. *Hyde Park, see p62 (www.wirelessfestival.co.uk).*

Early July Pride London
Huge annual gay and lesbian parade.
Oxford Street to Victoria Embankment (www.pridelondon.org).

Early July-mid Sept Watch This Space
Alfresco theatre beside the Thames.
*National Theatre, see p216
(www.nationaltheatre.org.uk/wts).*

7-15 Big Dance 2012
Royal Ballet's Wayne McGregor will work with 2,000 dancers in Trafalgar Square (*www.bigdance2012.com*).

Mid July Somerset House Series
A dozen concerts in the fountain court.
*Somerset House, see p85
(www.somerset-house.org.uk/music).*

Mid July-mid Sept The Proms (BBC Sir Henry Wood Promenade Concerts)
The world's biggest classical music festival, packed with top performers.
*Royal Albert Hall, see p193
(www.bbc.co.uk/proms).*

21-27 London 2012 Torch Relay
The Olympic Torch arrives in London for the end of its 70-day tour of the UK (*www.london2012.com*).

27 July-12 Aug London 2012 Olympic Games
Let the Games commence, *see pp50-67 for venues and schedule of events (www.london2012.com).*

27 July-12 Aug The Olympic Journey: the Story of the Games
Free exhibition of every medal since 1896 and every Torch since 1936.
*Royal Opera House, see p193
(www.roh.org.uk/theolympicjourney).*

31 July-16 Sept Another London
150 images of the city by photographer Henri Cartier-Bresson and others. *Tate Britain, see p113 (www.tate.org.uk).*

August 2012

Ongoing Damien Hirst, Shakespeare Festival (*see April*); Opera Holland Park,

London 2012 Festival, Edvard Munch, LIFT, City of London Festival (*see June*); Watch This Space, The Proms, London 2012 Olympic Games, The Olympic Journey, Another London (*see July*).

Early Aug Great British Beer Festival
Earls Court Exhibition Centre, see p59 (gbbf.camra.org.uk).

25-26 Notting Hill Carnival
Europe's biggest street party.
Notting Hill (www.nottinghillcarnival.biz).

27 Summer Bank Holiday

29 Aug-9 Sept London 2012 Paralympic Games
See pp50-67 for venues and schedule of events (www.london2012.com).

September 2012
Ongoing Damien Hirst, World Shakespeare Festival (*see April*); London 2012 Festival, Edvard Munch (*see June*); Watch This Space, The Proms, Another London (*see July*); London 2012 Paralympic Games (*see August*).

Early Sept London Mela
South Asian music and street arts.
Gunnersbury Park, Ealing (www.londonmela.org).

From 12 Pre-Raphaelites: Victorian Avant-Garde
The first British modern art movement.
Tate Britain, see p113 (www.tate.org.uk).

Mid Sept Mayor's Thames Festival
Westminster & Tower Bridges (www.thamesfestival.org).

Mid Sept Open-City London
Access to 600 buildings normally closed to the public (*www.open-city.org.uk*).

October 2012
Ongoing Edvard Munch (*see June*); Dance Umbrella (*see September*).

Early Oct Pearly Kings & Queens Harvest Festival
St Martin-in-the-Fields, see p81 (www.pearlysociety.co.uk).

Early Oct-late Nov Dance Umbrella
The city's headline dance festival
(www.danceumbrella.co.uk).

Mid Oct-early Nov London Film Festival
BFI Southbank, see p198 (www.bfi.org.uk/lff).

Mid Oct Frieze Art Fair
Regent's Park (www.friezeartfair.com).

November 2012
Ongoing Dance Umbrella (*see September*).

5 Bonfire Night

11 Remembrance Sunday

Early Nov London to Brighton Veteran Car Run
Starts at Serpentine Road, Hyde Park (www.lbvcr.com).

Early Nov Lord Mayor's Show
Annual inauguration procession for the Lord Mayor of the City of London
(www.lordmayorsshow.org).

Mid Nov London Jazz Festival
Major knees-up which now attracts some of the world's top performers
(www.londonjazzfestival.org.uk).

December 2012
25 Christmas Day
26 Boxing Day
31 New Year's Eve Celebrations

Transport

ARRIVING & LEAVING

By air

Gatwick Airport
0844 335 1802,
www.gatwickairport.com. About
30 miles south of central London.
Of the three rail services to London, by far
the quickest is the **Gatwick Express**
(*8528 2900, www.gatwickexpress.com*) to
Victoria; it takes 30mins and runs 3.30am-
12.30am daily. Tickets cost £17.90 single
or £30.80 for an open return (valid for 30
days). Under-15s pay £8.45 for a single
and £11.50 for returns; under-5s go free.
Discounts of £1-£2 on all fares for online
bookings. Assisted travel advice is
available (*0800 138 1016*).

  Southern (*0845 748 4950, www.
southernrailway.com*) also runs a rail
service between Gatwick and Victoria,
with trains every 5-10mins (every 30mins
between 1am and 4am). It takes about
35mins, and costs £11.30 for a single,
£11.40 for a day return (after 9.30am) and

£23.60 for an open-period return (valid for
one month). Under-16s get half-price
tickets; under-5s go free. **Assisted travel
advice** is available (*0800 138 1016*), and
accessibility guides to stations are
available online (*bit.ly/iKMB5H*).

  If you're staying in the King's Cross or
Bloomsbury areas, consider taking the
trains run by **Thameslink** (*0845 748
4950, www.firstcapitalconnect.co.uk*) to St
Pancras. Tickets are £9.40 single, £9.50
day return (after 9.32am). Assisted travel
advice is available (*0800 058 2844,
bit.ly/mvhayw*). A **taxi** to central London
costs about £100 and takes at least an hour.

Heathrow Airport
0844 335 1801,
www.heathrowairport.com. About
15 miles west of central London.
The **Heathrow Express** train (*0845
600 1515, www.heathrowexpress.co.uk*)
runs to Paddington every 15mins (5.10am-
11.25pm daily), and takes 15-20mins. The
train can be boarded at the station that
serves Terminals 1, 2 and 3 (aka Heathrow

Central), or the separate station serving Terminal 5. Tickets cost £16.50 single or £32 return (£1 less online, £2 more if you buy on board); under-16s go half-price. Many airlines have check-in desks at Paddington. **Assisted travel advice** is available (*0845 600 1515*).

The journey by tube into central London is longer but cheaper. The 50-60min **Piccadilly line** ride into central London costs £4.50 one way with an Oyster card or £5 cash (£2.50 under-16s. *See Public Transport, p18*). Trains run every few minutes from about 5am to 11.57pm daily (6am-11pm Sun).

The **Heathrow Connect** (*0845 678 6975, www.heathrowconnect.com*) rail service offers direct access to Hayes, Southall, Hanwell, West Ealing, Ealing Broadway and Paddington stations in west and north-west London. The trains run every half-hour, terminating at Heathrow Central (Terminals 1 and 3). From there to Terminal 4 get the free shuttle; between Central and Terminal 5, there's free use of the Heathrow Express. A single from Paddington is £8.50; an open return is £16.50. Assisted travel advice is available (*0845 678 6975*).

National Express (*0871 781 8181, www.nationalexpress.com*) runs daily coach services to London Victoria (90mins, 5am-9.35pm daily), leaving Heathrow Central bus terminal every 20-30mins. It's £5 for a single (£2.50 under-16s) or £9 (£4.50 under-16s) for a return. For information on accessibility, or to organise assistance, contact the National Express Disabled Person Travel Helpline at least 48 hours before travel (*08717 818181, bit.ly/kuBT71*).

A **taxi** into town will cost £45-£65 and take 30-60mins.

London City Airport
7646 0000, www.londoncityairport.com. About 9 miles east of central London.
The **Docklands Light Railway** (DLR) runs to London City Airport. The journey to Bank station in the City takes around 20mins, and trains run 5.30am-12.30am Mon-Sat or 7.30am-11.30pm Sun. By road, a **taxi** costs around £30 to central London; less to the City or to Canary Wharf.

Luton Airport
01582 405100, www.london-luton.com. About 30 miles north of central London.
It's a short bus ride from the airport to Luton Airport Parkway station. From here, the **Thameslink** rail service (*see xxxx*) calls at many stations (St Pancras International and City among them); journey time is 35-45mins. Trains leave every 15mins or so and cost £13.50 single and £23 return, or £14.50 for a cheap day return (after 9.30am Mon-Fri, all day weekends). Trains between Luton and St Pancras run at least hourly all night.

By coach, the Luton to Victoria journey takes 60-90mins. **Green Line** (*0870 608 7261, www.greenline.co.uk*) runs a 24hr service. A single is £14 and returns cost £19; under-16s £11 single, £15 return. A **taxi** to London costs £70-£80.

Stansted Airport
0844 335 1803, www.stanstedairport.com. About 35 miles north-east of central London.
The **Stansted Express** train (*0845 748 4950, www.stanstedexpress.com*) runs to and from Liverpool Street station; the journey time is 40-45mins. Trains leave every 15mins, and tickets cost £21 single, £29.30 return; under-16s travel half-price, under-5s free.

Several companies run coaches to central London. The **Airbus** (*0871 781 8181, www.nationalexpress.com*) coach service from Stansted to Victoria takes at least 80mins. Coaches run roughly every 30mins (24hrs daily), more at peak times. A single is £10 (£5 for under-16s), return is £17 (£8.50 for under-16s).

A **taxi** into the centre of London costs around £100 and the journey takes at least an hour.

By coach

Coaches run by **National Express** (*0871 781 8181, www.nationalexpress.com*), which is the biggest coach company in the UK, arrive at Victoria Coach Station (*164 Buckingham Palace Road, SW1W 9TP, 0843 222 1234, www.tfl.gov.uk*), a good 10min walk from Victoria tube station. This is where companies such as Eurolines (*01582 404511, www.eurolines.com*) dock their European services.

By rail

Trains from mainland Europe are operated by **Eurostar** (*0843 218 6186, www.eurostar.com*) and arrive at **St Pancras International** (*Pancras Road, King's Cross, NW1 2QP, 7843 7688, www.stpancras.com*).

GETTING AROUND

Public transport

Getting around London on public transport is easy – but not cheap.

Information

Details on timetables and a host of other travel information are provided by **Transport for London** (*0843 222 1234, www.tfl.gov.uk/journeyplanner*). Complaints or comments on most forms of public transport can also be taken up with **London TravelWatch** (*7505 9000, www.londontravelwatch.org.uk*).

TfL's **Travel Information Centres** provide help with the tube, buses and Docklands Light Railway (DLR; see p23). You can find them in **Camden Town Hall**, opposite St Pancras (9am-5pm Mon-Fri), and in the stations below. Call 0843 222 1234 for more information.

Euston station 7.15am-9.15pm Mon-Fri; 7.15am-6.15pm Sat; 8.15am-6.15pm Sun.
Heathrow Terminals 1, 2 & 3 tube station 6.30am-9pm daily.
Liverpool Street tube station 7.15am-9.15pm Mon-Sat; 8.15am-8pm Sun.

Piccadilly Circus tube station 9.15am-7pm daily.
Victoria station 7.15am-9.15pm Mon-Sat; 8.15am-8.15pm Sun.

Fares & tickets

Tube and DLR fares are based on a system of six zones, stretching 12 miles out from the centre of London. A flat cash fare of £4 per journey applies across zones 1-4 on the tube, and £4.50 for zones 1-6; customers save up to £2.50 per journey with a pre-pay Oyster card (*see below*). Anyone caught without a ticket or Oyster card is subject to a £50 on-the-spot fine (reduced to £25 if paid within three weeks).

Oyster cards A pre-paid smart-card, Oyster is the cheapest way of getting around on public transport. You can charge up standard Oyster cards at tube stations, Travel Information Centres (*see above*), some rail stations and newsagents. There is a £5 refundable deposit payable on each card; to collect your deposit, call 0845 330 9876.

Visitor Oyster cards are available from Gatwick Express outlets, National Express coaches, Superbreak, visitlondon.com, visitbritaindirect.com, Oxford Tube coach service and on Eurostar services. The only difference between Visitor Oysters and 'normal' Oysters is that they come pre-loaded with money.

A tube journey in zone 1 using Oyster pay-as-you-go costs £1.90 (65p for under-16s), compared with the cash fare of £4. A single tube ride within zones 2, 3, 4, 5 or 6 costs £1.40 (65p for under-16s); single journeys from zones 1 through to 6 using Oyster are £4.20 (7am-7pm Mon-Fri) or £2.40 (all other times), or £1.10 for children. Up to four children pay just £1 each for their fares when accompanied by an adult with a Travelcard.

If you make a number of journeys using Oyster pay-as-you-go on a given day, the total fare deducted will always be capped at the price of an equivalent Day

Travelcard (*see below*). However, if you only make one journey using Oyster pay-as-you-go, you will only be charged a single Oyster fare.

Day Travelcards If you're only using the tube, DLR, buses and trams, using Oyster to pay as you go will always be capped at the same price as an equivalent Day Travelcard.

Anytime Day Travelcards can be used all day. They cost from £7.20 for zones 1-2 (£3.60 child), up to £14.80 for zones 1-6 (£7.40 child). Tickets are valid for journeys begun by 4.30am the next day. The cheaper Off-Peak Day Travelcard allows travel after 9.30am Mon-Fri and all day at weekends and public holidays. It costs from £5.60 for zones 1-2 up to £7.50 for zones 1-6.

Children

Under-5s travel free on buses and trams without the need to provide any proof of identity. Five- to 10-year-olds can also travel free on public transport, but need to obtain a 5-10 Oyster photocard. For details, see www.tfl.gov.uk/fares or call 0845 330 9876.

An 11-15 Oyster photocard is needed by 11- to 15-year-olds to pay as they go on the all tube/DLR lines, and to buy 7-Day, monthly or longer period Travelcards, and by 11- to 15-year-olds if using the tram to/from Wimbledon.

Photocards Photocards are not required for 7-Day Travelcards or Bus Passes, adult-rate Travelcards or Bus Passes charged on an Oyster card. For details of how to obtain 5-10, 11-15 or 16+ Oyster photocards, see www.tfl.gov.uk/fares or call 0845 330 9876.

London Underground

Delays are fairly common, with lines closing frequently at weekends for engineering works. Trains are hot and crowded in rush hour (8-9.30am and 4.30-7pm Mon-Fri). Even so, the 12 colour-coded lines that together comprise the underground rail system – also known as 'the tube' – remain the quickest way to get around London (for a map of the Underground system, *see p254*), carrying approximately 3.5 million passengers every weekday. Comments or complaints are dealt with by **LU Customer Services** on 0845 330 9880 (8am-8pm daily); for lost property, *see p228*.

Using the system You can get Oyster cards from www.tfl.gov.uk/oyster, by calling 0845 330 9876, at tube stations, Travel Information Centres, some rail stations and newsagents (*see left*). Single or day tickets can be bought from ticket offices or machines. You can buy most tickets and top up Oyster cards at self-service machines. Some ticket offices close early (around 7.30pm); carry a charged-up Oyster card to avoid being stranded.

To enter and exit the tube using an Oyster card, simply touch it to the yellow reader, which will open the gates. Make sure you also touch the card to the reader when you exit the tube, or you'll be charged a higher fare when you next use your card to enter a station. On certain lines, you'll see a pink 'validator' – touch this reader in addition to the yellow entry/exit readers and on some routes it will reduce your fare.

To enter using a paper ticket, place it in the slot with the black magnetic strip facing down, then pull it out of the top to open the gates. Exiting is done in much the same way; however, if you have a single journey ticket, it will be retained by the gate as you leave.

Timetables Tube trains run daily from around 5am (except Sunday, when they start an hour or so later, and Christmas Day, when there's no service). You shouldn't have to wait more than 10mins for a train; during peak times, services should run every 2-3mins. (*cont. p23*)

Assisted travel

General assistance

Direct Enquiries *01344 360101, www.directenquiries.com.* This nationwide database of accessible sites also features a complete accessible guide to Underground stations (*bit.ly/l4uQLa*).

Disabled Persons' Transport Advisory Committee (DPTAC) *7944 8011, dptac.independent.gov.uk.* The official body that advises the UK government on disabled travel has a site packed with links.

Transport for All *7737 2339, www.transportforall.org.uk.* This pressure group has been campaigning for accessible transport for over 20 years. The website is a mine of useful information.

Traveline *0871 200 2233, www.traveline.info.* This is a partnership of transport operators and local authorities which provides impartial advice on public transport services nationwide, and journey-planning.

Public transport

London is committed to making its transport system accessible to as many people as possible. Nevertheless, much of the underground rail system is more than 100 years old, so modifications and improvements can be difficult and occasionally impossible. At the time of writing, 60 of the Underground's 270 stations have **step-free access** from platform to street level, and stations with car parks offer free parking to drivers with Blue Badges

(*see p22*). Accessible maps are available online (*bit.ly/kCOZP*), as are detailed text descriptions and audio descriptions of selected stations (*bit.ly/aweLKh*).

The newer **Docklands Light Railway** is completely accessible, with lifts or ramps at all stations to platforms (the gap between the platform edge and the train is approximately 7.5cm wide and the step up or down from the platform to the train is approximately 5cm high), but travellers should check that everything is working as it should before heading out. A free SMS text alert service is available (*bit.ly/iB6OvF*).

All London buses (except Heritage routes 9 and 15) are now accessible to wheelchair users via lowered floors or retractable ramps, making overground routes around the capital a simpler proposition for passengers with impaired mobility. The online Transport for London Journey Planner (*bit.ly/mEknSV*) includes options to guide passengers with impaired mobility.

Up to the minute **information on London's bus routes** is available by phone (*0843 7222 1234*).

A **large-print accessibility guide** to getting around London is available to download online (*bit.ly/mc7xlE*).

Older Londoners and disabled residents may be entitled to a **Freedom Pass**, which gives free travel (subject to certain restrictions) across London. If you are eligible, you must contact your local council. Full details are available online (*bit.ly/lesBVb*) and by phone (*0845 275 7054, Mon-Fri 9am-5pm*).

Railways

Travelling with a wheelchair

Most trains can accommodate wheelchairs within the dimensions prescribed in government regulations (700mm wide, 1200mm long). A small number of older trains can only carry wheelchairs with a maximum width of 670mm.

The maximum combined weight of a person and their wheelchair that can be conveyed is limited by the capabilities of the individual member of staff assisting the passenger and the stated maximum safe-working load of the ramp (between 230kg and 300kg).

Powered scooters

Because scooters come in a wide variety of shapes and sizes, many tip backwards on ramps, are heavier than a ramp's safe working load, or are the wrong shape to manoeuvre safely inside a carriage.

Some companies, therefore, have trains that cannot carry scooters. If you are a scooter-user who wants to travel by rail, you should contact the relevant train company (*see p24*) to check it can safely accommodate your scooter.

Disabled person's railcard

Many disabled people are eligible for the Disabled Person's Railcard, which gives a third off rail fares for the cardholder and a companion (*0845 605 0525, textphone 0845 601 0132, www.disabledpersons-railcard.co.uk*).

Railway enquiries

National Rail Enquiries *0845 748 4950, textphone 0845 605 0600, www.nationalrail.co.uk.*
National Rail Enquiries is the first point of contact for all information on accessible rail travel. It provides up-to-date information on train timetables, fares, disruptions to services and also has information on the accessibility of individual stations. To check the accessibility of the stations you will be using go to the 'Stations and Destinations' page, click on 'Stations Facilities Search', type in the name of the station and then click on 'Stations Made Easy'. Individual train companies also produce their own information. Check their websites before travelling.

Train companies can provide users with assistance, though 24 hours' advance notification is usually required. Staff cannot escort customers throughout a journey, provide personal care (for example, help with eating and drinking, taking medication or using the toilet) or carry heavy luggage.

Taxis

All **London black cabs** are wheelchair accessible, and assistance dogs and wheelchairs are carried for no extra charge. Black cabs are metered, and charge according to distance travelled, time of day and time taken. There is a minimum fare of £2.20. Only licensed black cabs can be hailed in the street, and can be booked by phone in advance (*0871 871 8710*).

Licensed minicabs provide a ▶

Assisted travel cont.

cheaper alternative, with flat-rate fares to destinations, but must be booked in advance. Passengers with special requirements should advise the controller at the time of booking to ensure a suitable vehicle is dispatched. **Transport for London** offers a free online minicab search (*bit.ly/iFTVfJ*), and a paid-for GPS-based text service (*text CAB to 60835 to receive details of three minicab companies near your location, cost 35p*).

Private cars

Disabled drivers eligible for a **European Blue Badge** (*see bit.ly/ikvKB4 for information*) can also qualify for exemption from the London Congestion Charge of £10 per day. To claim exemption, drivers must fill out a form (*available at bit.ly/krgLBv*) and pay a one-off fee of £10.

Blue Badge holders should note that in the central London areas of Westminster, the City, Kensington and Chelsea, and parts of Camden, the usual right to park for free at metered bays or on double- or single-yellow lines does not apply. These areas offer their own dedicated Blue Badge parking spaces. A complete map and guide to these spaces is available online (*bit.ly/miwaAW*).

Assisted transport

London has three membership-based schemes for residents unable to use public transport: Dial-a-Ride; Taxicard; and Capital Call.

Dial-a-Ride uses accessible vehicles such as people carriers and minibuses to transport people directly to their destinations. The service is provided free of charge, but at least 24 hours' prior booking is required. Passengers can be accompanied by friends or family (*0845 999 1 999 or 020 7309 8900 for details*). **Taxicard** provides a limited number of subsidised trips in black cabs per year. People who receive the higher rate mobility component of the Disability Living Allowance, the registered blind and recipients of a war pension monthly supplement are automatically eligible (*to apply, call 7484 2929, email taxicard@londoncouncils.gov.uk or fax 7484 2919*).

Capital Call is similar to Taxicard, but operates in the boroughs of Bexley, Ealing, Enfield, Haringey, Hillingdon, Hounslow, Kingston, Lambeth, Lewisham, Merton and Southwark. The scheme, which uses licensed minicabs to offer discounted fixed-price fares, is open only to Taxicard holders in these boroughs (*7275 2446 for membership information*).

During the London 2012 Games

All Olympic and Paralympic Games events will have a limited number of Blue Badge parking spaces, which will need to be booked in advance. Additional Blue Badge spaces will be provided at stations near the venues, and Dial-a-Ride minibuses will transport disabled spectators directly to the venue from nearby accessible stations (*see pp50-67*).

For information on **accessible sightseeing tours**, *see p151*.

(from p19) Times of last trains vary; they're usually around 12.30am daily (11.30pm on Sun). The tubes run all night only on New Year's Eve; otherwise, you're limited to night buses *(see p24)*.

Fares The single fare for adults across the network is £4. Using Oyster pay-as-you-go, the fare varies by zone: zone 1 costs £1.90; zones 1-2 costs £1.90 or £2.40, depending on the time of day; zones 1-6 is £2.40 or £4.20. The single fare for children aged 5-15 is 65p for any journey. Under-5s travel free *(see also p18)*.

National Rail & London Overground services

Independently run commuter services co-ordinated by **National Rail** (*0845 748 4950, www.nationalrail.co.uk*) leave from the city's main rail stations. Travelcards are valid on these services within the right zones, but not all routes accept Oyster pay-as-you-go; check before you travel.

Operated by Transport for London, meaning it does accept Oyster, the **London Overground** is a fabulously useful service. Crystal Palace, West Croydon and New Cross are now connected (via brand-new intermediate stations such as Shoreditch High Street) to Dalston Junction and the northerly extent of the Overground. Trains run every 20mins (every 30mins on Sun).

For lost property, *see p228*.

Docklands Light Railway (DLR)

DLR trains (*7363 9700, www.tfl.gov.uk/dlr*) run from Bank station (where they connect with the tube system's Central and Waterloo & City lines) or Tower Gateway, close to Tower Hill tube (Circle and District lines). At Westferry station, the line splits east and south via Island Gardens to Greenwich and Lewisham; a change at Poplar can take you north to Stratford. The easterly branch forks after Canning Town to either Beckton or London City Airport; the latter is due to extend across the river to Woolwich Arsenal this year. Trains run 5.30am-12.30am daily. For lost property, *see p228*.

Fares Adult single fares on the DLR are the same as for the tube *(see p18)* except for DLR-only journeys in zones 2-3, which cost £3.50 (£1.30 with Oyster pay-as-you-go) or £1.40 for 11-15s (65p with Oyster pay-as-you-go).

The DLR also offers one-day **Rail & River Rover** tickets, which add one day's DLR travel to hop-on, hop-off travel on **City Cruises** riverboats (10am-6pm; *see p28*) between Westminster, Waterloo, Tower and Greenwich Piers.

Starting at Tower Gateway, trains leave hourly from 10am for a special tour, with a guide adding commentary. It costs £14.50 for adults or £7.25 for children; a family pass (two adults and up to three under-16s), which must be bought in person from the piers, costs £37. Under-5s go free.

Buses

You must have a ticket or valid pass before boarding any bus in zone 1, and before boarding any articulated, single-decker bus ('bendy buses', which are in the process of being phased out) anywhere in the city. You can buy a ticket (or a 1-Day Bus Pass) from machines at bus stops, although they're often not working; better to travel with an Oyster card or some other pass *(see p18)*. Inspectors patrol buses at random; if you don't have a ticket or pass, you may be fined £50.

For lost property, *see p228*.

Fares Using Oyster pay-as-you-go costs £1.20 a trip; your total daily payment, regardless of how many journeys you take, will be capped at £3.90. Paying with cash at the time of travel costs £2 for a single trip. Under-16s travel for free (using an Under-11 or 11-15 Oyster photocard; *see p18*). A 1-Day Bus Pass gives unlimited bus and tram travel for £3.90.

Night buses Many bus routes operate 24hrs a day, seven days a week. There are also some special night buses with an 'N' prefix, which run from about 11pm to 6am. Most night services run every 15-30mins, but busier routes run a service around every 10mins. Fares are the same as for daytime buses; Bus Passes and Travelcards can be used at no extra fare until 4.30am of the morning after they expire.

Green Line buses Green Line buses (*0844 801 7261, www.greenline.co.uk*) serve the suburbs within 40 miles of London. Its office is opposite **Victoria Coach Station** (*see p18*); services run 24hrs.

Train operators

Chiltern Railways *0845 600 5165, textphone: 0845 707 8051, bit.ly/lVitHw*

C2C *operated by National Express. See below*

CrossCountry Trains *0844 811 0125, textphone 0844 811 0126, bit.ly/khYXck*

East Coast *0845 722 5444, textphone 0845 120 2067, bit.ly/m9Ugfq*

European Passenger Services *(for Eurostar) 08705 186186, bit.ly/iHzrii*

First Capital Connect *0800 058 2844, textphone 0800 975 1052, bit.ly/mvhayw*

First Great Western *0800 197 1329, typetalk 018001 0800 197 1329, bit.ly/lU3RPb*

First Scotrail *0800 912 2901, typetalk 18001 0800 912 2 901, bit.ly/kuc9QC*

Gatwick Express Ltd *0845 850 1530, www.gatwickexpress.com*

Grand Central *0844 811 0072, textphone 0845 305 6815, bit.ly/kw3Jdb*

Heathrow Connect *0845 678 6975, textphone 0845 330 3729, www.heathrowconnect.com*

Tramlink

In south London, trams run between Beckenham, Croydon, Addington and Wimbledon. Travelcards that cover zones 3, 4, 5 or 6 are valid, as are Bus Passes. Cash fares are £2 (£1.20 with Oyster pay-as-you-go).

For lost property, *see p228*.

Water transport

Most river services operate every 20-60mins between 10.30am and 5pm, and may run more often and later in summer. For commuters, **Thames Clippers** (*0870 781 5049, www.thamesclippers.com*) offers a service between Embankment Pier and Royal Arsenal Woolwich Pier; stops include Blackfriars, Bankside, London Bridge, Canary Wharf and Greenwich. A standard day roamer ticket (valid 10am-5pm) costs £12, while a single from Embankment to Greenwich is £5.30, or £4.80 for Oyster cardholders.

Thames Executive Charters (*www.thamesexecutivecharters.com*) also offers Travelcard discounts on its River Taxi between Putney and Blackfriars, calling at Wandsworth, Chelsea Harbour, Cadogan Pier and Embankment, meaning a £4.50 standard single becomes £3.

Westminster Passenger Service Assocation (*7930 2062, www.wpsa.co.uk*) runs a daily service from Westminster Pier to Kew, Richmond and Hampton Court from April to October. At around £12 for a single, it's not cheap, but it is a lovely way to see the city, and there are discounts of 30-50% for Travelcard holders.

Thames River Services (*www.westminsterpier.co.uk*) operates from the same pier, offering trips to Greenwich, Tower Pier and the Thames Barrier. A trip to Greenwich costs £9.50, though £13 buys you a Rivercard, which allows you to hop on and off at will. Travelcard holders get a third off.

For commuter service timetables, plus a full list of leisure operators and services, *see www.tfl.gov.uk.*

For lost property, *see p228.*

Taxis

The licensed **London taxi**, aka 'black cab' (although, since on-car advertising, they've come in many colours), is a much-loved feature of London life. Drivers must pass a test called 'the Knowledge' to prove they know every street in central London, and the shortest route to it.

If a taxi's orange 'For Hire' sign is lit, it can be hailed. If a taxi stops, the cabbie must take you to your destination if it's within seven miles. It can be hard to find an empty cab, especially when it's raining or just after the pubs close. Fares rise after 8pm on weekdays and at weekends.

You can book black cabs from the **24hr Taxi One-Number** (*0871 871 8710*, a £2 booking fee applies, plus 12.5% if you pay by credit card), **Radio Taxis** (*7272 0272*) and **Dial-a-Cab** (*7253 5000*; credit cards only, with a booking fee of £2). Comments or complaints about black cabs should be made to the **Public Carriage Office** (*0845 602 7000, www.tfl.gov.uk/pco*). Note the cab's badge number, which should be displayed in the rear of the cab and on its back bumper.

For lost property, *see p228.*

Heathrow Express *0845 600 1515, textphone 0845 330 3729, www.heathrowexpress.com*

London Midland *0800 092 4260, textphone 0844 811 0134, bit.ly/kl6uDf*

London Overground *0845 601 4867, bit.ly/mcwF25*

National Express East Anglia *0800 028 2878, textphone 0845 606 7245, bit.ly/kxkCDh*

Northern Rail *0845 600 8008, textphone 0845 604 5608, www.northernrail.org*

Southeastern Railway *0800 783 4524/01732 770099, textphone 0800 783 4548, bit.ly/kOjMbh*

Southern Trains *0800 138 1016, textphone: 0800 138 1018, bit.ly/iKMB5H*

South West Trains *0800 528 2100, textphone 0800 692 0792, bit.ly/iVH7w9*

Stansted Express *0845 600 7245, www.stanstedexpress.com*

Transport For London *7222 1234, www.tfl.gov.uk*

Virgin Trains *0845 744 3366, textphone 08457 443367, bit.ly/llcsDe*

Minicabs (saloon cars) are generally cheaper than black cabs, but can be less reliable. Only use licensed firms (look for a disc in the front and rear windows), and avoid those that illegally tout for business in the street: drivers may be unlicensed, uninsured and dangerous.

Trustworthy and fully licensed firms include **Addison Lee** (7387 8888), which will text you when the car arrives, and **Lady Cabs** (7272 3300), **Ladybirds** (8295 0101) and **Ladycars** (8558 9511), which employ only women drivers. Otherwise, text HOME to 60835 ('60tfl'). Transport for London will then text you the numbers of the two nearest licensed minicab operators and the number for Taxi One-Number, which provides licensed black taxis in London. The service costs 35p plus standard call rate.

Motorbike taxis A minimum charge of £25 is levied by both **Passenger Bikes** (0844 561 6147, www.passengerbikes.com) and rival **Taxybikes** (7255 4269, www.addisonlee.com/services/taxybikes). Bikes are equipped with panniers, and can carry a small to medium suitcase. You pay a premium for the thrill: central London to Gatwick currently costs £110-£120.

Driving

London's roads are clogged, and parking is a nightmare. Walking or using public transport are better options. If you hire a car, you can use any valid licence from outside the EU for up to a year after arrival. Speed limits in the city are generally 20mph or 30mph on most roads. Don't use a mobile phone while driving or you risk a £1,000 fine.

Car hire All firms below have branches at the airport; several also have offices in the city centre. Shop around for the best rate; always check the level of insurance included in the price.

Alamo UK 0870 400 4562, www.alamo.co.uk. US: 1-877 222 9075, www.alamo.com.

Avis UK 0844 581 0147, www.avis.co.uk. US: 1-800 331 1212, www.avis.com.

Budget UK 0844 544 3439, www.budget.co.uk. US: 1-800 472 3325, www.budget.com.

Enterprise UK 0870 350 3000, www.enterprise.co.uk. US: 1-800 261 7331, www.enterprise.com.

Europcar UK 0871 384 1087, www.europcar.co.uk. US: 1-877 940 6900, www.europcar.com.

Hertz UK 0870 844 8844, www.hertz.co.uk. US: 1-800 654 3001, www.hertz.com.

National UK 0870 400 4552, www.nationalcar.co.uk. US: 1-800 222 9058, www.nationalcar.com.

Thrifty UK 01494 751500, www.thrifty.co.uk. US: 1-800 847 4389, www.thrifty.com.

Congestion charge Drivers coming into central London between 7am and 6pm Monday to Friday must pay £10, a fee known as the congestion charge. The congestion charge zone is bordered by Marylebone, Euston and King's Cross (N), the Old Street roundabout (NE), Tower Bridge (E), Elephant & Castle (S), Vauxhall Bridge (SW), and Hyde Park Corner (W). You'll know when you're about to drive into the charging zone from the red 'C' signs on the road. Enter the postcode of your destination at bit.ly/iYrmSG to see if it's within the zone.

There are no tollbooths – the scheme is enforced by numberplate recognition from CCTV cameras. Passes can be bought from some newsagents, garages and NCP car parks; you can also pay online at www.cclondon.com, by phone on 0845 900 1234 or by SMS (online pre-registration required). You can pay any time during the day; payments are also accepted until midnight on the next charging day, though the fee rises to £12. Expect a fine of £50 if you fail to pay, rising to £100 if you delay payment.

Breakdown services
AA (Automobile Association) *0870 550 0600 information, 08457 887766 breakdown, www.theaa.com.*
ETA (Environmental Transport Association) *0845 389 1010, www.eta.co.uk.*
RAC (Royal Automobile Club) *0870 572 2722 information, 0800 828282 breakdown, www.rac.co.uk.*

Parking Central London is dotted with parking meters, but free spots are rare. Meters cost £1.10 for 15mins, and are limited to 2hrs. Parking on a single or double yellow line, a red line or in reserved residents' parking bays during the day is illegal, and your car may be fined, clamped or towed.

However, in the evening (from 6pm or 7pm in much of central London) and at various times at weekends, parking on single yellow lines is legal and free. If you find a clear spot on a single yellow line during the evening, look for a sign giving the local regulations. Take particular care when parking in Westminster in the evening and at weekends: from late 2011 the council will expand paid parking hours to weekends and evenings.

NCP 24hr car parks (*0845 050 7080, www.ncp.co.uk*) are numerous but pricey (£2-£7.20 for 2hrs). Central ones include Arlington House, Arlington Street, St James's, W1; Snowsfields, Southwark, SE1; and 4-5 Denman Street, Soho, W1.

Clamping & vehicle removal The immobilising of illegally parked vehicles with a clamp is common in London. There will be a label on the car telling you which payment centre to phone or visit. You'll have to stump up an £80 release fee and show a valid licence. The payment centre will de-clamp your car within four hours. If you don't remove your car, it may get clamped again, so wait by your vehicle.

If your car has disappeared, it's either been stolen or, if it was parked illegally,

towed to a car pound by the local authority. A release fee of £200 is levied for removal, plus £40 per day from the first midnight after removal. To add insult to injury, you'll also probably get a parking ticket of £60-£100 when you collect the car (reduced by a 50% discount if paid within 14 days). To find out how to retrieve your car, call the **Trace Service** hotline (*7747 4747*).

Cycling
London isn't the friendliest city for cyclists, but the growing **London Cycle Network** (*www.londoncyclenetwork.org.uk*) and the **London Cycling Campaign** (*7234 9310, www.lcc.org.uk*) help make it better. **Transport for London** (*0843 222 1234*) offers a printable route-finder for cyclists, and Mayor Boris Johnson has put a lot of weight behind developing cycling. His 'Cycle Superhighways' have had a mixed reception and, designed for residents to use for getting into central London, are of limited use for tourists looking to get between the major sights. The **TFL Cycle Hire** ('Boris Bikes') scheme has been hugely popular, however. After a shaky start, it is now open to anyone with a credit or debit card, though membership for regular users is cheaper. There's a £1 access fee, and the first 30 minutes are free. See *bit.ly/9nJ1ZV* for details. Commercial London **cycle hire** companies include the **London Bicycle Tour Company** (*7928 6838, londonbicycle.com*) and **Velorution** (*7637 4004, www.velorution.biz*).

Walking
The best way to see London is on foot, but the city's street layout is very complicated – even locals often carry maps. Basic maps of central London are in the back of this book (*see pp244-253*), with essential locations clearly marked; the standard Geographers' *London A-Z* and Collins' *London Street Atlas* are useful supplements. There's also route advice at *www.tfl.gov.uk/gettingaround.*

Guided tours

By bicycle

The **London Bicycle Tour Company** (*see p27*) runs a range of tours in central London.

By boat

City Cruises: Rail River Rover

7740 0400, www.citycruises.com. **Rates** *£14.50; £7.25 reductions.*

Combines hop-on, hop-off travel on any regular City Cruise route (pick-ups at Westminster, London Eye, Tower and Greenwich Piers) with free DLR travel. All piers are accessible to wheelchair users.

Jason's Trip Canal Boats

www.jasons.co.uk. **Rates** *£8.50 return; £7.50 reductions.*

Popular 90min narrowboat tours between Little Venice and Camden. Not accessible to wheelchair users.

Thames RIB Experience

7930 5746, www.thamesribexperience.com. **Rates** *£29-£45; £16-£27 reductions.*

Our favourite of the growing number of Thames RIB tours (a RIB is a powerful speedboat) zooms you straight from the Embankment, either to Canary Wharf (50mins) or the Thames Barrier (80mins), and back. Book in advance, and inform them of any special needs.

By bus

Big Bus Company

7233 9533, www.bigbustours.com. **Rates** *£26; £10 reductions; free under-5s.*

These open-top buses (8.30am-6pm, or until 4.30pm in winter) cover more than 70 stops in town, among them Haymarket, Green Park and Marble Arch. There's live commentary in English, and recorded commentary in eight other languages. Passengers can hop on and off as much as they like. Tickets include a river cruise.

Original London Sightseeing Tour

8877 1722, www.theoriginaltour.com. **Rates** *£25; £12 reductions; £86 family; free under-5s.*

OLS's hop-on, hop-off bus tours cover 90 stops in central London. Commentary in seven languages. Tickets include a river cruise. One-third of buses now accessible to wheelchair users.

London Duck

7928 3132, www.londonducktours.co.uk. **Rates** *£20; £14-£16 reductions; £58 family.*

Tours of Westminster in an amphibious vehicle. The 75min road/river trip starts on Chicheley Street (behind the London Eye) and enters the Thames at Vauxhall. Not accessible to wheelchair users.

By helicopter

Cabair *8953 4411, www.cabair helicopters.com.* **Rates** *£150/person.*

Cabair runs half-hour tours (Sun, some Sat) that depart from Elstree Aerodrome in north London and follow the Thames.

By car

Black Taxi Tours of London

7935 9363, www.blacktaxitours.co.uk. **Rates** *£100-£115.* Tailored 2hr tours for up to five people. Accessible to wheelchair users.

Small Car Big City

7585 0399, www.smallcarbigcity.com. **Rates** *£99-£179.* Tour in a classic Mini Cooper.

On foot

Head to **www.walklondon.org.uk** in search of free walks and events. Good choices for paid group tours include the following organisations: **And Did Those Feet** (*8806 3742, www.chr.org.uk*), **Performing London** (*01234 404774, www.performinglondon.co.uk*), **Silver Cane Tours** (*07720 715295, www.silvercanetours.com*) and **Urban Gentry** (*8149 6253, www.urbangentry.com*). **Original London Walks** (*7624 3978, www.walks.com*) provides an astonishing 140 different walks on a variety of themes. Walks are available for wheelchair users by arrangement. A range of idiosyncratic walk suggestions can also be downloaded from **www.citiesinsound.com**.

For more on accessible tours, *see p151.*

Guided tours

By bicycle

The **London Bicycle Tour Company** (*see p27*) runs a range of tours in central London.

By boat

City Cruises: Rail River Rover
7740 0400, www.citycruises.com.
Rates *£14.50; £7.25 reductions.*
Combines hop-on, hop-off travel on any regular City Cruise route (pick-ups at Westminster, London Eye, Tower and Greenwich Piers) with free DLR travel. All piers are accessible to wheelchair users.

Jason's Trip Canal Boats
www.jasons.co.uk. **Rates** *£8.50 return; £7.50 reductions.*
Popular 90min narrowboat tours between Little Venice and Camden. Not accessible to wheelchair users.

Thames RIB Experience *7930 5746, www.thamesribexperience.com.*
Rates *£29-£45; £16-£27 reductions.*
Our favourite of the growing number of Thames RIB tours (a RIB is a powerful speedboat) zooms you straight from the Embankment, either to Canary Wharf (50mins) or the Thames Barrier (80mins), and back. Book in advance, and inform them of any special needs.

By bus

Big Bus Company *7233 9533, www.bigbustours.com.* **Rates** *£26; £10* reductions; free under-5s.
These open-top buses (8.30am-6pm, or until 4.30pm in winter) cover more than 70 stops in town, among them Haymarket, Green Park and Marble Arch. There's live commentary in English, and recorded commentary in eight other languages. Passengers can hop on and off as much as they like. Tickets include a river cruise.

Original London Sightseeing Tour
8877 1722, www.theoriginaltour.com.
Rates *£25; £12 reductions; £86 family;* free under-5s.
OLS's hop-on, hop-off bus tours cover 90 stops in central London. Commentary in seven languages. Tickets include a river cruise. One-third of buses now accessible to wheelchair users.

London Duck *7928 3132, www.londonducktours.co.uk.* **Rates** *£20; £14-£16 reductions; £58 family.*
Tours of Westminster in an amphibious vehicle. The 75min road/river trip starts on Chicheley Street (behind the London Eye) and enters the Thames at Vauxhall. Not accessible to wheelchair users.

By helicopter

Cabair *8953 4411, www.cabair helicopters.com.* **Rates** *£150/person.*
Cabair runs half-hour tours (Sun, some Sat) that depart from Elstree Aerodrome in north London and follow the Thames.

By car

Black Taxi Tours of London
7935 9363, www.blacktaxitours.co.uk.
Rates *£100-£115.* Tailored 2hr tours for up to five people. Accessible to wheelchair users.

Small Car Big City *7585 0399, www.smallcarbigcity.com.* **Rates** *£99-£179.* Tour in a classic Mini Cooper.

On foot

Head to **www.walklondon.org.uk** in search of free walks and events. Good choices for paid group tours include the following organisations: **And Did Those Feet** (*8806 3742, www.chr.org.uk*), **Performing London** (*01234 404774, www.performinglondon.co.uk*), **Silver Cane Tours** (*07720 715295, www. silvercanetours.com*) and **Urban Gentry** (*8149 6253, www.urbangentry.com*). **Original London Walks** (*7624 3978, www.walks.com*) provides an astonishing 140 different walks on a variety of themes. Walks are available for wheelchair users by arrangement. A range of idiosyncratic walk suggestions can also be downloaded from **www.citiesinsound.com**.

For more on accessible tours, *see p151*.

Accommodation

London has rooms to suit every budget and every need, but book early.

Andaz Liverpool Street

40 Liverpool Street, EC2M 7QN (7961 1234, www.london.liverpoolstreet. andaz.com). Liverpool Street tube/rail. **Rates** £240-£300 double. **Rooms** 267.

A faded railway hotel until its £70m Conran overhaul in 2000, the red-brick Great Eastern became in 2007 the first of Hyatt's new Andaz portfolio. The fresh approach means out with gimmicky menus, closet-sized minibars and even the lobby reception desk, and in with down-to-earth, well-informed service and eco-friendliness. The bedrooms still wear style-mag uniform – Eames chairs, Frette linens – but free services (local calls, wireless internet, healthy minibar) and savvy efforts to connect with the vibey local area are appreciated: witness the Summer Garden, temporarily installed at the base of the atrium as a place to lounge over cocktails or enjoy the Designer Jumble Sale, and entertainment in the hotel's wonderfully gothic Freemasons' Temple.

Notes *Bars/cafés (5). Business centre. Concierge. Gym. Internet: wireless & high-speed (free). Restaurants (5). Room service. Smoking rooms. TV. Drop-off point outside main entrance. There is an automatic revolving door and an adjacent accessible door on either side. Lifts located in lobby provide access to all upper floors. A ramp is available for access to the bar and staff are happy to assist. Accessible toilet on ground floor. Accessible toilet in the standard male and female toilets on first floor. Four accessible rooms with adapted en suite bathrooms located on first and second floors.*

Britannia International

162 Marsh Wall, E14 9SJ (7712 0100, www.britanniahotels.com). South Quay DLR or Canary Wharf DLR/tube. **Rates** from £69. **Rooms** 442.

Great views from the upper floors of this consistently good high-rise hotel in futuristic Canary Wharf.

Andaz Liverpool Street.

Notes *Two designated parking spaces. Six rooms with specially adapted en suite facilities adjacent to lifts. Roll-in showers are available. Access to the hotel is by ramp, and the hotel is accessible to wheelchair users throughout, with the restaurant offering ample space to manoeuvre. No hearing loop, large print or Braille menus. Assistance dogs welcome. Notify staff of any special needs prior to arrival via main number.*

Brown's

Albemarle Street, W1S 4BP (7493 6020, bit.ly/9Nftzg). Green Park tube. **Rates** £327-£587. **Rooms** 117.
Brown's was opened in 1837 by James Brown, butler to Romantic poet, hedonist and freedom-fighter Lord Byron. The first British telephone call was made from here in 1876, five years after Napoleon III and Empress Eugenie took refuge in one of the considerable suites after fleeing the Third Republic. The Ethiopian Emperor Haile Selassie and Rudyard Kipling were also guests. The bedrooms are all large and extremely comfortable, furnished with original art, collections of books and, in the suites, fireplaces; the elegant, classic British hotel restaurant, the Albemarle, gives a nod to modernity with a series of contemporary British artworks, including pieces by the likes of Tracey Emin and Bridget Riley, but the public spaces of the hotel thrum with history. Non-residents can visit: try the £37 afternoon tea in the English Tea Room or sip a cocktail in the classily masculine Donovan Bar.

Notes *Bar/café. Business centre. Concierge. Gym. Internet: wireless (free), high-speed (£15/day). Restaurant accessible to wheelchair users. Room service. Spa facilities. TV: pay movies. Two accessible rooms.*

The Chamberlain Hotel

130-135 Minories, EC3N 1NU (7680 1500, www.thechamberlainhotel.com). Tower Hill tube or Fenchurch St rail. **Rates** from £145. **Rooms** 64.
London brewer Fuller's owns and operates this charming, small hotel which comes with its own pub on the ground floor.

Notes *Ramp available to main entrance, with four rooms on floors 1-4 with specially adapted en suite facilities. No Braille or large print menus in restaurant, but ample room for wheelchair users to manoeuvre. Assistance dogs welcome.*

Copthorne Tara Hotel

Scarsdale Place, Wrights Lane, W8 5SR (7937 7211, bit.ly/lnWCYO). High Street Kensington tube. **Rates** £90-£215. **Rooms** 833.
The winner of a 2006 award for accessibility, the well located Copthorne Tara has recently begun an overdue refurbishment of its rooms, which should be completed in 2012.

Notes *Ten specially adapted single, twin and double rooms rooms with bathrooms featuring level-access showers or baths with hoists. Front desk has a lowered section for wheelchair users, and there is level access to all areas. Staff are happy to help. Assistance dogs welcome.*

Crowne Plaza Docklands

Royal Victoria Dock, Western Gateway, E16 1AL (7055 2000, www.crowneplazadocklands.co.uk). Royal Victoria DLR. **Rates** from £230. **Rooms** 210.
Functional if uninspiring four-star hotel in the heart of Docklands.

Notes *Ramped entrance with designated parking and step-free access to entrance from car park, which has designated disabled spaces. 11 rooms with adapted en suite bathrooms and adjoining rooms for carers on request. Assistance dogs welcome.*

Crowne Plaza London

19 New Bridge Street, EC4V 6DB (7438 8000, www.ichotelsgroup.com). Blackfriars tube/rail. **Rates** from £300. **Rooms** 203.

Upmarket hotel perched on the edge of the City, with impressive facilities and prices to match.

Notes *10 rooms with specially adapted en suite facilities, located on floors 1-5 adjacent to fire escape. On-street Blue Badge parking with one bay. Restaurant has ample room for wheelchair users to manoeuvre. Assistance dogs welcome.*

The Cumberland

Great Cumberland Place, off Oxford Street, W1H 7DL (7262 1234, www.guoman.com). Marble Arch tube. **Rates** £160-£363 double. **Rooms** 1,019.

Perfectly located by Marble Arch tube (turn the right way and you're there in seconds), the Cumberland is a bit of a monster: in addition to the 900 rooms in the main block, there are another 119 in an annexe down the road. The echoing, rather chaotic lobby has some dramatic modern art and sculptures, as well as an impressive but somewhat severe waterfall. The rooms are minimalist, featuring acid-etched headboards, neatly modern bathrooms and plasma TVs – nicely designed, but rather small. The hotel's excellent dining room is the exclusive Rhodes W1, but there are also a barbrasserie and boisterous, trash-industrial style, late-night DJ bar. Weekend breakfasts can feel like feeding the 5,000.

Notes *Bars/cafés (3). Concierge. Gym. Internet: wireless & high-speed (£15/day). Restaurants (3). Room service. TV: pay movies. Public car park in Bryanston Street 350m (approx) away. Drop-off point outside main entrance. There is level access to automatic double door. Reception has a hearing induction loop. Six passenger lifts provide access to all floors. Ten accessible rooms have en suite accessible bathrooms, six of these have a bath with shower over. A transfer area is provided along with a bath seat. Four rooms are available with a roll in shower. All bathrooms have assistance alarms and grab rails. Accessible toilet facilities located on the lower ground floor.*

DoubleTree by Hilton

92 Southampton Row, WC1B 4BH (7242 2828, bit.ly/f72Xue). Russell Square tube. **Rates** from £175. **Rooms** 215.

The former Bonnington (later Park Inn) Hotel reopened after extensive refurbishment by its new owners in February 2011. The refurbishment has improved access for wheelchair users throughout the hotel by removing steps to meeting areas. Rooms are spacious and well appointed, with just enough design flair to be interesting. The hotel is brilliantly located to allow visitors to explore such sites as the British Museum.

Business centre. Free wireless internet. Bar. Fitness centre. Restaurant. Three adapted rooms. One dual-door lift, so wheelchair users can enter on one side and exit on the other. Two toilets accessible to wheelchair users, on ground and lower ground floors. Level access to ground-floor meeting rooms. Induction loop at reception and in meeting rooms. Assistance dogs welcome.

Crowne Plaza Docklands. *See p33.*

Guoman Tower Hotel

St Katharine's Way, E1W 1LD (7481 2575, www.guoman.com). Tower Hill tube or Fenchurch St rail. **Rates** from £130. **Rooms** 801.

Once voted one of the buildings Londoners would most like to demolish by readers of the *Sunday Times*, this 1970s concrete monolith has a pleasant interior and fabulous views of Tower Bridge. Nearby St Katharine Docks are worth a look.

Notes *The car park has one designated space for disabled drivers. Level access to main entrance, with doorman to assist. Three rooms with adapted en suite bathrooms. Restaurant and bar have ample room for wheelchair users to manoeuvre. Assistance dogs welcome.*

The Hempel

31-35 Craven Hill Gardens, W2 3EA (7298 9000, www.the-hempel.co.uk).

Lancaster Gate or Queensway tube or Paddington tube/rail. **Rates** from £144. **Rooms** 50.

Since the mid 1990s, the serried white stucco façades of a quiet backwater square in Bayswater have concealed a dramatic alternative universe dreamed up by the actress turned hotelier Anoushka Hempel. Though no longer under her ownership, this boutique hotel started a design revolution, and the original vision still works. The rooms are all different, but defiantly black and white, and minimal to the point of being barely furnished. The upstairs restaurant serves a menu of European and Japanese fish dishes.

Notes *Access to main entrance via ramp. Five rooms with adapted en suite bathrooms. Lift has tactile markings. Restaurants have ample room for wheelchair users to manoeuvre. Assistance dogs welcome.*

The Cumberland. *See p34.*

Hilton Hotel

53 Upper Street, N1 0UY (7354 7781, www.hilton.co.uk). Highbury & Islington tube/rail. **Rates** *from £164.* **Rooms** 184.

Functional branch of the ever-growing Hilton chain designed for business travellers. Rooms are light and pleasant.

Notes *12 rooms with adapted en suite bathrooms. Access by ramp to the right of main entrance. Car park belongs to adjacent Business Design Centre, but is available to guests and has eight designated bays for disabled drivers. Assistance dogs welcome.*

Hyatt Regency London The Churchill

30 Portman Square, W1H 7BH (7486 5800, www.london.churchill.hyatt.com). Bond Street or Marble Arch tube. **Rates** *from £460.* **Rooms** 434.

Worth a visit for high tea if you can't afford to stay there, this five-star hotel was the recipient of a Tea Guild Award of Excellence for 2011. Also hosts the Michelin-starred restaurant Locanda Locatelli.

Notes *Four rooms with adapted en suite bathrooms, with wheel-in shower. Route from car park to entrance accessible to wheelchair user with assistance. Restaurant has ample room for wheelchair users to manoeuvre, and large-print menus.*

Marriott Grosvenor Square

Grosvenor Square, W1K 6JP (7493 1232, www.marriott.com). Bond Street tube. **Rates** *from £409.* **Rooms** 236.

Situated in a converted old townhouse near the American Embassy, the Marriott has been refurbished in a contemporary style heavily influenced by Japanese design, complete with paper screens.

Hyatt Regency London The Churchill. *See p37*.

&♍☕♿🚾♿L🐕

Notes *Five rooms with adapted en suite bathrooms. Hoist and manual wheelchairs on request. Adapted changing rooms on floor LG2. Access to main area by gentle ramp, with level access to reception and restaurant from entrance. Lift has tactile markings. Assistance dogs welcome.*

Le Meridien
21 Piccadilly, W1J 0BH (7734 8000, www.lemeridienpiccadilly.co.uk). Piccadilly Circus tube. **Rates** *from* £350. **Rooms** 266.
Slightly old-fashioned five-star hotel on Piccadilly. Standard bathrooms are on the small side, though fixtures and fittings are of a high quality.

&♍☕♿🚾♿🐕

Notes *Three rooms with adapted en suite bathrooms, all located on third floor. Adapted changing rooms on floor LG2. Assistance dogs welcome.*

Milestone Hotel & Apartments
1-2 Kensington Court, W8 5DL (7917 1000, www.milestonehotel.com). High Street Kensington tube. **Rates** £280-£322 double. **Rooms** 57.
Wealthy American visitors make annual pilgrimages here, their arrival greeted by the comforting, gravelly tones of their regular concierge, as English as roast beef and the glass of sherry in the room. Yet amid the trappings of old-school luxury (such as butlers on 24-hour call) thrives inventive modernity (such as the resistance pool in the spa). The rooms that overlook Kensington Gardens feature the inspired decor of South African owner Beatrice Tillman: the Safari suite contains tent-like draperies and leopard-print upholstery; the Tudor Suite has an elaborate inglenook fireplace, minstrels' gallery and a pouffe concealing a pop-up TV.

🧑♿♍☕🚾🐕

Notes *Bar/café. Business centre. Concierge. Gym. Internet: wireless & high-speed (free). Pool: indoor. Restaurant. Room service. Smoking rooms. Spa facilities. TV: DVD and pay movies. The hotel does not have a car park but on-street Blue Badge bays are adjacent. There is five-step or ramp access to the entrance. The heavy single-width door pushes open to a second set of heavy double-width doors that pull open. A lift, adjacent to reception, accesses all floors. Once inside the restaurant, there is level access and full table service available. There is ample room for a wheelchair user to manoeuvre. Menus are available in large print. One accessible room with accessible en suite facilities. There is also an accessible toilet 7m from the accessible entrance adjacent to reception. Staff receive disability awareness training and are Typetalk aware. Documents available in large print. Assistance dogs welcome.*

Millennium Gloucester Hotel
4-18 Harrington Gardens, SW7 4LH (7373 6030, www.millenniumhotels.com). Gloucester Road tube. **Rates** from £239. **Rooms** 610.
Slightly tired four-star hotel that offers exemplary services for disabled guests.

&♍☕♿🅿🚾♿L🐕

Notes *Car park has no designated bays for disabled drivers, but the route to the entrance is accessible to wheelchair users unaided. There is also a designated drop-off point by the entrance. Ramp to entrance. Six rooms with adapted en suite facilities, and adjoining rooms for carers if needed. Charging facilities for scooters and electric chairs. Lift has tactile markings. Level access to restaurant, which has space for wheelchair users to manoeuvre. Assistance dogs welcome.*

Milestone Hotel & Apartments. *See p39.*

Mint Hotel
Tower of London

7 Pepys Street, EC3N 4AF (7709 1000, www.minthotels.com). Tower Hill tube or Fenchurch Street rail.
Rates from £149. **Rooms** 583.
The newest addition to the growing Mint chain is smart and welcoming, and all rooms are equipped with Apple computers that double as TVs. Decor is bland modern, but rooms are spacious by London standards and the views from the popular Skylounge bar are something else.

♿ 🚶 ♿ 🅿️ 🛏️ 🐾 ✈️

Notes *29 accessible rooms and one accessible suite with adapted en suite bathrooms with roll-in power showers. All public areas, including café and Skylounge, accessible to wheelchair users. Parking priority given to disabled drivers. Assistance dogs welcome.*

Radisson Edwardian
Grafton Hotel

130 Tottenham Court Road, W1T 5AY (7388 4131, bit.ly/4zRMS2). Warren Street tube. **Rates** from £199.
Rooms 330.
Smart, well located branch of upmarket chain. When booking, ask for a room at the rear to avoid traffic noise.

♿ 🚶 ♿ 🅿️ 🛏️ 😊 🐾 ✈️

Notes *Two rooms with adapted en suite bathrooms, one of which has a roll-in shower. Level access to hotel from street, valet parking service and drop-off point. Assistance dogs welcome.*

Ramada Hotel & Suites
London Docklands

2 Festoon Way, Royal Victoria Dock, E16 1RH (7540 4820, www.ramadadocklands.co.uk). Prince Regent DLR. **Rates** from £91. **Rooms** 224.
A functional business hotel that gains a little something special thanks to its waterside location, right in the middle of Docklands. Can get very busy when the nearby ExCel centre has an exhibition on. The hotel has 153 rooms, and 71 suites designed for long-term stays.

♿ 🚶 ♿ 🅿️ 🛏️ 😊 ✈️

Notes *Bar. Gym. Restaurant. On site designated parking. Eight accessible standard rooms and four accessible suites. Adapted rooms feature showers with seating and self-raising toilet seats.*

Royal Horseguards

2 Whitehall Court, SW1A 2EJ (7839 3400, www.guoman.com). Embankment tube or Charing Cross tube/rail. **Rates** £360-£400.
Rooms 281.
The Royal Horseguards occupies a French château discreetly located off Whitehall. The building was designed by Alfred 'Natural History Museum' Waterhouse for the National Liberal Club in 1887, and the club founder, William Gladstone, great reformer that he was, probably would have approved of the recent refurb of the interior by the Guoman group. It's immaculately clean, 'classic but modern' in style, with welcoming staff. The bedrooms have useful dressing tables, iPod docks and wonderfully comfortable Hypnos beds, and bathrooms come with flatscreen TV and Elemis products. The buffet-style breakfasts are ordinary, but from the upper floors the river views of County Hall and the London Eye – whisper it – rival those of the Savoy.

🚶 ♿ 🐾 📶 🛏️ ✈️

Notes *Bars/cafés (2). Business centre. Concierge. Gym. Internet: wireless (free). Restaurant. Room service. TV. Drop-off point directly outside the entrance. The concierge staff will, by prior arrangement, take a guest's car to the local NCP Car Park, which is approximately 500m away. Level access to entrance, double doors lead directly*

Mint Hotel Tower of London. *See p41.*

*into lobby. Staff happy to offer
assistance. There is an induction loop.
Three accessible en suite bedrooms
(shower/bath facility). Lifts to all floors.
Portable ramp gives access from the
reception lobby to all other areas, staff
will assist with this service. The
accessible toilet is located near the
passenger lifts. Assistance dogs welcome.*

Thistle City Barbican
*120 Central Street, EC1V 8DS
(7956 6000, www.thistle.com).
Old Street tube/rail.* **Rates** *from £199.*
Rooms 463.
Functional and largely charmless big
business hotel in the intriguing and
historic Clerkenwell district. The hotel
distinguishes itself by its attention to
detail. Call ahead to arrange any special
requirements, including specific diets.

Notes *One designated Blue Badge
parking space. Steep ramp to hotel
entrance, then level access to reception.
Steps to bar. Assistance available.
One accessible double room with
adapted en suite bathroom (lowered
bath, but no shower), and adjacent
room for carer if needed. Three portable
induction loops available. Designated
disabled toilet on first floor. Vibrating
alarm clocks available on loan.
Information and menus available in
large print and Braille. Assistance dogs
welcome. Full accessibility guide online
at bit.ly/pOHxVS.*

Threadneedles
*5 Threadneedle Street, EC2R 8AY
(7657 8080, www.theetoncollection.com).
Bank tube/DLR.* **Rates** *from £225.*
Rooms 69.
Threadneedles boldly slots some contemporary style into a fusty old dame of a
building, formerly the grand Victorian HQ
of the Midland Bank, next door to the
Bank of England and the Royal Exchange.

The etched glass-domed rotunda of the
lobby soars on columns over an artful
array of designer furniture amd shelving
that looks like the dreamchild of some
powerful graphics software. It's a calm
and stunning space. The bedrooms are
individual. coherent and soothing examples of City-boy chic, in muted beige and
textured tones, with limestone bathrooms
and odd view of St Paul's, Tower 42 and
the Lloyds Building. It's all well run and
well thought out.

Notes *Level access to entrance,
but not to reception. Four rooms
with adapted en suite bathrooms.
Motorised scooters allowed
throughout. Lift has Braille and
raised markings and a mirror to aid
reversing out. Level access to
restaurant, with ample space for
wheelchair users to manoeuvre.
Assistance dogs welcome.*

YHA London Central
*104 Bolsover Street, W1W 5NU
(0845 371 9154, www.yha.org.uk).
Great Portland Street tube.*
Rates *from £20 adult.* **Beds** 294.
The Youth Hostel Association's newest
hostel is one of its best – as well as being
one of the best hostels in London. The
friendly and well-informed receptionists
are stationed at a counter to the left of the
entrance, in a substantial café-bar area.
The basement contains a well-equipped
kitchen and washing areas; above it, five
floors of clean, neatly designed rooms,
many en suite. Residents have 24hr access
(by individual key cards) and the location – in the shadow of the giant BT
Tower – is quiet but an easy walk from
most of central London.

Notes *Bar/café. Internet: wireless
(free). TV. No accessible rooms.
Assistance dogs welcome.*

Royal Horseguards. *See p41.*

CARAVANNING

Abbey Wood
Caravan Club Site

*Federation Road, SE2 0LS (8311
7708, www.caravanclub.co.uk). Abbey
Wood rail.* **Pitches** 210.
Rates £15.70-£29.30.
It feels positively rural when you reach
this verdant, gently sloping site with its
mature trees and spacious grounds. This
location is the ideal base for exploring the
capital or nearby Greenwich, which offers
its own blend of fascinating attractions.

Notes *Manually operated barrier with
keypad code at entrance. Keypad not
reachable from inside vehicle. No
vehicular access to pitches after 10pm,
at which time pedestrian gate is also
locked. Entryphone at a height of 1.5
metres. Dropped kerb to reception for
wheelchair users. Call bell for assistance
near the reception door at a height of
1.3m. No pitches designated for disabled
people, though six hard pitches and
three grass pitches, located nearest the
toilet block, are often recommended.
The nearest of these pitches is 160
metres away from the reception
building and between 20 and 60 metres
from the toilet block. There are three
toilet blocks on the site. Toilet block A
contains an accessible WC and
shower and has level access to laundry
facilities. A hoist is available on request.
In both male and female toilets, one
shower cubicle, one privacy cubicle and
one WC cubicle is fitted with grabrails
to assist ambulant disabled people. One
urinal is lower at 520mm high and is
fitted with a grabrail. The taps to the
washbasins are lever type to assist
people with limited manual dexterity.
There is a combined accessible shower
and toilet located adjacent to other
toilets and accessed using a RADAR
key, available at reception.*

Threadneedles. *See p43.*

CHAIN HOTELS

London's many budget chain hotels are often in modern, purpose-built buildings, so what you lose in old-fashioned luxury you gain in the latest facilities. Below are the branches we have chosen for their combination of accessibility and location, but other hotels in the same chains may do the job, too. As a rule, the earlier you book, the cheaper the room. Online booking is preferred. Where possible, standard rate or Freephone telephone numbers are provided.

Holiday Inn
Coram Street, WC1N 1HT (7923 6601, www.holiday-inn.co.uk). Russell Square tube. **Rates** from £100. **Central booking** online, or via 0800 434040

Notes *This branch has eight accessible rooms with adapted en suite bathrooms.*

Ibis
47 Lillie Road, SW6 1UD (7610 0880, www.ibishotel.com). West Brompton tube. **Rates** from £98. **Central booking** online, or via 0871 702 9469.

Crystal Palace Caravan Club Site
Crystal Palace Parade, SE19 1UF (8778 7155, www.caravanclub.co.uk). Gispy Hill rail or Crystal Palace Overground/rail. **Pitches** 84. **Rates** Caravan £5-£8. Tent £5-£15.
A busy but friendly site on the edge of a pleasant park with many attractions for children. The park is famous for its Victorian plaster models of dinosaurs, which have recently been restored. More recently, the opening of the East London Overground line has made access to the centre of London a cinch.

Notes *Visitor and late-arrivals parking area near reception, but no bays are marked out. The road and visitor parking areas have a tarmac finish; the late-arrivals area has firm gravel. No designated pedestrian route between reception and the visitor car parking. Additional parking adjacent to the reception block. Vehicle entry barrier is controlled by key-pad control set at approximately one metre height. Reception near site entrance with dropped kerb from the road. No designated accessible pitches though six of the pitches, with a gravel surface, are recommended for disabled people. The nearest of these pitches is 170 metres from the reception block and 20 to 60 metres from the toilet block, on a level route. The toilet block has space for parking. Male and female facilities have one shower and one WC with support grabrails to assist ambulant disabled people. One urinal has a vertical grabrail. A combined WC and shower for wheelchair users is in a separate room with ramped access. Lever taps assist people with limited manual dexterity. The shower has level access and there is a fold-down shower seat and a freestanding shower chair.*

YHA London Central. See p43.

Notes *12 accessible rooms with adapted en suite bathrooms.*

Premier Inn
1 Dukes Road, WC1H 9PJ (7554 3400, www.premierinn.com). Euston tube/rail. **Rates** from £69 if booked online in advance. **Central booking** online, or via 01582 567890.

Notes *12 accessible rooms with adapted en suite bathrooms.*

Novotel
53-61 Southwark Bridge Road, SE1 9HH (7089 0400, www.novotel.com). London Bridge tube/rail. **Rates** from £99. **Central booking** online or 8283 4500.

Notes *12 accessible rooms with adapted en suite bathrooms.*

Travelodge
1-23 City Road, EC1Y 1AE (7638 5501, www.travelodge.co.uk). Barbican tube/rail. **Rates** from £19 if booked online 21 days in advance. **Central booking** online, or via 01844 358500

Notes *19 accessible rooms with adapted en suite bathrooms.*

The London 2012 Shop

Make your London day out even better

Great Team GB and ParalympicsGB clothes and accessories are available at the accessible London 2012 Shops, conveniently located at Paddington and St Pancras International railway stations, Stansted Airport, Heathrow Terminals 3 and 5, John Lewis Oxford Street and John Lewis Stratford City.

london2012.com/shop

London 2012

London 2012 Olympic Games and Paralympic Games

THE LIE OF THE LAND

The London 2012 Games are divided into three principal areas – the Olympic Park, the Central Zone and the River Zone – with a number of satellite venues radiating out from them all over the capital.

The **Olympic Park** (*see p54*) is staggering – as an architectural, environmental and logistical achievement, for sure, but also in its sheer scale. More than half the planned bridges were complete by summer 2010, and planting in the parklands was well under way – the 'golden meadow', carefully seeded to flower in July and August 2012, first bloomed in summer 2010.

In this chapter, we provide information on the sporting venues and the events they will host in 2012, but there are many other significant structures in the Park. The innovative, eco-friendly Energy Centre is now operational, while the 'brown roof' of the Main Press Centre is being made out of wood and seeds recycled from the developing parkland habitat around it.

In Stratford City, to the east of the Olympic Park, Phase I of the development of the vast Westfield shopping mall (soon to be the biggest City shopping centre in Europe) should be complete in 2011, while the apartment blocks that will house some 17,000 athletes and officials during the Games have taken shape in the Athletes' Village. It is a rare boon for competitors that they'll be staying within walking dis-

tance of the major competition venues for London 2012. Everything will be connected to central London by the new Javelin shuttle service, promising journey times of just seven minutes to St Pancras International come the Games.

The **Central Zone** (*see p59*) brings events for the 2012 Games into the heart of 'tourist London': **Horse Guards Parade** is just down the road from Buckingham Palace (*see p73*), while **Hyde Park** is handy for the posh shops of Mayfair. People interested in getting a flavour of London 2012 venues prior to the events themselves are able to explore all three areas and more – given good weather, a day spent watching a cricket match at **Lord's Cricket Ground** (*see p118*), for example, is a treat.

The Olympic Park has transformed a vast, once-neglected area of east London, but the **River Zone** (*see p63*) may prove to have a subtler long-term influence on how Londoners understand their city. Locals generally conceive of London as divided by the River Thames into south and north, but infrastructure improvements linking south bank venues such as **Greenwich Park** and the **North Greenwich Arena** (*see p65*) to **ExCeL** (*see p63*) on the north bank may encourage people to consider the Thames as less of an absolute barrier, especially when the proposed cross-river cable car cranks into action. Whatever your level of interest in the Games, the UNESCO World Heritage Site of Maritime Greenwich (*see p127*), is a must-see.

Beyond these three major zones, the 2012 Games will visit two further historic London venues – **Wembley Stadium and Wimbledon** (*see pp65-66*), respectively the heart of English football and the centre of world tennis along with a number of improved or purpose-built sites **outside London** (*see p66*).

For details on general transportation around London, and for accessible transport information to and from the London 2012 Games, *see p16* **Transport**. For the accessible tube map, *see p254*.

Accessibility at the Games

The London 2012 Games aim to set a new standard for accessibility, with all venues accessible to all spectators, and assistance readily available if required. Wheelchair users lucky enough to be allocated tickets for Olympic events were invited to reserve designated spaces at the time of booking. In addition to **shuttle services** from key train and bus stations (*see p22*), all venues will have limited Blue Badge parking (by arrangement at the time of booking) and numerous accessible toilets, one of which will include adult changing facilities, complete with hoist. Space for assistance dogs to relieve themselves during events will also be provided.

Once inside a venue, disabled spectators will be able to use a free, easy-to-find service called **Games Mobility** for help with getting around. The service will loan wheelchairs and mobility scooters and guide visually impaired people to their seats.

Oscar Pistorius.

Indicative map of the Olympic Park at Games time

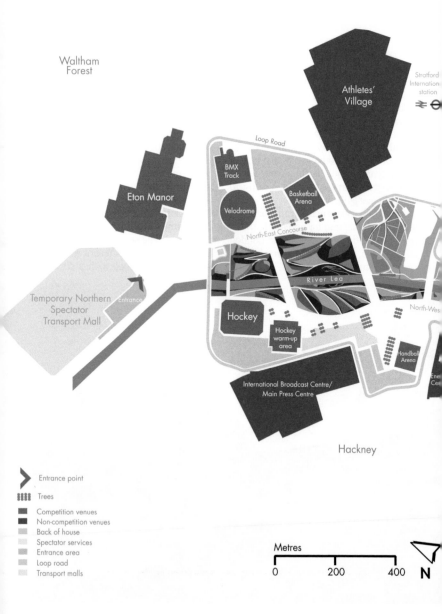

Waltham Forest

Stratford International station

Athletes' Village

Loop Road

BMX Track

Eton Manor

Basketball Arena

Velodrome

North-East Concourse

Temporary Northern Spectator Transport Mall

Entrance

River Lea

North-Wes

Hockey

Hockey warm-up area

Handball Arena

International Broadcast Centre/ Main Press Centre

Ener Cen

Hackney

> Entrance point

Trees

Competition venues
Non-competition venues
Back of house
Spectator services
Entrance area
Loop road
Transport malls

Metres
0   200   400   N

Spectator information will be provided in accessible formats, and audio description and commentary will be available at all venues. Audio augmentation for hearing-aid users will also be provided.

Olympic Park

Stratford tube/DLR/rail or West Ham tube/rail.

The centre of the 2012 Games is the combination of permanent stadia and temporary venues that make up the Olympic Park in east London. One year in advance of the Games, this has already become a major destination for locals and tourists. A self-guided tour is the best way to enjoy the last stages of the Park's development. The raised Greenway foot- and cyclepath, and towpaths north and south along the River Lea, make casual viewing from outside the perimeter fence a pleasure, with the View Tube near Pudding Mill Lane DLR supplying fine vistas over the Park and good-quality café food

Olympic Stadium

On Stadium Island, in the south section of the Park, across the Central Concourse from the Aquatics Centre.

The focal venue in the Olympic Park – host to the Opening and Closing Ceremonies, as well as both the Olympic and Paralympic Games Athletics – looks like a giant mechanical lotus flower, especially when you see its 14 stanchions of floodlights, open like 60m-long petals, reflected in the junction of the Lee Navigation and Hertford Union Canal. It sits on an island between three rivers, crossed by no fewer than five bridges. The stadium's top layer will be covered by material stretched over a cable-net roof to provide perfect conditions for the competitors and shelter from the elements for two-thirds of the seats.

Within the Stadium, there are 700 rooms (medical facilities, changing rooms, toilets) and a 60m warm-up track, but most of the normal stadium functions have been

Parklands.

London 2012 venues: Greater London area

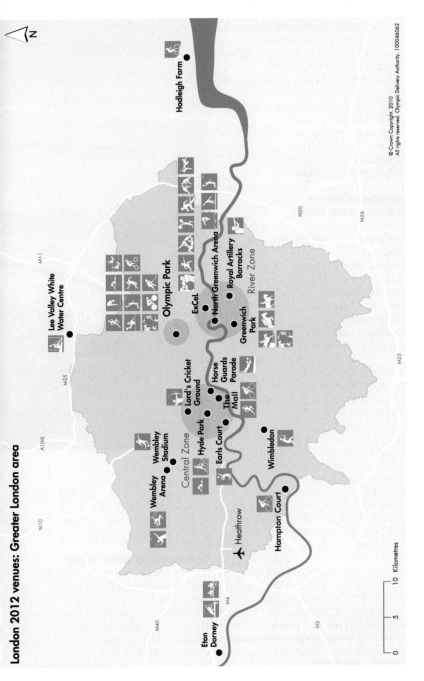

Hadleigh Farm

Lee Valley White Water Centre

Olympic Park

ExCeL

North Greenwich Arena

Royal Artillery Barracks

River Zone

Greenwich Park

Wembley Stadium

Wembley Arena

Lord's Cricket Ground

Horse Guards Parade

The Mall

Central Zone

Hyde Park

Earls Court

Wimbledon

Heathrow

Hampton Court

Eton Dorney

Kilometres

0   5   10

moved outside: refreshments, merchandising and information desks are to be stationed in a 'village' around the perimeter, giving the Park a festival feel.

This – and the division of seating – has allowed the total weight of the materials involved in the construction of this huge project to be kept low, reducing the carbon footprint created by both their manufacture and transportation.

Athletics
Paralympic Athletics

Aquatics Centre & Water Polo Arena

In the south-east of the Park, between the Olympic Stadium and Stratford City.

Another of the Olympic Park's iconic buildings, the Aquatics Centre will be the first building many spectactors see – it's on the approach from Stratford International station, with visitors crossing a vast bridge that conceals the training pool, a river and a railway line.

The Aquatics Centre was designed by Iraqi-born architect Zaha Hadid in typically uncompromising style. Its talking point is the huge, wave-shaped roof – steel and glass on the outside, treated timber within – that is flanked by 42m-high temporary stands on either side. These will accommodate the majority of spectators, with a smaller number seated on permanent concrete terracing. Inside, there are a 50m competition pool, 25m competition diving pool and a 50m warm-up pool. The first of 180,000 pool tiles was laid by world record-holding swimmer Mark Foster on 23 September 2010; the last of them by Paralympic gold medal winning swimmer Liz Johnson on 21 April, 2011; the venue as a whole will use more than 800,000 ceramic tiles.

Located next door to the Aquatics Centre, the Water Polo Arena is to be one of several of the temporary structures throughout the Olympic Park. Work on it began in spring 2011.

Aquatics – Diving
Aquatics – Swimming
Aquatics – Synchronised Swimming
Aquatics – Water Polo
Modern Pentathlon – swimming
Paralympic Swimming

Velodrome & BMX Track

At the northern end of the North-East Concourse, between the Basketball Arena and Eton Manor.

This venue, shaped like a giant Pringle crisp, is a stunner. Sir Chris Hoy – four career golds and a major part of the UK's cycling triumph at Beijing 2008 – helped to select the winning design team for the

Olympic Stadium. *See p54.*

Velodrome. Inside, the slope of the track and the best temperature have been carefully worked out to produce the optimal conditions for fast rides. The track is made of sustainable Siberian pine wood and the whole structure built from lightweight materials (including another cable-net roof) to keep transport and manufacture emissions low. Great pains have been taken to use daylight, rather than artificial lighting, and natural ventilation. The Velodrome even catches rainwater for recycling. Unimpressed by the engineering? Aesthetes will get great views of east London via a glass wall between upper and lower seating.

Work started on the BMX Track, right next door, in spring 2011. There will be temporary seating during the Games, and afterwards the track is to be relocated to form part of the VeloPark.

Cycling – BMX
Cycling – Track
Paralympic Cycling – Track

Basketball Arena

In the north-east of the Park, between the Velodrome and the Athletes' Village, on the North-East Concourse.

The Olympic Park's third-largest venue, this is going to be one of the busiest parts of the Park, with events happening daily

Paralympian Liz Johnson lays the last tile of the competition pool.

throughout the Games. Nevertheless, the Basketball Arena is only temporary. In fact, it's one of the largest impermanent structures built for any Games. Erected in only three months, it is covered with a stretched white material that will be used for light projections during London 2012, in a style perhaps reminiscent of the Beijing 2008 Water Cube.

- Basketball (preliminary rounds; women's quarter-finals)
- Handball (men's quarter-finals; men's & women's semi-finals, finals)
- Wheelchair Basketball
- Wheelchair Rugby

Eton Manor

In the most northerly section of the Olympic Park.

Perhaps the lowest profile of the Park's new, permanent constructions, this venue is on the site of the early 20th-century Eton Manor Sports Club, which had fallen into disuse by 2001. For the Games themselves, it will contain three 50m training pools for the Swimming and smaller pools for the other Aquatics disciplines, as well as an impressive show court set aside for Wheelchair Tennis.

Memorials to those sportsmen from the original club who died in World War I and II, which were moved off-site during construction, will return once the work is complete – and remain here after the Games, when Eton Manor will become a sports centre with facilities for tennis, hockey and five-a-side football.

- Wheelchair Tennis

Handball Arena

West side of the Park, just off the North-West Concourse, between the Olympic Stadium and the Hockey Centre.

The Handball Arena is a sleek, boxy modernist structure, but its appearance is designed to change over time: the exterior is adorned with around 3,000sq m of copper cladding that is intended to age and weather. Green initiatives include 88 pipes through the roof to let in natural light and reduce the need for artificial lighting, and pipes for harvesting rainwater. Spectators will enter directly on to the concourse level that encircles the building. This 'concourse' level is glazed, which will enable visitors to the Olympic Park to view the sport taking place inside, and illuminate the venue when lit at night. The athletes might be more excited about the sprung wood floor in the competition area. After the Games, a combination of permanent and retractable seating will enable the venue to be converted into a flexible indoor sports centre.

■ *Handball (preliminary rounds; women's quarter-finals)*
■ *Modern Pentathlon – Fencing*
■ *Goalball*

Hockey Centre
At the north end of the North-West Concourse, west of the Velodrome.
The Hockey Centre will have two pitches: the main one will have the larger capacity for spectators, while the smaller will be principally intended to allow players to warm up. It is hoped that, after the Games, both hockey pitches will be moved north to Eton Manor (*see left*).

■ *Hockey*
■ *Paralympic 5-a-side & 7-a-side Football*

CENTRAL ZONE
Taking the 2012 Games into the heart of London, the Central Zone mixes **sightseeing** (*see also pp72-151*) (**Horse Guards Parade**, **Hyde Park**) and sporting history (**Lord's Cricket Ground**, **Earls Court**).

Earls Court
Warwick Road, SW5 9TA. Earl's Court or West Brompton tube.
More usually associated in the minds of Londoners with trade shows and concerts (this is where Pink Floyd built *The Wall*), the concrete Exhibition Centre has a strong Olympic past: it hosted the Boxing, Gymnastics and Wrestling for the 1948 Games. Built in 1937, the building has a certain retro flair: its architect also designed grand 1920s cinemas.

■ *Volleyball*

Horse Guards Parade
Horse Guards Road, SW1A 2BJ. Charing Cross tube/rail or Westminster tube.
Best known for the Changing of the Guard and Trooping the Colour, this large parade

Goalball.

London 2012 Olympic Games Schedule

SPORT	VENUE	
Opening Ceremony	Olympic Stadium p54	
Closing Ceremony	Olympic Stadium p54	
Archery	Lord's Cricket Ground p62	
Athletics	Olympic Stadium p54	
Athletics – Marathon	The Mall	
Athletics – Race Walk	The Mall	
Badminton	Wembley Arena p66	
Basketball	Basketball Arena p57	
	North Greenwich Arena p65	
Beach Volleyball	Horse Guards Parade p59	
Boxing	ExCeL p63	
Canoe Slalom	Lee Valley White Water Centre p67	
Canoe Sprint	Eton Dorney p67	
Cycling – BMX	BMX Track	
Cycling – Mountain Bike	Hadleigh Farm p67	
Cycling – Road	London	
Cycling – Track	Velodrome p56	
Diving	Aquatics Centre p56	
Equestrian – Dressage	Greenwich Park p63	
Equestrian – Eventing	Greenwich Park p63	
Equestrian – Jumping	Greenwich Park p63	
Fencing	ExCeL p63	
Football	City of Coventry Stadium, Coventry	
	Hampden Park, Glasgow	
	Millennium Stadium, Cardiff	
	Old Trafford, Manchester	
	St James' Park, Newcastle	
	Wembley Stadium p65	
Gymnastics – Artistic	North Greenwich Arena p65	
Gymnastics – Rhythmic	Wembley Arena p66	
Gymnastics – Trampoline	North Greenwich Arena p65	
Handball	Handball Arena p58	
	Basketball Arena p57	
Hockey	Hockey Centre p59	
Judo	ExCeL p63	
Modern Pentathlon	Handball Arena p58	
	Aquatics Centre p56	
	& Greenwich Park p63	
Rowing	Eton Dorney p67	
Sailing	Weymouth & Portland p67	
Shooting	Royal Artillery Barracks p65	
Swimming	Aquatics Centre p56	
Swimming – Marathon	Hyde Park p62	
Synchronised Swimming	Aquatics Centre p56	
Table Tennis	ExCeL p63	
Taekwondo	ExCeL p63	
Tennis	Wimbledon p66	
Triathlon	Hyde Park p62	
Volleyball	Earls Court p59	
Water Polo	Water Polo Arena p56	
Weightlifting	ExCeL p63	
Wrestling – Freestyle	ExCeL p63	
Wrestling –Greco-Roman	ExCeL p63	

NOTES
For more information, see www.london2012.com.

	JULY								AUGUST										
	W 25	Th 26	F 27	Sa 28	Su 29	M 30	Tu 31		W 1	Th 2	F 3	Sa 4	Su 5	M 6	Tu 7	W 8	Th 9	F 10	Sa 11	Su 12
			•																	
			•	•	•	•	•		•	•	•									
											•	•	•	•	•	•	•	•	•	
													•						•	•
				•	•	•	•		•	•	•	•	•							
				•	•	•	•		•	•	•	•	•	•	•					
																•	•	•	•	•
				•	•	•	•		•	•	•	•	•	•	•	•				
				•	•	•	•		•	•	•	•		•	•					
					•	•	•		•	•										
																•	•	•	•	•
																•	•	•		
																			•	•
				•	•				•											
				•	•	•	•		•	•	•	•	•	•	•	•	•	•	•	
										•	•				•		•			
				•	•	•	•						•	•	•					
																•				
				•	•	•	•		•	•	•	•	•	•				•		
				•	•												•			
	•	•		•	•		•		•		•									
	•	•		•	•				•											
	•	•	•						•				•		•	•			•	
		•			•		•		•	•	•	•								•
	•				•		•		•	•	•	•					•		•	
					•								•	•	•		•		•	
				•	•	•	•		•	•				•	•					•
												•	•							
				•	•		•		•	•	•		•	•	•			•	•	•
				•	•	•	•		•	•	•		•	•	•			•	•	
				•	•	•	•		•	•	•								•	•
				•	•	•	•		•	•	•	•								
					•	•	•		•	•	•	•	•	•		•	•	•	•	
				•	•	•	•		•	•	•	•	•							
				•	•	•	•		•	•	•	•								
														•	•	•		•	•	
													•	•	•	•		•	•	
				•	•	•	•		•	•	•	•	•	•	•	•				
																•	•	•	•	
				•	•	•	•		•	•	•	•	•							
											•			•		•				
				•	•	•	•		•	•	•	•	•	•	•	•	•	•	•	•
				•	•	•	•		•	•	•	•	•	•	•	•	•	•		•
				•	•	•	•		•		•	•	•	•	•	•	•	•	•	•
													•	•	•					

London 2012 Paralympic Games Schedule

ZONE	VENUE	SPORT	DISCIPLINE
Olympic Park	Olympic Stadium	Opening/Closing Ceremony	
		Athletics	Track and Field
	Aquatics Centre	Swimming	
	Basketball Arena	Wheelchair Rugby	
		Wheelchair Basketball	
	Handball Arena	Goalball	
	Hockey Centre	Football Seven-a-side	
		Football Five-a-side	
	Eton Manor	Wheelchair Tennis	
	Velodrome	Cycling	Track
River Zone	ExCel	Boccia	
		Judo	
		Powerlifting	
		Table Tennis	
		Volleyball (sitting)	
		Wheelchair Fencing	
	Greenwich Park	Equestrian	Dressage
	North Greenwich Arena	Wheelchair Basketball	
	Royal Artillery Barracks	Archery	
		Shooting	
Other	Eton Dorney	Rowing	
	Weymouth and Portland	Sailing	
	Central London	Marathon	
	Brands Hatch	Cycling	Road

ground is open along its eastern side to sleepy St James's Park. For London 2012, it will act as a temporary venue for Beach Volleyball – which might even bring a smile to the lips of the legendarily deadpan Horse Guards.
 Volleyball – Beach

Hyde Park
Hyde Park, W2 2UH. Hyde Park Corner, Lancaster Gate, Knightsbridge or Queensway tube.
London's largest Royal Park will provide one of the most scenic backdrops for London 2012. Triathletes will swim 1,500m in the Serpentine boating lake, cycle 40km over seven laps of the park's perimeter, taking in Constitution Hill and Buckingham Palace, and then run 10km around the lake in four equal laps. A special grandstand will have a clear view of the finish line. The Marathon Swimming 10km event will see athletes complete six laps of the Serpentine.
 Aquatics – Swimming (Marathon Swimming)
 Triathlon

Lord's Cricket Ground
St John's Wood Road, NW8 8QN.
St John's Wood tube.
Established in 1814, Lord's (*see p118*) is the spiritual home of cricket. But, while much of the world remains immune to the charms of our summer sport, the 2012 Games will use this splendid setting instead to showcase a sport of far longer pedigree: Archery. The juxtaposition of the regal Victorian pavilion and the strikingly modern white pod of the media centre should be enjoyed by all spectators.
 Archery

AUGUST			SEPTEMBER								
Wed 29	Thurs 30	Fri 31	Sat 1	Sun 2	Mon 3	Tue 4	Wed 5	Thu 6	Fri 7	Sat 8	Sun 9
•											•
		•	•	•	•	•	•	•	•	•	
	•	•	•	•	•	•	•	•	•	•	
							•	•	•	•	•
		•	•	•	•						
	•	•	•	•	•						
			•		•	•	•	•	•		•
		•		•	•	•	•	•	•	•	
	•	•	•	•	•		•	•			
			•		•	•	•	•	•	•	
	•	•	•	•	•						
	•	•	•	•	•	•	•		•	•	
	•	•	•	•	•	•	•	•	•	•	
						•	•	•	•	•	
	•	•	•	•	•	•					
	•	•	•	•	•	•	•	•	•	•	
	•	•	•	•	•	•	•	•			
		•	•	•							
			•	•	•	•	•	•			
											•
							•	•	•	•	
Day 0	Day 1	Day 2	Day 3	Day 4	Day 5	Day 6	Day 7	Day 8	Day 9	Day 10	Day 11

RIVER ZONE

This selection of venues is scattered north and south across the divide of the River Thames, with **Greenwich Park**, **North Greenwich Arena** *and the* **Royal Artillery Barracks** *on the southern side, and* **ExCeL** *among the docks to the north.*

ExCeL

1 Western Gateway, Royal Victoria Dock, E16 1XL. Custom House or Prince Regent DLR.
Located between Canary Wharf and London City Airport, this convention centre is right on Royal Victoria Dock. For the London 2012 Games, ExCeL's 45,000sq m and two halls will be divided into five arenas accommodating 13 sports – it is to host the largest number of events of any venue outside the Olympic Park.

Boxing
Fencing
Judo
Table Tennis
Taekwondo
Weightlifting
Wrestling
Boccia
Paralympic Judo
Powerlifting
Paralympic Table Tennis
Volleyball – Sitting
Wheelchair Fencing

Greenwich Park

Greenwich Park, Greenwich, SE10 8XJ. Cutty Sark DLR or Greenwich DLR/rail.
Greenwich Park was, appropriately enough, a former royal hunting ground. Spectators will pack an arena set behind the National Maritime Museum (*see p132*)

Make your London day out even better

Great London 2012 clothes and accessories are available at the accessible London 2012 Shops, conveniently located at Paddington and St Pancras International railway stations, Stansted Airport, Heathrow Terminals 3 and 5, John Lewis Oxford Street and John Lewis Stratford City.

london2012.com/shop

ExCeL.

and the grand colonnades of the Old Royal Naval Hospital.

- 🔳 *Equestrian – Dressage*
- 🔳 *Equestrian – Eventing*
- 🔳 *Equestrian – Jumping*
- 🔳 *Modern Pentathlon – riding, combined event*
- 🔳 *Paralympic Equestrian*

North Greenwich Arena
Millennium Way, North Greenwich, SE10 OPH. North Greenwich tube.
Derided as an exorbitant New Labour vanity project when it opened in 2000, Richard Rogers' striking Millennium Dome has made a major comeback under the guise of the O2 Arena, a vast live music venue and shopping complex. As the North Greenwich Arena, it will also play a major role in London 2012. A proposed cable car link with ExCeL on the north side of the river looks set to become reality.

- 🔳 *Basketball (men's quarter-finals; men's & women's semi-finals, finals)*
- 🔳 *Gymnastics – Artistic*
- 🔳 *Gymnastics – Trampoline*
- 🔳 *Wheelchair Basketball*

Royal Artillery Barracks
Greenwich, SE18 4BH. Woolwich Arsenal rail.
Built in 1776, the Royal Artillery Barracks has the country's longest Georgian façade. To convert the area for Shooting and Paralympic Archery, a 62ft-high safety screen will be erected. Outdoor ranges are being constructed for Trap and Skeet; the Pistol and Rifle shooting will be held indoors. Grandstand will be specially built for each range.

- 🔳 *Shooting*
- 🔳 *Paralympic Archery*
- 🔳 *Paralympic Shooting*

WEMBLEY & WIMBLEDON
*Providing a counterweight to the east London focus of the 2012 Games, these iconic venues are in the city's north-west (**Wembley**) and west (**Wimbledon**).*

Wembley Stadium
Stadium Way, Wembley, Middx HA9 0WS. Wembley Park tube or Wembley Stadium rail.
Lord Foster's reworked Wembley Stadium (*see p201*) will be a grand setting for

Wembley Stadium.

several games during the London 2012 Football competition, including the finals. With a capacity of 90,000, it is Europe's second-largest stadium, and its 317m arch became an instant landmark when the new stadium opened in 2007.

Football

Wembley Arena
Arena Square, Engineers Way, Wembley, Middx HA9 0DH.
Wembley Park tube.

Most Londoners know Wembley Arena as one of the capital's most prestigious music venues, but it was built in 1934 to host the Empire Games (forerunner of the Commonwealth Games). It has good Games credentials, having been the location for the Swimming in 1948.

Badminton
Gymnastics – Rhythmic

Wimbledon
All England Lawn Tennis Club, Church Road, Wimbledon, SW19 5AE.
Southfields tube or Wimbledon tube/rail.

There could only be one setting for the London 2012 Tennis competition: the only world-class grass-court venue on the planet, home of the game's most prestigious Grand Slam tournament (*see p122*). The revamped Centre Court with its ingenious retractable roof was rebuilt in 2009, and now seats 15,000 spectators. Number 1 and number 2 courts will also be in use during the Games. Strawberries and cream are a certainty.

Tennis

OUTSIDE LONDON
The following venues range from those on the fringes of London **(Hadleigh Farm; Eton Dorney; Lee Valley White Water Centre)** *to the south coast, a hundred miles away* **(Weymouth & Portland)**. *The Olympic Football competition might take you further yet: portions of the event will take place in Scotland* **(Hampden Park, Glasgow)** *and Wales* **(the Millennium Stadium, Cardiff)**, *as well as the north of England* **(Old Trafford, Manchester; St James' Park, Newcastle)** *and the Midlands* **(City of Coventry Stadium)**.

Eton Dorney

Dorney Lake, off Court Lane, Dorney, Windsor, Berks SL4 6QP. Maidenhead, Slough or Windsor & Eton Riverside rail (approx 15-45mins from London Paddington station).

The 2012 Games should liven things up at Eton College, posh alma mater of Prime Minister David Cameron and London Mayor Boris Johnson. The lake, set in 400 acres of park, had a dry run for the Games when it hosted the 2006 Rowing World Championships, but subsequent improvements to the eight-lane, 2,200m course and the warm-up lanes were completed in summer 2010, along with a new cut-through and two bridges.

◢ *Canoe Sprint*
◣ *Rowing*
◤ *Paralympic Rowing*

Hadleigh Farm

Castle Lane, Benfleet, Essex SS7 2AP. Leigh-on-Sea or Benfleet rail (approx 45-50mins from London Fenchurch Street station).

Hadleigh Farm is a mix of woodland, pasture, hay meadow and marsh, with glorious views of the Thames Estuary and a ruined 13th-century castle. The hilly terrain is ideal for hosting the Mountain Bike competition and will have a temporary stadium for spectators.

◢ *Cycling – Mountain Bike*

Lee Valley
White Water Centre

Station Road, Waltham Cross, Herts EN9 1AB. Waltham Cross rail (approx 30mins from Liverpool Street station).

The brand-new White Water Centre is located at the far northern end of Lee Valley Regional Park. The first new London 2012 venue to open to the public in spring 2011, it has two white-water courses. The 300m competition course and 160m training course are both fed from a starting lake filled with 25,000 cubic metres of water – enough to fill 5,000

Olympic-sized swimming pools. The lake pumps 15 cubic metres of water per second down the course, with parts of the course reaching 7mph.

◢ *Canoe Slalom*

Weymouth & Portland

Weymouth & Portland National Sailing Academy, Osprey Road, Portland, Dorset DT5 1SA. Weymouth rail (approx 2hrs 40mins to 3hrs from London Waterloo station).

Improvements to the Weymouth & Portland National Sailing Academy were ready for competition by 2008 – making this the first London 2012 venue of any type to be finished. The new slipway, moorings and other facilities have already been used for several international events.

◢ *Sailing*
◣ *Paralympic Sailing*

Wimbledon.

Going out

Going out

Above all, London is to be enjoyed; here's how to make the most of it.

This section of the book is about getting out to explore what makes London such an enjoyable city for everyone, from the city's world-famous landmarks, to its thousands of pubs and shops.

If you wish to escape the queues and overcrowding at some of these places, plan your journey carefully. To minimise stress, we recommend avoiding major tourist attractions at the weekend, and only taking the tube outside rush hour (8-9.30am and 4.30-7pm Mon-Fri). Our opening times were accurate at the time of going to press, but always call ahead to check.

Finally, if you are on a budget, but determined to see every sight in the capital, the London Pass (www.londonpass.com) might just save you money. The six-day ticket (£95, £68 under-15s) is the best value, though it's by no means cheap.

Sightseeing, p72

The heart of this book deals with the sights, museums and galleries that help make London great.

There's so much to see and do in London that we have divided the city into compass points, North, South, East and West, and further divided the sights into Attractions (such as the London Eye) and Museums and Galleries.

Each location has an expert review from *Time Out*'s team of guide writers, coupled with an extensive accessibility guide, in which we cover such topics as car parking, the location of entrances and exits, level access and toilets.

Eating & Drinking, p152

What would London be without its restaurants and world-famous pubs? In recent years, eating and drinking in this city have undergone a renaissance so remarkable that London can now undoubtedly claim to be one of the great gastronomic destinations of the world. Anything you want to eat, from anywhere in the world, is here, on a plate.

In the process, the city has not left its roots behind. Around almost any corner lies an old, traditional pub where locals mix with newcomers in frequently boisterous, beer-fuelled discussion.

Our choice of restaurants and bars has been influenced by both accessibility and family-friendliness. In addition to some of London's finest restaurants and watering holes, we also recommend selected chains where the food is reliable and the facilities often superior to those at longer established venues. *The Time Out Eating & Drinking Guide* gives a complete picture.

Our selection of restaurants, cafés and bars comes complete with a neat summary of access symbols (*see p7*), plus comprehensive notes on practical aspects of getting into and getting around a venue. Although we have made a point of highlighting features for families and children, for a fuller picture we suggest our companion guidebook, *London for Children*.

Shopping & entertainment, p188

If you can't buy it or see it in London, then it probably doesn't exist. Our selection of shops reflects the fact that many of London's smaller, idiosyncratic stores don't offer great access or facilities for people with special requirements. If you are determined to unleash your inner shopaholic, the *Time Out Guide to London's Best Shops* should be your bible.

London, of course, wouldn't be London without its theatres, and our entertainment guide comes complete with contact information for all major venues, plus useful pointers to websites that can book you tickets and ensure you're seated in comfort. For good measure, we've included details of cinemas and top sports grounds.

Rolling down the river, p208

William Forrester, a professional tour guide and wheelchair user, offers his first-hand experience of London's most accessible and spectacular pathway.

Appy talk

Five smartphone apps to complement the information in this section.

Time Out *free (iPhone/Android).*
The best 'what's on' guide to London, if we say so ourselves. Locates nearby points of interest, and offers random suggestions to inspire and delight.

Toilet Map *£1.49 (iPhone/Android).*
Find your nearest public convenience. Online search at www.toiletmap.co.uk. Can search for accessible toilets only.

Pill Reminder Pro *69p (iPhone/Android).*
Set up audio alerts to remind you to take necessary medication.

Pharmacies *£1.49 (iPhone).*
Find your nearest chemist in London (*see p226*). Useful in emergencies.

WalkExplorer *free (iPhone/Android).*
Over 1,000 informative walking tours across the UK, some paid, some free.

Sightseeing

Sample the long history and enduring mysteries of the capital.

Buckingham Palace.

CENTRAL LONDON

Attractions

Banqueting House

Whitehall, SW1A 2ER (0844 482 7777, fax 3166 6310, www.hrp.org.uk). Westminster tube or Charing Cross tube/rail. **Open** 10am-5pm Mon-Sat. **Admission** £4.80; £4 reductions (carer free); free under-16s.

This Italianate mansion, designed by Inigo Jones and constructed in 1620, was London's first true Renaissance building. The sole surviving part of the Tudor and Stuart monarchs' Whitehall Palace, the Banqueting House features a lavish painted ceiling by Rubens, glorifying James I, 'the wisest fool in Christendom'. James's successor, Charles I, did not rule so wisely. After losing the English Civil War to Cromwell's Roundheads, he was executed in front of the Banqueting House in 1649 (the event is marked every 31 Jan). Lunchtime concerts are held on the first Monday of each month except August. Call before you visit: the mansion is sometimes closed for corporate functions.

♿ ♿ ♿ ♿ ⠿ Braille

Notes *Parking in busy Whitehall is not easy and there is no designated drop-off point. Moderate ramp to the entrance with heavy double-width doors. Level access to reception from the entrance. Induction loop hearing assistance system with specially trained staff. There is a moderate ramp/slope to gain access over three medium steps. The floors accessible by stairs are LG-G-1. The accessible toilet is located on the lower ground floor. The Main Hall of the Banqueting House is accessible via a lift, which is located in an adjoining property. The Banqueting House does not manage the adjoining property, so call 3166 6155/6152 in advance, especially if you plan to visit on a Saturday. A portable or standard-size wheelchair is required. Braille guide and induction loops are available; request on arrival.*

Buckingham Palace
& Royal Mews

*The Mall, SW1A 1AA (7766 7300
Palace, 7766 7302 Royal Mews,
7766 7301 Queen's Gallery,
www.royalcollection.org.uk).*
Green Park tube or Victoria tube/rail.
Open *State Rooms* mid July-Sept
9.45am-6pm (last entry 3.45pm) daily.
Queen's Gallery 10am-5.30pm daily.
Royal Mews Mar-July, Oct 11am-4pm
Mon-Thur, Sat, Sun; Aug, Sept 10am-
5pm daily; Nov-Dec 11am-4pm Mon-Fri.
Admission *Palace* £17; £9.75-£15.50
reductions; £45 family; free under-5s.
Queen's Gallery £8.75; £4.50-£7.75
reductions; £22 family; free under-5s.
Royal Mews £7.75; £5-£7 reductions;
£20.50 family; free under-5s.

Although nearby St James's Palace
remains the official seat of the British
court, every monarch since Victoria has
used Buckingham Palace as their primary
home. The palace was constructed as a
private house for the Duke of Buckingham
in 1703, but George III liked it so much he
purchased it for his German bride
Charlotte in 1761. George IV decided to
occupy the mansion after taking the
throne in 1820 and John Nash was hired
to convert it into a palace befitting a king.
Construction was riddled with problems,
and Nash – whose expensive plans had
always been disliked by Parliament – was
dismissed in 1830. When Victoria came to
the throne in 1837, the building was barely
habitable. The job of finishing the palace
fell to the unimaginative Edward Blore.
The neoclassical frontage now in place
was the work of Aston Webb in 1913.

As the home of the Queen, the palace is
usually closed to visitors, but you can
view the interior for a brief period each
year while the Windsors are on holiday;
you'll be able to see the State Rooms, still
used to entertain dignitaries and guests of
state, and part of the garden. At any time
of year, you can visit the Queen's Gallery
to see the monarch's personal collection of

treasures, including paintings by Rubens
and Rembrandt, Sèvres porcelain and the
Diamond Diadem crown. Further along
Buckingham Palace Road, the Royal
Mews is a grand garage for the royal fleet
of Rolls-Royces and home to the splendid
royal carriages and the horses, individu-
ally named by the Queen, that pull them.

Notes *The following buses run close
to Buckingham Palace and are
accessible for wheelchair users: 2, 8, 11,
16, 36, 52, 73, 148, 211, C1 and C10.
The nearest accessible tube is
Westminster. The* **State Rooms** *have
parking for visitors who require the
alternative access route with step-free
access, parking, and tours must be
booked in advance on 7766 7324. A
platform lift provides access to the
principal floor. Mobility scooters are not
permitted in the State Rooms but can be
used on the gardens' gravel paths. All
visitors should be aware that long
distances have to be covered during the
tour. Most rooms are carpeted and
some have polished wooden floors.
Induction loops are fitted and BSL
video tours are available free of charge.
At the* **Royal Mews***, parking is not
available. The nearest public parking is
on Palace Street. Manual wheelchairs
are available to borrow free of charge
on a first come, first served basis. All
areas of the Royal Mews have level
access but it is an historic building, so
floors are uneven and cobbled in places.
Benches are available throughout the
visitor route. Assistance dogs welcome.
The ticket sales desks, shop till counters
and the audio tour collection and return
points are equipped with induction
loops. A free audio tour is available and
neck loops available on request. British
Sign Language Interpreted and
Lipspeaking guided tours of the State
Rooms and Royal Mews run on selected
dates – call 7766 7323 for details.*

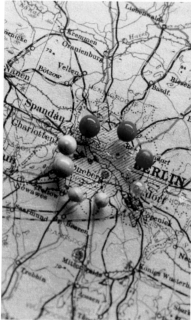

Churchill War Rooms.

Churchill War Rooms

Clive Steps, King Charles Street,
SW1A 2AQ (7930 6961, fax 7839
5897, textphone 7839 4906,
www.iwm.org.uk). St James's Park or
Westminster tube. **Open** 9.30am-6pm
daily. **Admission** £15.95; £8-£12.80
reductions; Disabled visitors £9.60
(carer free); free under-16s.

Out of harm's way beneath Whitehall, this cramped, spartan bunker was where Winston Churchill planned the Allied victory in World War II. Open to the public since 1984, the rooms powerfully bring to life the reality of a nation at war. The cabinet rooms were sealed on 16 August 1945, keeping the complex in a state of suspended animation: every pin stuck into the vast charts was placed there in the final days of the conflict. The humble quarters occupied by Churchill and his deputies give a tangible sense of wartime hardship, an effect reinforced by the wailing sirens and wartime speeches on the audio guide (free with admission).

Notes *No parking available. Wheelchair users should note that there are steps at the end of King Charles Street. Great George Street is a more accessible route. For security reasons a cloakroom is not available. Churchill War Rooms is fully accessible to mobility-impaired users. There is a lift to the basement level (single level display and exhibition area). Churchill War Rooms is wheelchair accessible throughout – the entire site is without stairs. The main entrance is on Horse Guards Road. There is a set of glass double doors (1240mm in total width), which open inwards. The historic nature of the site means that there are some narrow points within the corridors and doorways. The narrowest width is 763mm, enough for a standard wheelchair to pass. Due to the historic nature of the site, there is limited*

seating. There are seats in the Churchill Museum, one third of the way through the tour. There are seats in the café, which is approximately halfway through the tour. The café is fully wheelchair accessible. Two wheelchairs are available for use by any visitor. The Museum has two accessible toilets on the museum level accessed by lift. A family guide and a descriptive guide for visitors with visual impairment are also available. Assistance dogs welcome.

Enchanted Palace
at Kensington Palace

Kensington Gardens, W8 4PX (0844 482 7777 information, 0844 482 7799 reservations, www.hrp.org.uk). High Street Kensington tube or Queensway tube. **Open** *Mar-Oct* 10am-6pm daily. *Nov-Feb* 10am-5pm daily. **Admission** £12.50; £6.25-£11 reductions; £34 family; free under-5s.

Sir Christopher Wren extended this Jacobean mansion to palatial proportions on the instructions of William III. Until June 2012, the palace is undergoing renovations. During this period, the 'Enchanted Palace' show is bringing different rooms of the State Apartments to life with stories from the palace's history. This 'animated exhibition' combines live performance, courtesy of Wildworks theatre company, with high-fashion installations. You'll hear ghostly arguments from long-dead princesses, encounter the 'wild boy' who was kept here as a pet, and enter a 'whirling ballroom'.

Notes *Liberty Drives is a seasonal initiative by The Hyde Park Appeal to provide a free electric buggy service to aid mobility around the park's 760 acres, including Kensington Gardens where Kensington Palace is situated. The buggies seat up to five people and can give half-hour rides* *around the park, as well as offer drop off and pick up. For enquiries call 07767 498096. From June 2010 onwards, Kensington Palace has been undergoing major building works as part of an ambitious project to increase accessibility for all, ensuring that the new extension, entrance and East Front Garden are accessible, and includes the construction of a lift serving all floors – rendering all the palace levels open and accessible to visitors for the first time. Enchanted Palace is mainly located on the first floor of this historic building, so please note it is only accessible to those visitors with some degree of mobility up and down stairs, until the building works to improve access for all are complete in 2012. There is currently no lift, as this is being constructed as part of the building works and will therefore be available in 2012. Once in the State Apartments there are no level changes. Manual wheelchairs are available for use within Enchanted Palace; these are provided on a first come, first served basis and cannot be booked in advance. A Rooms Describer tours take place every Thursday. Tours of Enchanted Palace with an Explainer accompanied by a BSL interpreter can be arranged in advance. A temporary accessible toilet is available outside the entrance to the palace.*

Guildhall

Gresham Street, EC2P 2EJ (7606 3030, fax 7332 1996, www.guildhall.cityoflondon.gov.uk). St Paul's tube or Bank tube/DLR. **Open** *May-Sept* 10am-5pm daily. *Oct-Apr* 10am-5pm Mon-Sat. Closes for functions; phone ahead. **Admission** free.

The City of London and its progenitors have been holding grand ceremonial dinners in this hall for eight centuries. Memorials to national heroes line the walls, shields of the 100 livery companies grace the ceiling, and every Lord Mayor since 1189 gets a namecheck on the windows. Many famous trials have taken place here, including the treason trial of 16-year-old Lady Jane Grey, 'the nine days' queen', in 1553. Above the entrance to the Guildhall are statues of Gog and Magog. Born of the union between demons and exiled Roman princesses, these mythical giants are said to protect the City of London. The current statues replaced 18th-century originals destroyed during the Blitz.

Notes *Parking bays for Blue Badge Holders are located in Aldermanbury and Basinghall Street. Maximum stay 3hrs Mon-Fri, all day Sat, Sun. There is level access at the entrance. Access to most floors by lift or stair lift.*

HMS Belfast

Near Morgan's Lane, Tooley Street, SE1 2JH (7940 6300, www.iwm.org.uk). London Bridge tube/rail. **Open** *Mar-Oct* 10am-6pm daily. *Nov-Feb* 10am-5pm daily. **Admission** with voluntary donation included adult £13.50 (£12.25 without), £10.80 (£9.80 without), reductions; free under-16s (must be accompanied by an adult).

This 11,500-ton 'Edinburgh' class large light cruiser is the last surviving big gun World War II warship in Europe. A floating branch of the Imperial War Museum, it makes an unlikely playground for children, who tear around its gun turrets, bridge, decks, and engine room. The Belfast was built in 1938, ran convoys to Russia, and supported the Normandy Landings. She also helped UN forces in Korea, before being decommissioned in 1965.

Notes *Parking in Tooley Street area only. No designated parking spaces. The nature of the ship makes some of the areas below decks inaccessible to wheelchair users. Some modifications*

HMS Belfast.

have been made to provide a limited tour of the ship including the Quarterdeck, the Boat Deck and the Walrus Café. Large sections of '2 Deck' are also accessible. '2 Deck' is on the same level as the Quarterdeck and houses the main passages through the ship, the laundry, chapel, bakery, galley and prep areas, Petty Officers' mess, sick bay, dental surgery, Arctic mess deck and exhibitions Life at Sea and War & Peace.

Access to the ship is via a gangway with a wheelchair lift to lower on board. Loan wheelchairs are available, as are key-operated toilets. A virtual tour is available at www.hmsbelfasttours.org.uk. Assistance dogs for the deaf and sight impaired are welcome. Assistance dogs should not have any difficulty in accessing the areas listed above. However, the nature of the ship will make access to some of the areas below decks extremely difficult for a dog. All visitors are provided with a free handheld personal 'Acoustiguide'. There is an earpiece available, and prerecorded tours are offered in English (adult and family version), French, German and Spanish. Visitors unable to use the sound guide system can request a transcript.

Houses of Parliament

Parliament Square, SW1A 0AA (7219 4272 Commons information, 7219 3107 Lords information, www. parliament.uk). Westminster tube. **Open** *(when in session) House of Commons Visitors' Gallery* 2.30-10.30pm Mon, Tue; 11.30am-7.30pm Wed; 10.30am-6.30pm Thur; 9.30am-3pm Fri. *House of Lords Visitors' Gallery* 2.30-10.30pm Mon, Tue; 3-10pm Wed; 11am-7.30pm Thur; from 10am Fri. Tours summer recess only; see website for details. **Admission** Visitors' Gallery free. Tours £14; £6-£9 reductions; free under-5s.

After strict security checks at St Stephen's Gate (the only public access to Parliament),

visitors are welcome to observe the debates at the House of Lords and House of Commons. The experience is usually soporific, but an exception is Prime Minister's Questions at noon on Wednesday, when the incumbent PM fields a barrage of hostile questions from the opposition (and occasionally some of his own rebellious backbenchers) and soft questions from loyal backbenchers eager to present the government in a good light. Tickets must be arranged in advance through your embassy or MP, who can also arrange tours. The best time to visit Parliament is during the summer recess, when the main ceremonial rooms, including Westminster Hall and both Houses, are open to the public as part of an organised tour (book in advance online).

The first parliamentary session was held in St Stephen's Chapel in 1275, but Westminster only became the permanent seat of Parliament in 1532, when Henry VIII moved to a new des-res in Whitehall. Designed by Charles Barry, the Palace of Westminster is now a wonderful mishmash of styles, dominated by Gothic buttresses, towers and arches. It looks much older than it is: the Parliament buildings were created in 1860 to replace the original Houses of Parliament, destroyed by fire in 1834. The compound contains 1,000 rooms, 11 courtyards, eight bars and six restaurants, plus a small cafeteria for visitors. Of the original palace, only the Jewel Tower and the ancient Westminster Hall remain.

♿ 👤 ♿ 🛍 🦯 🚶

Notes *All tours are accessible by wheelchair users. Alternative routes and viewing points exist for visitors with large motorised wheelchairs. One stop (of 17) on the tour requires a slight detour before rejoining the main group. The public galleries of both Houses and committee rooms are fully wheelchair accessible or have space set aside for wheelchairs. Guide dogs can accompany owners on tours. They are also welcome* in the public galleries and committee rooms, but only two at a time within the galleries. If there is no space, visitors may leave their dog with the police. An interpreter (BSL signer) may accompany you on a tour. Parliament staff will arrange this through the charity Action on Hearing Loss (formerly the RNID, see p223) if given advance notice – but be aware there is heavy demand. Visitors to the public galleries and committee rooms must arrange their own interpreters and give advance notification of attendance: contact the Admission Order Officer on 7219 3700. The public galleries and committee rooms are fitted with induction loops. Within Parliament accessible toilets are located off the central lobby. Tours last around 75 minutes and there are no facilities at the starting point. Accessible public toilets also at nearby Westminster tube station.

London Dungeon

28-34 Tooley Street, SE1 2SZ (0871 423 2240, www.thedungeons.com). London Bridge tube/rail.
Open times vary; check website for details. **Admission** prices vary depending on visit date and time. On door prices: adult £23 £17-£21 reductions. Concessions available for disabled people.

Enter the atmospheric Victorian railway arches of London Bridge for this jokey and rather expensive celebration of torture, death and disease. Visitors are led through a dry-ice fog past gravestones and rotting corpses to experience nasty symptoms from the Great Plague exhibition: an actor-led medley of corpses, boils, projectile vomiting, worm-filled skulls and scuttling rats. The death-dealing exploits of Bloody Mary are explored alongside those of Sweeney Todd and, of course, Jack the Ripper. As a finishing touch, Extremis: Drop Ride to Doom re-enacts an execution – with you playing the part of the victim.

Notes No car park, and no car park for public use within 200m. No on-street Blue Badge bays or designated drop-off point. There is level access to the entrance on Tooley Street. The high reception desk is 20m from the main entrance and does not have level access. There is a turnstile, 50cm wide, to the right of the ticket desk leading to the start of the tour. Wheelchair users can use the corridor, to the left of the ticket desk, to access the tour. Motorised scooters are allowed in public parts (no re-charging facility). The floor for parts of the tour has a cobbled surface. The tour comprises several shows. There is space for wheelchair users to view all shows. Only two wheelchair users are able to take the tour at one time. A booklet is available from the ticket desk to guide visitors with hearing impairments. A shallow step leads out from the Great Fire of London area. Some areas of the tour are accessed by several steps, but have routes available to bypass the steps, accompanied by a member of staff. There are steps to the Boat Ride (middle of tour); visitors who cannot manage these steps are guided around and reunited with the group on the other side of the Boat Ride. There is ramped access to the ride, but visitors need to be able to transfer to the seats. Assistance dogs are not permitted to ride with visitors, and a member of the party must be with the dog at all times. The accessible toilet, with level access, is 42m from the main entrance. Staff receive disability awareness training. Information in large print on request.

London Eye

Riverside Buildings, County Hall, Westminster Bridge Road, SE1 7PB (0870 500 0600, disabled booking line 0871 222 0188, fax 0870 400 2006, www.londoneye.com). Westminster tube

London Eye.

or Waterloo tube/rail. **Open** daily *Sept-Mar* 10am-8.30pm. *Apr-June* 10am-9pm. *July& Aug* 10am-9.30pm.

At the hub of the South Bank's millennial makeover rolls the London Eye, here only since 2000 but already up there with Tower Bridge and the Houses of Parliament as the capital's most postcard-friendly asset. Assuming you choose a clear day, a 30min circuit affords great views of the city. Take a few snaps from the comfort of your pod and that's your sightseeing done. The London Eye was the vision of husband-and-wife architects Julia Barfield and David Marks, who entered a 1992 competition to design a structure auspicious enough to mark the millennium. The Barfield-Marks giant wheel idea came second in the contest; the winning entry is conspicuous by its absence. The Eye was planned as a temporary structure but its removal now seems unthinkable. Indeed, the wheel's popularity is such that owner Merlin Entertainments has seen fit to future-proof its investment with a three-year renovation for London 2012. Each of the wheel's 32 pods (one for every London borough) will be removed and upgraded by the summer of 2012.

Notes *There are three car parks on the South Bank, all with designated parking. Ticket hall and capsules wheelchair accessible. Disabled visitors pay discounted rate with one carer free of charge; proof of disability is not required. Assistance dogs welcome. Groups of less than four are fast-tracked to the front of the queue. T-Loops are available in the ticket office. Staff receive in-house disability awareness training. Wheelchairs available (refundable £350 deposit required). The facilities for the London Eye, including the ticket office and toilets (there is an accessible toilet situated next to the café), are located in County Hall, opposite the London Eye on the South Bank.*

Old Bailey
(Central Criminal Court)

Corner of Newgate Street & Old Bailey, EC4M 7EH (7248 3277). St Paul's tube. **Open** *Public gallery* 10am-1pm, 2-4.30pm Mon-Fri. **Admission** free. No under-14s; 14-16s only if accompanied by adults. **No credit cards**.

A gilded statue of blind (meaning impartial) justice stands atop London's most famous criminal court. The current building was completed in 1907; the site itself has hosted some of the most famous trials in British history, including that of Oscar Wilde. Anyone is welcome to attend a trial, but bags, cameras, dictaphones, mobile phones and food are banned, and no storage facilities are provided.

Notes *Wheelchair access is via main door or side door.*

St Martin-in-the-Fields

Trafalgar Square, WC2N 4JJ (7766 1122, fax 7389 0773 www.smitf.org). Leicester Square tube or Charing Cross tube/rail. **Open** 8am-7pm Mon-Wed; 8am-9pm Thur-Sat; 11.30am-6pm Sun. *Services* 8am, 1.15pm, 6pm Mon, Tue, Thur, Fri; 8am, 1.15pm, 5.30pm, 6pm Wed; 8am, 10am, 5pm, 6.30pm Sun. *Brass Rubbing Centre* 10am-6pm Mon-Wed; 10am-8pm Thur-Sat; 11am-5pm Sun. **Admission** free. Brass rubbing £4.50.

There's been a church 'in the fields' between Westminster and the City since the 13th century, but the current one was built in 1726 by James Gibbs, using a fusion of neoclassical and Baroque styles. The parish church for Buckingham Palace (note the royal box, situated to the left of the gallery), St Martin's benefited from a £36m Lottery-funded refurbishment, completed in 2008. The bright interior has been fully restored, with Victorian furbelows removed and the impressive addition of a brilliant altar window that shows the cross, stylised as if rippling on water. The crypt, its fine, atmospheric café and the London Brass Rubbing Centre have all been modernised.

♿ 👫 👪 ♿

Notes *The accessible entrance is by signed ramp on the north side. A lift is available between crypt and church and from the street to crypt level. The concert area is fully accessible.*

St Paul's Cathedral

Ludgate Hill, EC4M 8AD (7236 4128, www.stpauls.co.uk). St Paul's tube.
Open 8.30am-4pm Mon-Sat. *Galleries, crypt & ambulatory* 9.30am-4.15pm Mon-Sat. Special events may cause closure; check before visiting. *Tours of cathedral & crypt* 10.45am, 11.15am, 1.30pm, 2pm Mon-Sat. *Services* 7.30am, 8am, 12.30pm, 5pm Mon-Sat; 8am, 10.15am, 11.30am, 3.15pm, 6pm Sun.
Admission *Cathedral, crypt & gallery* £12.50; £4.50-£11.50 reductions; £29.50 family; free under-6s. *Tours* £3; £1-£2.50 reductions.

The first cathedral to St Paul was built on this site in 604, but fell to Viking marauders. Its Norman replacement, a magnificent Gothic structure with a 490ft spire (taller than any London building until the 1960s), burned in the Great Fire, although its spire had been destroyed by lightning more than 100 years earlier. The current church was commissioned in 1669 from Sir Christopher Wren as the centrepiece of London's rise from the ashes, and the first stone was laid six years later. Modern buildings now encroach on the cathedral from all sides, but the passing of three centuries has done nothing to diminish the appeal of Wren's design.

Start with the exterior. Over the last decade, a £40m restoration project has removed most of the Victorian grime from the walls and the extravagant main façade looks as brilliant today as it must have when the last stone was placed in 1708. On the south side of the cathedral, an austere park has been laid out, tracing the outline of the medieval chapter house whose remains lie 4ft beneath it.

The vast open spaces of the interior contain memorials to such national heroes as Wellington and TE Lawrence (of Arabia). The statue of John Donne, Metaphysical poet and former Dean of St Paul's, is often overlooked, but it's the only monument to have been saved from Old St Paul's. There are also more modern works, including a Henry Moore sculpture and temporary Arts Project displays of major modern art. The Whispering Gallery, inside the dome, is reached by 259 steps from the main hall; the acoustics here are so good that a whisper can be bounced clearly to the other side of the dome. Steps continue up to first the Stone Gallery (119 tighter, steeper steps), with its high external balustrades, then outside to the Golden Gallery (152 steps), with its giddying views. Come here to orient yourself before setting off in search of other monuments.

Before leaving, head down to the maze-like crypt (through a doorframe decorated with skull and crossbones), which contains a shop and café, and memorials to Alexander Fleming, William Blake and Admiral Lord Nelson, whose grand tomb (purloined from Wolsey by Henry VIII but never used by him) is beneath the centre of the dome. To one side is the small, plain tombstone of Christopher Wren himself, inscribed by his son with the epitaph, 'Reader, if you seek his monument, look around you'; at their request, Millais and Turner were buried near him.

As well as tours of the main cathedral and self-guided audio tours (£4, £3.50 reductions), you can join special tours of the Triforium, visiting the library and Wren's 'Great Model', at 11.30am and 2pm on Monday and Tuesday and at 2pm on Friday (pre-book on 7246 8357, £16 including admission).

♿ 👫 👪 ♿ 🚻 🐕

St Paul's Cathedral.

Notes *On-street Blue Badge parking is located by the coach park on the south side. There is a further designated bay on Paternoster Row, to the north of the Cathedral. The cathedral has two entrances at the west end which are accessed by 24 steps. The accessible south entrance is step-free; from here there is direct lift access to the cathedral floor and the crypt. Wheelchair users can access all part of the cathedral floor.* **The Quire and Sacrarium** *has a small chairlift that can be operated by the user. Wheelchair users can access all areas in the crypt including the shop, café and restaurant. There are a few wheelchairs to borrow. Access to the* **Whispering, Stone and Golden Galleries** *is via stair only; visitors with pre-existing medical conditions, mobility difficulties or concerns with heights and confined spaces should not attempt this climb. For people who have difficulty climbing the stairs to the dome,* **Oculus: An Eye into St Paul's** *(located in the crypt) has a virtual access 'fly-through' film of the dome. An audio guide is included with admission. (Touch Tour is available, book in advance on 7246 8357). Touch-screen multi-media BSL signed tour with subtitles is included in cost of admission. The cathedral is equipped with an induction loop system that covers the cathedral floor. This is used at all services. To arrange wheelchair access for services, call 7246 8320. The accessible toilet is 45m from the main lift within the standard toilets in the crypt. Assistance dogs welcome.*

Sea Life London Aquarium
County Hall, Riverside Building, Westminster Bridge Road, SE1 7PB (0871 663 1678, www.sealife.co.uk). Westminster tube or Waterloo tube/rail. **Open** 10am-6pm Mon-Thur, 10am-7pm Fri-Sun. **Admission** at door £19.02, children 3-15 £14.04 (free under 3s); £18 reductions; £60 family; free under-3s. Discounted tickets online, and after 3pm. Concession for disabled visitors.

This is one of Europe's largest aquariums and a huge hit with children. The inhabitants are grouped by geographical origin, beginning with the Atlantic, where blacktail bream swim alongside the Thames Embankment. The 'Rainforests of the World' exhibit has introduced poison arrow frogs, crocodiles and piranha. The Ray Lagoon is still popular, though touching the friendly flatfish is no longer allowed (it's bad for their health). Starfish, crabs and anenomes can be handled in special open rock pools instead, and the clown fish still draw crowds hoping to encounter the elusive Nemo. There's a mesmerising Seahorse Temple and a tank full of turtles. The centrepieces, though, are the two massive Pacific and Indian Ocean tanks, with menacing sharks quietly circling fallen Easter Island statues and dinosaur bones.

Notes *No parking available and no designated drop-off point. The aquarium is located on 3 levels, starting on level -2 and continuing on level -1 and on to the Shark Walk, before exiting on level 0. There is full disabled access with lifts to all levels. There are also accessible toilets available on every floor. Motorised scooters are allowed in public parts of the venue. Loan wheelchairs are available, on a first come first served basis, subject to availability, and require a deposit of £200 using a credit card. Wheelchairs cannot be pre-booked. The* **Sea Life Theatre** *has designated spaces for wheelchair users in the front row, which is 79m from the nearest accessible toilet. Assistance dogs are allowed in the auditorium. The theatre is on level -1, on the far side of the Thames Path exhibit. Staff receive disability awareness training and are Typetalk aware. Assistance dogs welcome.*

Shakespeare's Globe

21 New Globe Walk, SE1 9DT (7401 9919, www.shakespeares-globe.org). Southwark tube or London Bridge tube/rail. **Open** *Exhibition* 10am-5pm daily. *Globe Theatre tours Oct-Apr* 10am-5pm daily. *May-Sept* 9.30am-12.30pm Mon-Sat; 9.30-11.30am Sun. *Rose Theatre tours May-Sept* 1-5pm Mon-Sat; noon-5pm Sun. Tours every 30mins. **Admission** £10.50; £8.50 reductions; £6.50 children; £28 family.

The original Globe Theatre, where many of William Shakespeare's plays were first staged and which he co-owned, burned to the ground in 1613 during a performance of *Henry VIII*.

Nearly 400 years later, it was rebuilt not far from its original site, using construction methods and materials as close to the originals as possible, and is now open to the public for 90-minute tours throughout the year. During matinées, the tours go instead to the site of the Rose (21 New Globe Walk, SE1 9DT, 7261 9565, www.rosetheatre.org.uk), built by Philip Henslowe in 1587 as the first theatre on Bankside; red lights show the position of the original theatre. Funds are being sought to continue excavations and preserve the site.

Under the adventurous artistic directorship of Dominic Dromgoole, the Globe is also a fully operational theatre. From 23 April, conventionally regarded as the Bard's birthday, into early October, seasons of Shakespeare's plays and the odd new drama are performed.

大点大点 wc 点 点点 点 点 L 点 点

Notes *Car park at the side of the venue has two designated bays; parking is free for Blue Badge holders, but should be booked in advance. The cobbled route from the car park to the entrance is accessible to a wheelchair user with assistance. No designated drop-off point. Blue Badge holders can also park on New Globe Walk. The Shakespeare's*

Globe site includes an open-air theatre, exhibition space; Swan at the Globe Bar and Brasserie. Access to all areas is via lift from the main foyer on **New Globe Walk**. *A separate entrance to the Exhibition is accessed via a ramp on Bankside. A dedicated* **access information line** *operates from 10am-5pm, Monday to Friday: 7902 1409 (this is not a booking service). A printed* **access guide** *is also available. There are accessible toilets 6m from the main lift; on the piazza level, opposite the main foyer lift; on the mezzanine level 50m from the exhibition entrance. There is an induction loop in the* **Education Studios**. *Motorised scooters are allowed in public parts of the venue. Staff receive disability awareness training and are Typetalk aware. Documents can be requested in Braille and large print. Registered assistance dogs welcome. For more information, see p212.*

Somerset House & the Embankment Galleries

The Strand, WC2R 1LA (7845 4600, www.somersethouse.org.uk). Temple tube or Charing Cross tube/rail. **Open** 10am-6pm (last entry 5.15pm) daily. *Tours* phone for details. **Admission** *Courtyard & terrace* free. *Embankment Galleries* £6; reductions £5; under 12s free. website for details. *Tours* phone for details.

The original Somerset House was a Tudor palace commissioned by the Duke of Somerset. In 1775, it was demolished to make way for a new building, effectively the first purpose-built office block in the world. The architect Sir William Chambers spent the last 20 years of his life working on the neoclassical edifice overlooking the Thames, built to accommodate learned societies such as the Royal Academy. Various governmental offices also took up residence.

The taxmen are still here, but the rest of the building is open to the public.

Attractions include a formidable art gallery (the wonderful Courtauld, *see p95*), the handsome fountain court, and a terraced café and a classy restaurant, both taken over in 2010 by Tom Aikens. The Embankment Galleries explore connections between art, architecture and design in temporary exhibitions, and at Christmas usually host an adventurous market; downstairs, a ceremonial Thames barge and information boards explain the place's history.

In summer, overheated children never tire of running through the choreographed fountains; in winter, an ice-skating rink is erected on top of them.

Notes *Parking is available at Somerset House for Blue Badge holders. To check availability and book, call 7845 4600. Somerset House is accessible to wheelchair users. A limited number of wheelchairs are available to borrow. Assistance dogs welcome.*

Southwark Cathedral

London Bridge, SE1 9DA (7367 6700, www.southwark.anglican.org). London Bridge tube/rail. **Open** 9am-5pm daily (closing times vary on religious holidays). *Services* 8am, 8.15am, 12.30pm, 12.45pm, 5.30pm Mon-Fri; 9am, 9.15am, 4pm Sat; 8.45am, 9am, 11am, 3pm, 6.30pm Sun. *Choral Evensong* 5.30pm Mon, Thur (girls); 5.30pm Tue (boys & men); Fri (men only). **Admission** free; suggested donation £4.

The oldest bits of this building date back more than 800 years. The retro-choir was the setting for several Protestant martyr trials during the reign of Mary Tudor. The courtyard is one of the area's prettiest places for a rest, especially during the summer. Inside, there are memorials to Shakespeare, John Harvard (benefactor of the American university) and Sam Wanamaker (the force behind the recon-

struction of the Globe); Chaucer features in the stained glass. The Millennium Buildings, including a refectory, engage visitors with the building's history. The cathedral offers welcome respite from the crowds attracted by the fresh produce on sale at the neighbouring Borough Market.

Notes *There is a bus stop within 150m. The Cathedral does not have its own car park and there are no on-street Blue Badge bays. There is no designated drop off point. The stretch of Montague Close between the cathedral and London Bridge is owned by the cathedral, so parking can be reserved here if requested in advance. There are ramp/slope options for access to the Main, Cathedral and Refectory entrances. Inside there is no level access to the service. Induction loops are fitted in the cathedral and all of the conference rooms; staff are trained to use the hearing assistance system. Motorised scooters are allowed in public parts of the venue (no re-charging facility). There is a platform lift to access a small level-change 20m from the Cathedral entrance. Seating in the cathedral can be moved, so wheelchair users can sit anywhere for services. There is a standard lift for public use located 17m from the main entrance. In the restaurant there is ample room for a wheelchair user to manoeuvre. The refectory can also be accessed internally, from Lancelot's Link. Accessible toilets are available in the basement and at the top of Lancelot's Link, next to the entrance off Cathedral Street where access is by lift. Staff receive disability awareness training. Assistance dogs welcome. A raised or tactile plan of the building is available on request. Wheelchairs are available for visitors to borrow. A handheld audio tour of the cathedral is available from the cathedral shop for a small fee.*

Tower Bridge Exhibition

*Tower Bridge, SE1 2UP (7403 3761, fax
7357 7935, www.towerbridge.org.uk).
Tower Hill tube or Tower Gateway
DLR.* **Open** *Apr-Sept* 10am-6.30pm
daily. *Oct-Mar* 9.30am-6pm daily.
Admission £7; £3-£5 reductions; £11
family; free under-5s.

Opened in 1894, this is the 'London Bridge'
that wasn't sold to America. Originally
powered by steam, the drawbridge is now
opened by electric rams when big ships
need to venture upstream (check when the
bridge is next due to be raised on its website and Twitter feed). An entertaining
exhibition on the history of the bridge is
displayed in the old steamrooms and the
west walkway, which provides a superb
crow's-nest view along the Thames.

The main entrance of the Tower Bridge
Exhibition is located at the North West
Tower of the bridge; allowing entrance
into the bridge's secret underbelly. On
exiting the bridge, follow the painted blue
line on the floor which leads you directly
to the glorious Victorian engine rooms and
the second part of the tour, located on the
south side of the bridge at river level on
Shad Thames.

♿ 🧑‍🦽 ♿ 🧑‍🦼 ♿ 🚻 🚌 🧳 🦮

Notes *There is no car park for public
use within 200m, nor is there a
designated drop-off point. Access is by
ramp/slope to a single width door
138cm wide; the door will be opened by
a member of staff. There is a lift for
public use (North Tower) which is
situated just inside the main entrance.
The lift is always operated by an
attendant, and is the only way for
visitors to access level 4 from the main
entrance. There is level access to the
reception from the entrance. There is
also a lift in the South Tower. Motorised
scooters are allowed in public parts of the
venue (no re-charging facility). The
museum has an induction loop which
staff are trained to use. There is a*

*wheelchair available, ask at the ticket
office. Rolling videos describe the history
of the bridge. These videos have subtitles,
scripts are available from the ticket office
on request. Tour guides are available on
both walkways to answer questions and
offer assistance. The accessible toilet is
5m from the South Tower Lift and
located on level 2. Access to the Engine
Rooms is via ramps/slopes. The
accessible toilet is 10m from the Engine
Rooms entrance. Staff receive disability
awareness training. Assistance dogs
welcome.*

Tower of London

*Tower Hill, EC3N 4AB (0844 482
7777, fax 3166 6310 www.hrp.org.uk).
Tower Hill tube or Tower Gateway
DLR.* **Open** *Mar-Oct* 10am-5.30pm
Mon, Sun; 9am-5.30pm Tue-Sat. *Nov-
Feb* 10am-4.30pm Mon, Sun; 9am-
4.30pm Tue-Sat. **Admission** £17;
£9.50-£14.50 reductions; £47 family;
free under-5s.

If you haven't been to the Tower of
London, go now. Despite the exhausting
crowds and long climbs up inaccessible
stairways, this is one of the finest historical attractions in the whole of the British
Isles. The impressive buildings of the
Tower span over 900 years of history and
the bastions and battlements house a
series of interactive displays on the lives
of British monarchs, and the often excru-
ciatingly painful deaths of traitors.
There's easily enough to do here to fill a
whole day, and it's well worth joining one
of the entertaining free tours led by the
Yeoman Warders (or Beefeaters).

Make the Crown Jewels your first stop,
and as early in the day as you can: if you
wait until you've pottered around a few
other things, the queues are immense.
Beyond satisfyingly solid vault doors, you
get to glide along a set of travelators past
such treasures of state as the Monarch's
Sceptre, mounted with the Cullinan I diamond, and the Imperial State Crown,

which is worn by the Queen each year for the opening of Parliament.

The other big draw is the Royal Armoury in the central White Tower, with its swords, poleaxes, halberds, morning stars (spiky maces) and other gruesome tools for separating human beings from their body parts. For children, there are swordsmanship games, coin-minting and even a child-sized long bow. The garderobes (medieval toilets) also seem to appeal.

Back outside, Tower Green – where executions of prisoners of noble birth were carried out until 1941 – is marked by a poem and a stiff glass pillow, sculpted by poet and artist Brian Catling. Overlooking the green, Beauchamp Tower, dating to 1280, has an upper floor full of intriguing graffiti by the prison inmates (including Anne Boleyn, Rudolf Hess and the Krays).

Towards the entrance, the 13th-century Bloody Tower is another must-see that is always swamped later in the day. The ground floor is a reconstruction of Sir Walter Raleigh's study, the upper floor details the fate of the Princes in the Tower. In the riverside wall is the unexpectedly beautiful Medieval Palace, with its reconstructed bedroom and throne room, and spectacularly complex stained glass in the private chapel. The whole palace is deliciously cool if you've been struggling round on a hot summer's day.

♠♿🚻★🐾♫ L ⠿ 🐕

Notes *There is a car park for public use within 200m, behind the Welcome Centre, across Tower Hill. The car park has several designated bays, lift access and accessible toilets. No on-street Blue Badge bays or designated drop-off point. As with many historic buildings, access for wheelchair users is difficult owing to small passageways, stairs and cobbled walkways. The* **Jewel House** *is accessible. The access leaflet and more detailed access guide use a traffic-light rating system to help visitors get around, while the popular Yeoman Warder*

guided tour offers an alternative route for people unable to climb steps. British Sign Language (BSL) guided tours are available. Yeoman Warders on guided tours carry portable induction loops. Assisted descriptive tours of the Jewel House and **White Tower** *for blind and visually impaired visitors use raised 2D image cards. The* **Welcome Centre** *has magnifying sheets. Audio guides are available for blind and visually impaired visitors for an additional fee. White Tower information is provided in Braille and tactile format. The 'Hands on History' display is on the top floor, and there is a 'handling point' in the basement, which has a lift. There are tactiles in the* **Lower Salt Tower** *and the* **Wall Walk**. *The new* **Armouries Café** *has ample room for a wheelchair user to manoeuvre. The accessible toilet is 272m from the main entrance located in the toilet area, behind Jewel House. There is a moderate slope to the toilet.*

Westminster Abbey

20 Dean's Yard, SW1P 3PA (7222 5152 information, 7654 4900 tours, fax 7233 2072, www.westminster-abbey.org). St James's Park or Westminster tube. **Open** 9.30am-4.30pm Mon, Tue, Thur, Fri; 9.30am-7pm Wed; 9.30am-2.30pm Sat. *Abbey Museum, Chapter House & College Gardens 10am-4pm daily. Tours phone for details.* **Admission** £16; £13 reductions (carer free); free under-11s with adult; £32-£38 family. *Abbey Museum free. Tours £3.*

The cultural significance of Westminster Abbey is hard to overstate, but also hard to remember as you're shepherded around, forced to elbow fellow tourists out of the way to read a plaque or see a tomb – get here as early as you can. Edward the Confessor commissioned a church to St Peter on the site of a seventh-century version, but it was only consecrated on 28 December 1065, eight days before he died.

Westminster Abbey.

William the Conqueror subsequently had himself crowned here on Christmas Day 1066 and, with just two exceptions, every English coronation since has taken place in the abbey.

Many royal, military and cultural notables are interred here. The most haunting memorial is the Tomb of the Unknown Warrior, in the nave, the only tombstone on which it is forbidden to walk. Elaborate resting places in side chapels are taken up by the tombs of Elizabeth I and Mary Queen of Scots. In Innocents Corner lie the remains of two lads believed to be Edward V and his brother Richard (their bodies were found at the Tower of London), as well as two of James I's children. Poets' Corner is the final resting place of Chaucer, the first to be buried here. Few of the other writers who have stones here are buried in the abbey, but the remains of Dryden, Johnson, Browning and Tennyson are all present. Henry James, TS Eliot and Dylan Thomas have dedications – on the floor, fittingly for Thomas.

In the vaulted area under the former monks' dormitory, one of the abbey's oldest parts, the Abbey Museum celebrated its centenary in 2008. You'll find effigies and waxworks of British monarchs, among them Edward II and Henry VII, wearing the robes they sported in life. The 900-year-old College Garden is one of the oldest cultivated gardens in Britain and a useful place to escape the crowds.

An ongoing refurbishment revealed the restored Cosmati Pavement to the public in spring 2010, but the abbey has ambitious plans to create more visitor facilities and a new gallery – the new refectory should be feeding hungry visitors from late 2011.

Notes *Abingdon Car Park, Great College Street is approx 200m to the south of the Abbey. No on-street Blue Badge bays. The area outside the Great West Door off Broad Sanctuary is used* *as a drop-off point for coaches and minibuses and can be used as a drop-off point for Blue Badge holders if requested in advance. Accessible entry is via Great North Door ramp. Marshals are available at this, and all entrances, to offer assistance to visitors. Once inside not all the Abbey is accessible and most of the floors are uneven. Motorised scooters allowed in public parts. An induction loop covers all of the main building and is used at all services. In the museum, exhibits can be audio described. Tactile and Braille signage is available, as are Touch Tours. A loan wheelchair is available. There are also Braille and large print versions of the welcome leaflet available from the Information Desk. The accessible toilet is 100m from the Great North Door just past Poets' Corner. The Coffee Club kiosk is located in the North Cloister and has ample room for wheelchair users to manoeuvre.*

Westminster Cathedral

42 Francis Street, SW1P 1QW (7798 9055, www.westminstercathedral.org.uk). Victoria tube/rail. **Open** *7am-6pm Mon-Fri; 8am-6.30pm Sat; 8am-7pm Sun. Exhibition 10am-5pm Mon-Fri; 10am-6pm Sat, Sun. Bell tower 9.30am-4.30pm daily. Services 7am, 8am, 10.30am, 12.30pm, 1.05pm, 5.30pm Mon-Fri; 8am, 9am, 10.30am, 12.30pm, 6pm Sat; 8am, 9am, 10.30am, noon, 5.30pm, 7pm Sun.* **Admission** *free. Exhibition £5; free-£2.50 reductions; £11 family. Bell tower & exhibition £8; free-£4 reductions; £17.50 family.*

With its domes, arches and soaring tower, the most important Roman Catholic church in England looks surprisingly Byzantine. There's a reason: architect John Francis Bentley, who built it between 1895 and 1903, was heavily influenced by the Hagia Sophia in Istanbul. Compared to the candy-cane exterior, the interior is surprisingly restrained (in fact, it's unfinished), but there are still some impressive marble columns and mosaics. Eric Gill's sculptures of the Stations of the Cross (1914-18) were dismissed as 'Babylonian' when they were first installed, but worshippers have come to love them. A permanent exhibition, 'Treasures of the Cathedral', opened in the upper gallery in 2010 to celebrate the centenary of the cathedral's consecration. It displays an impressive Arts & Crafts coronet, a Tudor chalice, holy relics and Bentley's amazing architectural model of his cathedral, complete with tiny hawks. A lift runs to the top of the 273ft bell tower.

Notes *No nearby parking. The accessible entrance is from the piazza. Side chapels are two steps up. The gift shop is down three very steep steps. The refectory is up two steep steps then down 19 steep steps. British Sign Language Mass first Sunday each month, 4.30pm. There is an accessible toilet in the Clergy House close to the accessible entrance.*

Winston Churchill's Britain at War Experience

64-66 Tooley Street, SE1 2TF (7403 3171, fax 7403 5104, www.britainatwar.co.uk). London Bridge tube/rail. **Open** *Apr-Oct* 10am-5pm daily. *Nov-Mar* 10am-4.30pm daily **Admission** £12.95; reductions £6.50; child (5-15) £5.50; under 5s free; £29 family.

This old-fashioned exhibition recalls the privations endured by the British during World War II. Visitors descend from street level in an ancient lift to a reconstructed tube station shelter. The experience continues with displays about London during the Blitz, including bombs, rare documents, photos and reconstructed shopfronts. The displays on rationing, food production and Land Girls are fascinating, and the set-piece walk-through bombsite is quite disturbing.

Notes *Coaches/cars can drop off and pick up outside the exhibition. There is an NCP car park close by. Level access at the entrance and disabled access to most areas. There is an accessible toilet. Contact the museum in advance for full information. Assistance dogs welcome.*

Museums & galleries

Bank of England Museum

Entrance on Bartholomew Lane, EC2R 8AH (7601 5545, www.bankofengland.co.uk/museum). Bank tube/DLR. **Open** 10am-5pm Mon-Fri. **Admission** free.

Housed inside the former Stock Offices of the Bank of England, this engaging and surprisingly lively museum explores the history of the national bank. As well as ancient coins and original artwork for British banknotes, the museum offers a rare chance to lift nearly 30lbs (13.5kg) of gold bar (you reach into a secure box, closely monitored by CCTV). One exhibit looks at the life of Kenneth Grahame, author of *The Wind in the Willows* and a long-term employee of the bank. Interactive videos add a touch of modernity. Child-friendly temporary exhibitions take place in the museum lobby.

Notes *The museum welcomes disabled visitors and tries to overcome the limitations of an historic building that lacks easy access for people with disabilities. Portable ramps give wheelchair users access to all areas of the museum, including the toilet for disabled visitors. Phone in advance so that ramps can be prepared. There are induction loops in the cinema. The main interactive video display has optional subtitles. Coaches and cars can stop briefly to set down and pick up outside the entrance to the museum.*

British Museum.

Bankside Gallery

48 Hopton Street, SE1 9JH (7928 7521, www.banksidegallery.com). Southwark or London Bridge tube/rail. **Open** 11am-6pm daily (closes between exhibitions). **Admission** free; donations appreciated.

In the shadow of Tate Modern, this tiny gallery is the home of the Royal Watercolour Society and the Royal Society of Painter-Printmakers. The gallery runs a frequently changing programme of delightful print and watercolour exhibitions throughout the year; many of the works on show are for sale. Both societies hold frequent events here, including talks and demonstrations.

Notes *Two parking bays on street. Ramp at main entrance and inside to allow wheelchair access to most areas of the gallery.*

Barbican Art Gallery

Barbican Centre, Silk Street, EC2Y 8DS (7638 8891, www.barbican.org.uk). Barbican tube or Moorgate tube/rail. **Open** 11am-8pm daily, 11am-6pm Tue, Wed, 11am-10pm Thur. **Admission** £10 (£8 online); concessions £8 (£7 online).

The art gallery at the Barbican Centre on the third floor isn't quite as 'out there' as it would like you to think, but the exhibitions on design, architecture and pop culture are usually pretty diverting, as are their often attention-grabbing titles. The conservatory on level 3 (open Sun and bank hols noon-4pm) is London's second largest and a little-known gem.

Notes *There is a car park and Blue Badge holders can obtain a voucher allowing free parking by presenting their Blue Badge at the box office/ticket desk. There are also wider accessible bays in car parks 3 and 5. These spaces*

can be booked by calling the box office on 0845 120 7500. The main entrance in Silk Street is ramped and lifts give access to all levels. All venues in the centre (two art galleries, two theatres, concert hall, restaurant and bars) have seating for wheelchair users: notify access requirements when booking. There are three wheelchairs for visitors' use, subject to availability. These can be reserved by calling the box office on 7638 8891. The conservatory has limited access for unassisted wheelchair users. Accessible toilets are on levels -2, -1, G, 1, 2, 3 & 4.

British Museum

Great Russell Street, WC1B 3DG (7323 8299, www.britishmuseum.org). Russell Square or Tottenham Court Road tube. **Open** *Galleries* 10am-5.30pm Mon-Wed, Sat, Sun; 10am-8.30pm Thur,Fri. *Great Court* 9am-6pm Mon-Wed, Sun; 9am-11pm Thur-Sat. *Multimedia guides* 10am-4.30pm Mon-Wed, Sat, Sun; 10am-7.30pm Thur, Fri. *Eye Opener tours (40mins)* phone for details. **Admission** free; donations welcome. *Temporary exhibitions* prices vary. *Multimedia guides* £4.50; £3-£4 reductions. *Eye Opener tours* free.

Officially the country's most popular tourist attraction, the British Museum opened to the public in 1759 in Montagu House, which then occupied this site. The current building is a neoclassical marvel built in 1847 by Robert Smirke, one of the pioneers of the Greek Revival style. The most high profile addition since was Norman Foster's popular if rather murky glass-roofed Great Court, open since 2000 and now claimed to be 'the largest covered public square in Europe'.

This £100m landmark surrounds the domed Reading Room (used by the British Library until its move to King's Cross), where Marx, Lenin, Dickens, Darwin, Hardy and Yeats once worked.

Star exhibits include ancient Egyptian artefacts – the Rosetta Stone on the ground floor (with a barely noticed, perfect replica in the King's Library), mummies upstairs – and Greek antiquities, including the marble friezes from the Parthenon known as the Elgin Marbles. The Celts gallery upstairs has Lindow Man, killed in 300BC and so well preserved in peat you can see his beard, while the Wellcome Gallery of Ethnography holds an Easter Island statue and regalia from Captain Cook's travels. The King's Library provides a calming home to a permanent exhibition entitled 'Enlightenment: Discovering the World in the 18th Century', a 5,000-piece collection devoted to the extraordinary formative period of the museum. The remit covers archaeology, science and the natural world; the objects displayed range from Indonesian puppets to a beautiful orrery.

You won't be able to see everything in one day, so buy a souvenir guide and pick out the show-stoppers, or plan several visits. Highlights tours focus on specific aspects of the huge collection; Eye Opener tours offer specific introductions to world cultures. There are also regular blockbuster exhibitions, for which it may be necessary to book. A planned extension is aimed in part to provide more spacious accommodation for such shows.

🧍‍♂️♿🧍‍♀️⚙️🚾♥️🎧👁️♿🔤 🐕‍🦺

Notes *There is no designated drop-off point, but there is a convenient spot outside the Montague Place entrance. There is a car park in the front forecourt, off Great Russell Street. Designated parking bays must be booked in advance. Parking is free for Blue Badge holders. The route from the car park to the entrance is accessible to a wheelchair user with assistance owing to slopes/ramps. There is a platform lift either side of the entrance steps and level access to reception from the entrance. Induction loop. Staff receive disability awareness training and are Typetalk aware. The accessible toilets are 50m from the Great Russell Street entrance situated either side of the Reading Room. Motorised scooters are allowed in public parts of the venue. Customers cannot charge scooters or electric wheelchairs. There are lifts at Great Russell Street and Montague Place entrances to access various floors while lift access to level 2 is via the North West lift from level 1. The* **BP Lecture Theatre** *has designated spaces for wheelchair users located in the back row. There is an induction loop. Assistance dogs are allowed in the auditorium. The accessible toilets are 25m from the South Lift situated either side of the Theatre.* **Restaurant** *has level access inside. No tables or chairs are permanently fixed. Menus available in Braille and large print. Blind and deaf visitors can use the museum's multimedia guide (audio description and signed videos) free of charge. A member of staff trained in BSL skills is usually on duty. Wheelchairs are available to borrow by the Great Russell Street and Montague Place entrances.*

Charles Dickens Museum
48 Doughty Street, WC1N 2LX (7405 2127, www.dickensmuseum.com). Chancery Lane, Holborn or Russell Square tube. **Open** 10am-5pm daily. *Tours* by arrangement.
Admission £7; £5 reductions; children £3, under-10s free.
London is scattered with plaques marking addresses where Dickens lived, but this is the only surviving building. He lived here from 1837 to 1840, writing *Nicholas Nickleby* and *Oliver Twist* while in residence. Ring the doorbell to gain access to four floors of Dickensiana, collected over the years from various former residences. Some rooms are arranged as they might have been when he lived here; others deal with different aspects of his life, from struggling hack to famous performer.

Notes *Work is taking place to improve access to the museum and its collection in time for the 2012 bicentenary of Dickens' birth. A wheelchair ramp is being fitted for better access. New projects involve a customer-care kit and an audio tour for visitors with impaired vision. There are weekly Handling Sessions during which visitors may write with Dickens' own quill pen, handle material and ask questions. Phone for details.*

Courtauld Gallery

The Strand, WC2R 1LA (7848 2526, www.courtauld.ac.uk/gallery). Temple tube or Charing Cross tube/rail. **Open** 10am-6pm daily. *Tours* phone for details. **Admission** £6; £4.50 reductions (carer free). Free Mon 10am-2pm except public holidays. Free students & under-18s daily.

Located for the last two decades in the north wing of Somerset House (*see p85*), the Courtauld has one of Britain's greatest collections of paintings, and contains several works of global importance. Although there are some outstanding early works (Cranach's wonderful *Adam & Eve*, for one), the collection's strongest suit is in Impressionist and Post-Impressionist paintings. Popular masterpieces include Manet's astonishing *A Bar at the Folies-Bergère*, alongside plenty of superb Monets and Cézannes, important Gauguins (such as *Nevermore*), and some Van Goghs and Seurats. On the top floor, there's a selection of gorgeous Fauvist works, a lovely room of Kandinskys and plenty more besides.

Hidden downstairs, the sweet little gallery café is frequently forgotten, but it feels delightfully separate from the rest of Somerset House. Make a free Monday morning visit to the art collection and finish with a relaxed lunch. Note that bulky backpacks must be carried, not worn, through the collection; there are a few coin-operated lockers downstairs.

Notes *There is one designated parking space on site which should be booked in advance on 7845 4671. The nearest NCPs are at Drury Lane and the South Bank Centre. There is level access to most parts of the Gallery with a lift to all floors, the café and toilet and locker facilities. Assisted ramp access is available to room 1.*

Design Museum

Shad Thames, SE1 2YD (7403 6933, www.designmuseum.org). Tower Hill tube or London Bridge tube/rail. **Open** 10am-5.45pm daily. **Admission** with charitable donation included £11 (£10 without); £10 (£9 without) reductions; £7 (£6 without) students; free under-12s.

Exhibitions in this white 1930s building, formerly a banana warehouse, focus on modern and contemporary design. The temporary shows run from major installations to prize-winning design artefacts, from architects' travel photographs to retrospectives of key modernist theorists of the built environment. The Blueprint Café has a balcony overlooking the Thames, and designer books and items relating to the current show are on sale in the museum shop.

Notes *No car park within 200m. Free on-street marked Blue Badge bays are available on Shad Thames, next to the entrance. No designated drop-off point. No level access to the front entrance of the museum, but there is a moderate ramp/slope with a level landing at the top. Level access to reception from the entrance. There is an induction loop, which staff are trained to use. Level access inside and motorised scooters are allowed in public parts of the venue. Access to other floors is by lift located 25m from the main entrance. The lift* has Braille and tactile markings. A loan wheelchair is available at the admissions desk. Some of the videos shown in the museum have subtitles. The café, once inside, has level access and there is ample room for wheelchair users to manoeuvre. Clearly written menus are available on the wall. The accessible toilet is 12m from the main entrance and located within the ground floor male and female standard toilets. Level access to the accessible toilet. Staff receive disability awareness training and a member of staff is trained to British Sign Language (BSL) Level 1. Information is available in large print. Assistance dogs welcome.

Florence Nightingale Museum

St Thomas' Hospital, 2 Lambeth Palace Road, SE1 7EW (7620 0374, www.florence-nightingale.co.uk). Westminster tube or Waterloo tube/rail. Buses include 12, 53, 77, 148, 159, C10 & RV1. The museum is situated in the ground of St Thomas' Hospital, at parking level. **Open** 10am-5pm daily. **Admission** £5.80; £4.80 reductions; £16 family.

The nursing skills and campaigning zeal that made Florence Nightingale a Victorian legend are honoured here. Reopened after refurbishment for the centenary of her death in 2010, the museum is a chronological tour through a remarkable life under three key themes: family life, the Crimean War, health reformer. Among the period mementoes – clothing, furniture, books, letters and portraits – are Nightingale's lantern and stuffed pet owl, Athena.

Notes *Public parking available at St Thomas' Hospital. The museum is located in the Congestion Charging Zone and there is a machine in the car park where you can pay the zone fee. The museum is fully accessible for wheelchair users and has an accessible*

toilet. There is an induction loop hearing assistance system.

Foundling Museum

40 Brunswick Square, WC1N 1AZ (7841 3600, http://bit.ly/3JgMY). Russell Square tube. **Open** 10am-5pm Tue-Sat; 11am-5pm Sun. **Admission** £7.50; £5 reductions; free under-16s.

The Foundling Museum recalls the social history of the Foundling Hospital, set up in 1739 by shipwright and sailor Thomas Coram. On his return to England from America in 1720, Coram was appalled by the number of abandoned children he saw. Securing royal patronage, he persuaded Hogarth and Handel to become governors; it was Hogarth who made the building Britain's first public art gallery; works by artists as notable as Gainsborough and Reynolds are on display. The most heartrending display is a tiny case of mementos that were all mothers could leave the children they abandoned here.

Notes *Ramp into museum, lift to all floors. Accessible toilet facilities.*

Garden Museum

Lambeth Palace Road, SE1 7LB (7401 8865, fax 7401 8869, www.gardenmuseum.org.uk). Lambeth North tube or Waterloo tube/rail. **Open** 10.30am-5pm Mon-Fri; 10.30am-4pm Sat. **Admission** £6; £5 reductions; free under-16s, full-time students and carers of visitors with access needs.

The world's first horticulture museum (formerly the Museum of Garden History) fits neatly into the old church of St Mary's. A 'belvedere' gallery (built from eco-friendly Eurban wood sheeting) contains the permanent collection of artworks, antique gardening tools and horticultural memorabilia, while the ground floor is used for temporary exhibitions. In the small back garden, the replica of a 17th-century knot garden was created in hon-

Garden Museum.

Handel House Museum.

our of John Tradescant (who is buried here), the intrepid plant hunter and gardener to Charles I. A stone sarcophagus contains the remains of William Bligh, the captain of the mutinous HMS Bounty. A charming café and shop.

♿ 🚶 ♿ 🚻 🅿️⭐⭐ 🐕

Notes *Paid car parks at Novotel Hotel and Black Prince Road. Blue Badge holders are allowed unlimited free parking in designated parking bays and up to three hours free parking on single and double yellow lines as long as the car is not causing an obstruction. The museum, gardens, café and shop are fully accessible for wheelchair users, with ramps to all parts and a lift to the collection on the mezzanine floor. The accessible toilet is situated on the ground floor. Assistance dogs welcome.*

Guards Museum

Wellington Barracks, Birdcage Walk, SW1E 6HQ (7414 3428, www.theguardsmuseum.com). St James's Park tube. **Open** 10am-4pm daily. **Admission** £4; £1-£2 reductions; free under-16s.

Just down the road from Horse Guards, this small museum tells the 350-year story of the Foot Guards, using flamboyant uniforms, period paintings, medals and intriguing memorabilia, such as the stuffed body of Jacob the Goose, the Guards' Victorian mascot, who was regrettably run over by a van in barracks. Appropriately, the shop is well stocked with toy soldiers of the British regiments.

♿ 🚶 ♿ 🚻 🏃 🐕

Notes *No nearby parking. There are 15+ steps to the entrance but step-free access is by a ramp/slope. There is a lift adjacent to the courtyard for public use. It gives access to the museum from the Wellington Barracks courtyard. There is level access from the entrance to the reception area. Inside there is level*

access and a fixed induction loop, which staff are trained to use. The accessible toilet is 30m from the accessible entrance located at the rear of the museum. Assistance dogs welcome.

Handel House Museum

25 Brook Street (entrance in Lancashire Court), W1K 4HB (7495 1685, www.handelhouse.org). Bond Street tube. **Open** 10am-6pm Tue, Wed, Fri, Sat; 10am-8pm Thur; noon-6pm Sun. **Admission** £6; £2-£5 reductions, carer free; free under-5s.

The composer George Frideric Handel moved to Britain from his native Germany aged 25 and settled in this house 12 years later, remaining here until his death in 1759. The house has been restored with original and recreated furnishings, paintings and a welter of the composer's scores (in the same room as photos of Jimi Hendrix, who lived in the attic, now the museum office). The programme of events includes Thursday recitals.

🚶♿ 🚶 ♿ 🚻 🅿️⭐⭐ 🐕 🐕

Notes *Accessible parking on Brook's Mews and wheelchair access to the museum from there. There is a slope to the entrance, the double-width doors pull open. The most accessible route to the entrance is from Brook's Mews on to Avery Court into Lancashire Court. Lift and accessible toilet adjacent to reception. One wheelchair may be borrowed, phone in advance. Workshops with audio description.*

Hayward Gallery

Southbank Centre, Belvedere Road, SE1 8XX (7960 4200, www.southbankcentre.co.uk). Embankment tube or Waterloo tube/rail. **Open** 10am-6pm Mon-Thur, Sat, Sun; 10am-10pm Fri. **Admission** varies, see website for details.

This versatile gallery continues its excellent programme of exhibitions, loaned from around the world. It's carved out a particular niche for itself with participatory installations – Antony Gormley's fog-filled chamber for 'Blind Light', the rooftop rowing boat for group show 'Psycho Buildings' and, in summer 2010, Ernesto Neto's swimming pool – but there's plenty of variety offered. Visitors can hang out in the industrial-look café downstairs (it's a bar at night), aptly called Concrete, before visiting free contemporary exhibitions at the inspired Hayward Project Space; take the stairs to the first floor from the glass foyer extension.

Notes *Wheelchair users and disabled visitors who require a carer may bring a companion free of charge. Unstepped access is via lift from the Southbank Centre Car Park – Hayward Gallery. Blue Badge holders receive a free voucher to use at Southbank Centre Car Park on production of a paid event ticket in the Hayward Gallery foyer. Access to both levels is by ramp or lift. For a walk along the South Bank, see p208.*

Household Cavalry Museum
Horse Guards, Whitehall, SW1A 2AX (7930 3070, http://bit.ly/GMjwv). Westminster tube or Charing Cross tube/rail. **Open** *Mar-Sept* 10am-6pm daily. *Oct-Feb* 10am-5pm daily. **Admission** £6; £4 reductions; £15 family ticket; free under-5s.
Household Cavalry is a workaday name for the military peacocks who make up the Queen's official guard. They tell their stories through video diaries at this small but entertaining museum, which also displays medals, uniforms and shiny cuirasses (breastplates). You'll also get a peek – and whiff – of the horses that parade just outside every day: the stables are separated from the museum by a glass screen.

Notes *The museum is accessible to all visitors. Call for specific information.*

Hunterian Museum
Royal College of Surgeons, 35-43 Lincoln's Inn Fields, WC2A 3PE (7869 6560, www.rcseng.ac.uk/museums). Holborn tube. **Open** 10am-5pm Tue-Sat. **Admission** free. **No credit cards**.
The collection of medical specimens once held by John Hunter (1728-93), physician to King George III, can be viewed in this museum. The sparkling glass cabinets of the main room offset the goriness or downright oddness of the selection of exhibits, which include Charles Babbage's brain and Winston Churchill's dentures, as well as shelf after shelf of diligently classified pickled body parts. The upper floor holds a brutal account of old-fashioned surgical techniques. Children's activities include occasional demonstrations by a 'barber surgeon'. Bookings for these should be made by phone.

Notes *Wheelchair access is at Nuffield entrance via lift. The College is happy to provide visitors with special access requirements with a 'buddy' to accompany them.*

ICA
(Institute of Contemporary Arts)
The Mall, SW1Y 5AH (7930 0493 information, 7930 3647 tickets, www.ica.org.uk). Piccadilly Circus tube or Charing Cross tube/rail. **Open** *Galleries (during exhibitions)* noon-7pm Wed, Fri-Sun; noon-9pm Thur. **Admission** Varies with event. Visitors with access needs are entitled to concessionary rates for most ICA events. Free tickets for companions. Founded in 1947 by a collective of poets, artists and critics, the ICA has recently found itself somewhat adrift. The institute moved to the Mall in 1968 and set itself up as a venue for arthouse cinema, perform-

ance art, philosophical debates, art-themed club nights and anything else that might challenge convention – but 'convention' is much harder to challenge now, when everyone's doing it. Artistic director Ekow Eshun resigned once threats of immediate closure had been averted, but his successor Gregor Muir is facing the same challenges.

♿ 🧍 ♿ 🚻 💬 🦯 L 🦮

Notes *No parking available but visitors can be dropped off and collected from the main entrance. There are parking meters in Waterloo Place and Carlton House Terrace, at the rear of the ICA. There are also car parks in Whitcombe Street and Spring Gardens, both off Trafalgar Square. Note that a journey from any of these would mean negotiating the Duke of York Steps (30 steps), or reaching the ICA via Pall Mall and Trafalgar Square. There is level access to the entrance from the Mall. There is one set of automatic sliding doors. The* **box office and bookshop** *are situated in the main foyer at ground level.* **Cinema 1,** **Cinema 2** *and the* **theatre** *are all accessible via permanent ramps. There is space for two wheelchair users in both cinemas and the theatre can accommodate up to six wheelchair users. The lower gallery has a platform lift located by the entrance to the gallery. The user can operate this independently or with the assistance of a member of staff. There is a lift available, but it requires visitors to transfer from their wheelchair into the lift. This option is not suitable for those using a motorised wheelchair. The assistance of a member of staff is required to access the lift as it is not in a public area. The lift also allows access to the* **Nash and Brandon rooms** *on the first floor. There is also a temporary ramp that can be erected at 12 Carlton House Terrace, the administrative entrance to the ICA. Accessing this entrance can be achieved*

by exiting from the main entrance, travelling along the Mall to Trafalgar Square, Pall Mall, Waterloo Place and then Carlton House Terrace. Ask on arrival if you would like to use this ramp. Assistance dogs are welcome and may be left with a member of staff. Large print versions of the ICA programme, other programmes and gallery guides are available on request. There is a text phone in the box office (7839 0737), which can be used for booking tickets as well as general enquiries. The box office has an induction loop system. The cinemas and theatre are equipped with an infrared hearing system. Headsets are available from the box office free of charge. Most talks at the ICA are also served by an infrared hearing system. There is one wheelchair available for use by visitors. Check with the box office when making a booking. Call the Centre Manager on 7766 1442 for more information.

London Film Museum

County Hall, SE1 7PB (7202 7040, www.londonfilmmuseum.com). Westminster tube or Waterloo tube/rail. **Open** 10am-5pm Mon-Fri; 10am-6pm Sat & Sun. **Admission** £13.50; £11.50 reductions; under 15s £9.50; under-5s free of charge. Concession for disabled visitors £11.50; for each paying visitor a carer or companion receives free admission.

Dedicated to British film (by which it means films that were made in Britain, which allows unexpected blockbusters such as *Star Wars* and the Indiana Jones movies to be sneaked in alongside the more obvious *Kind Hearts and Coronets* and *Brief Encounter*), the London Film Museum is at the heart of the former home of London's metropolitan government, County Hall. The interactive displays tell the stories of great studios such as Pinewood and Ealing, discussing David Lean and other major directors, and detail different types of movie that have come from these islands. The box-like offices lining the corridors contain sets and props – among thousands of original artefacts, you can see the Rank gong. 'Charlie Chaplin: The Great Londoner' explores the Tramp's life.

Notes *The road directly behind County Hall is private and can only be used for dropping off visitors with impaired mobility . There is no parking on this street. Blue Badge parking is available on Belvedere Road. The nearest NCP car park is 100m away on the other side of Jubilee Gardens. As the museum is on the first floor of County Hall, call in advance to arrange access by lift accompanied by a member of staff (takes 10 mins). Inside, all main areas are accessible to wheelchair users. Accessible toilets are situated on the ground and first floor. Staff are access trained. Assistance dogs are welcome.*

London Transport Museum
Covent Garden Piazza, WC2E 7BB (7379 6344, www.ltmuseum.co.uk). Covent Garden tube. **Open** 10am-6pm Mon-Thur, Sat, Sun; 11am-6pm Fri. **Admission** £10; £6-£8 reductions; free under-16s.

Reopened in 2007 after the most thorough refurbishment since its move to Covent Garden in 1980, the London Transport Museum traces the ways people have got about town from the horse age to the present day. As well as a remodelled interior, the museum emerged with a much more confident focus on social history and design, illustrated by a superb array of preserved buses, trams and trains, and backed up by temporary exhibitions.

The collections are in broadly chronological order, beginning with the Victorian gallery, where a replica of Shillibeer's first horse-drawn bus service in 1829 takes pride of place. Another gallery is dedicated to the museum's impressive collection of poster art. Under the leadership of Frank Pick in the early 20th century, London Transport developed one of the world's most coherent brand identities. The new museum also raises important questions about the future of public transport in the city, with a display on ideas that are 'coming soon'.

Notes *No Blue Badge parking bays. Standard parking bays in Tavistock and Wellington Streets. The area of the piazza outside the front of the museum can be used as a drop-off point by prior arrangement. The entrance in the south east corner of Covent Garden Piazza has a cobbled surface leading to a slope to double-width doors that open automatically. The reception has level access with an induction loop hearing assistance system. The museum is accessible for wheelchair users with ramps/slopes and lifts to all floors. Not all the vehicles on display are accessible. Exhibits can be audio described. Touch Tours are available. A loan wheelchair is available. The museum provides occasional described tours for visually impaired visitors; it also provides BSL interpreted gallery talks (advance booking essential). Large-print highlights tours are available from the ticket desk and information desk. Magnifiers can also be supplied by the ticket desk. Audio-visual exhibits in the are either subtitled or have induction loops. There are designated spaces for wheelchair users at the front and rear of the theatre. The nearest accessible toilet is 10m from the designated seating area. Assistance dogs are allowed in the auditorium. There is ample room for a wheelchair user to manoeuvre in the café. The accessible toilet is 32m from the main entrance.*

London Transport Museum.

Museum of London.

Museum of London

150 London Wall, EC2Y 5HN (7001 9844, www.museumoflondon.org.uk). Barbican, St Paul's or Moorgate tube. **Open** 10am-6pm daily. **Admission** free; suggested donation £3.

The Museum of London is a gem. A five-year, £20 million refurbishment unveiled a thrilling lower-ground-floor gallery that covers the city from 1666 to the present day. The new space features everything from a defused World War II bomb, suspended in a room where the understated and moving testimony of ordinary Blitz survivors is screened, to clothes by the late Alexander McQueen.

The museum's biggest obstacle has always been its tricky location: the entrance is two floors above street level, hidden behind a grim wall. To solve this, a new space was created on the ground floor, allowing one key exhibit – the Lord Mayor's gold coach – to be seen from the outside. The architects Wilkinson Eyre also managed to increase gallery space by a quarter, enabling the museum to focus on the city's relationship with the rest of the world and how it was changed by trade, war and empire. There are displays and thoughtful interactives on poverty (they've reconstructed an actual debtor's cell, complete with graffiti), finance, shopping and 20th-century fashion, including a re-created Georgian pleasure garden, with mannequins sporting Philip Treacy masks and hats.

Upstairs, the chronological displays begin with 'London Before London', where artefacts include flint axes from 300,000 BC, found near Piccadilly, and the bones of an aurochs. 'Roman London' includes an impressive reconstructed dining room complete with mosaic floor. Windows overlook a sizeable fragment of the City wall, whose Roman foundations have clearly been built upon many times over the centuries. Sound effects and audio-visual displays illustrate the medieval, Elizabethan and Jacobean city, with particular focus on the plague

and the Great Fire, which destroyed London in 1666.

♿ 🚶‍♀️ 👥 ᴡᴄ🚻 🅿️ ♿🚽 Ⓛ 🐕‍🦺

Notes *The Museum has disabled parking spaces for blue and orange badge holders. These should be booked in advance on 7814 5552. The entrance is on a pedestrian high walk which can be reached by stairs, escalators or lifts from Aldersgate Street; London Wall; or St Martins-le-Grand. Lift access to the museum from the car park. There is an accessible lift serving all floors and accessible toilets on most floors. Wheelchairs, disability scooters and folding seats are available to borrow; call 7814 5660. Magnifying glasses and a large-print event brochure available together with regular Touch Tours; phone to book.*

National Gallery

Trafalgar Square, WC2N 5DN (7747 2885, www.nationalgallery.org.uk). Leicester Square tube or Charing Cross tube/rail. **Open** 10am-6pm daily, 10am-9pm Fri. **Admission** free. Special exhibitions vary (reductions for disabled visitors).

Founded in 1824 to display 36 paintings, the National Gallery is now one of the world's great repositories for art. There are masterpieces from virtually every European school of art, from austere 13th-century religious paintings to the sensual delights of Caravaggio and Van Gogh.

Furthest to the left of the main entrance, the modern Sainsbury Wing extension contains the gallery's earliest works: Italian paintings by masters such as Giotto and Piero della Francesca, as well as the Wilton Diptych, the finest medieval English picture in the collection, showing Richard II with the Virgin and Child. The basement of the Sainsbury Wing is the setting for important temporary exhibitions.

In the West Wing (left of the main entrance) are Italian Renaissance master-

National Gallery. *See p105.*

pieces by Correggio, Titian and Raphael. Straight ahead on entry, in the North Wing, are 17th-century Dutch, Flemish, Italian and Spanish Old Masters, including works such as Rembrandt's *A Woman Bathing in a Stream* and Caravaggio's *Supper at Emmaus*. Velázquez's *Rokeby Venus* is one of the artist's most famous paintings, a reclining nude asking herself – and us – 'How do we look?' Also in this wing are works by the great landscape artists Claude and Poussin. Turner insisted that his *Dido Building Carthage* and *Sun Rising through Vapour* should hang alongside two Claudes here that particularly inspired him.

In the East Wing (to the right of the main entrance, and most easily reached via the new street-level entrance on Trafalgar Square) are some of the gallery's most popular paintings: works by the French Impressionists and Post-Impressionists, including Monet's *Water-Lilies*, one of Van Gogh's *Sunflowers* and Seurat's *Bathers at Asnières*. Don't miss Renoir's astonishingly lovely *Les Parapluies*. You shouldn't plan to see everything in one visit, but free guided tours, audio guides and the superb Art Start computer (which allows you to tailor and map your own itinerary of must-sees) help you make the best of your time.

♿ ♿ ♿ ♿ ♿

P★★ 🚆 ♿ L ⠿ 🐕

Notes *On street Blue Badge parking bays available on St Martin's Street. Four entrances have level access: the Getty, the Sainsbury Wing, National Café and Education Centre entrances. The main Portico entrance is not accessible. Wheelchairs are available at the Getty Entrance on level 0, the Sainsbury Wing cloakroom on level 0 and the Education Centre (street level). The* **Sainsbury Wing** *reception has an infrared hearing assistance system. Inside the gallery there is level access and an induction loop hearing assistance system. Motorised scooters are allowed in public parts of the venue.* **Upper floors** *are accessed by lifts. Exhibits can be audio described. Tactile and Braille signage and information packs are available. There are also tactile line diagrams and Braille interpretations of paintings. Verbal description sessions on paintings for blind and partially sighted visitors are held every last Saturday of the month. The audio guides have volume enhancement, and the exhibition videos and films have subtitles and transcripts for visitors with hearing impairments. The gallery also provides BSL-interpreted talks. Check and book events via the website. The* **Sainsbury Wing Theatre** *on Levels -1 and -2 has spaces for wheelchair users. Ramp access to the front of the theatre is on Level -2. Both the café and dining rooms have level access inside and ample room for wheelchair users to manoeuvre. There are accessible toilets near all entrances. Staff receive disability awareness training and are Typetalk aware. Assistance dogs welcome.*

National Portrait Gallery

St Martin's Place, WC2H 0HE (7306 0055, www.npg.org.uk). Leicester Square tube or Charing Cross tube/rail. **Open** 10am-6pm Mon-Wed, Sat, Sun; 10am-9pm Thur, Fri. **Admission** free. Special exhibitions vary (reductions for disabled visitors).

Portraits don't have to be stuffy. The excellent National Portrait Gallery has everything from oil paintings of stiff-backed royals to photographs of soccer stars and unflattering political caricatures. The portraits of musicians, scientists, artists, philanthropists and celebrities are arranged in chronological order from the top to the bottom of the building.

At the top of the escalator up from the main foyer, on the second floor, are the earliest works, portraits of Tudor and Stuart royals and notables, including Holbein's 'cartoon' of Henry VIII and the 'Ditchley Portrait' of his daughter, Elizabeth I, her pearly slippers placed firmly on a colourful map of England. On the same floor, the 18th-century collection features Georgian writers and artists, with one room devoted to the influential Kit-Cat Club of bewigged Whig (leftish) intellectuals, Congreve and Dryden among them. More famous names include Wren and Swift.

The second floor also shows Regency greats, military men such as Wellington and Nelson, plus Byron, Wordsworth and other Romantics. The first floor is devoted to the Victorians (Dickens, Brunel, Darwin) and to 20th-century luminaries, such as TS Eliot and Ian McKellen.

Notes *Blue Badge bays available on St Martin's Street. The main entrance does not have level access (two steps) but the shop and Orange Street entrance (at the rear) have moderate slopes to entrance doors. Reception has an induction loop hearing assistance system. Inside the gallery there is a portable induction loop; the audio guides desk is on floor 2, at the top of the escalator. Video guides are available. Motorised scooters are allowed in public parts of the venue. Upper floors are reached by lifts. Large-print captions for many portraits and temporary exhibitions are available at the information desk, as are magnifying glasses. Descriptive folders with tactile images are available throughout the gallery and from the main information desk. Visualising Portraits picture descriptions and workshops are also available; contact 7312 2483. BSL-interpreted talks are available each month. Loan wheelchairs are available. There are designated spaces (at the back) for wheelchair users in the theatre; these are 18m from the nearest accessible toilet. There is an induction loop. Both the café and restaurant have level access inside with ample room for wheelchair users to manoeuvre. Accessible toilets are 17m from the Orange Street entrance and 13m from the front lift on floor -2, by the entrance to the Ondaatje Wing Theatre. Staff receive disability awareness training. Assistance dogs welcome.*

Natural History Museum
Cromwell Road, SW7 5BD (7942 5000, www.nhm.ac.uk). South Kensington tube. **Open** 10am-5.50pm daily. **Admission** free; charges for special exhibitions. **Tours** free.
Both a research institution and a fabulous museum, the NHM opened in Alfred Waterhouse's purpose-built, Romanesque palazzo in 1881. Now joined by the splendid Darwin Centre extension, the original building looks magnificent, its pale blue and terracotta façade preparing you for the natural wonders within.

Taking up the full length of the vast entrance hall is the cast of a Diplodocus skeleton. A left turn leads into the west wing or Blue Zone, where long queues form to see animatronic dinosaurs – the ever-popular T Rex is back after hip surgery in 2010. A display on biology features an illuminated, adult-sized model of a foetus in the womb along with graphic diagrams of how it might have got there.

A right turn from the central hall leads past the 'Creepy Crawlies' exhibition to the Green Zone. Stars include a cross-section through a Giant Sequoia tree and an amazing array of stuffed birds, including the chance to compare the egg of a hummingbird, smaller than a little finger nail, with that of an elephant bird (now extinct), almost football-sized. Beyond is the Red Zone. 'Earth's Treasury' is a mine of information on a variety of precious metals, gems and crystals; 'From the Beginning' is a brave attempt to give the expanse of geological time a human perspective. Outside, the delightful Wildlife Garden (Apr-Oct only) showcases a range of British lowland habitats, including a 'Bee Tree', a hollow tree trunk that opens to reveal a busy hive.

Many of the museum's 22 million insect and plant specimens are housed in the new Darwin Centre, where they take up nearly 17 miles of shelving. This is also home to the museum's research scientists, who can be observed at work. But a great deal of this amazing institution is still hidden from public view, given over to labs and specialised storage.

Notes *On-site parking spaces for Blue Badge holders are limited. Book in advance on 7942 5888 (24 hours). A drop-off point is available for larger vehicles. There are challenges in making a Grade I-listed building accessible, but access to most public spaces has been improved. A new lift has been installed in the lobby by the museum's accessible entrance on Exhibition Road. There are two accessible toilets near the entrance. All floors of the Blue, Green and Red Zones and the Darwin Centre are accessible by lift and have accessible toilets. Information available in Braille and large print. Exhibits cannot be audio described, but touch tours are available. Large print maps of the museum available from the information desks. A loan wheelchair is available. Both the Deli Café and the restaurant have space for wheelchair users to manoeuvre. Staff receive disability awareness training. Assistance dogs welcome.*

Petrie Museum of Egyptian Archaeology

University College London, Malet Place, WC1E 6BT (7679 2884, www.petrie.ucl.ac.uk). Goodge Street, Warren Street or Euston Square tube. **Open** 1-5pm Tue-Sat. **Admission** free; donations welcome.

Set up in 1892 by eccentric traveller and diarist Amelia Edwards, the refurbished (and now much easier to find) museum is named after Flinders Petrie, tireless excavator of ancient Egypt. Where the British Museum's Egyptology collection is strong on the big stuff, the Petrie is dim case after dim case of minutiae: pottery shards, grooming accessories, beads. Highlights include artefacts from the heretic pharaoh Akhenaten's ancient capital Tell el Amarna. Wind-up torches illuminate gloomy corners and computers offer 3D views of selected objects.

Notes *Check before visiting to ensure works not taking place as this makes access more difficult. The museum may be able to arrange parking in the main university quadrangle (off Gower Street). There is a banner over the entrance to the museum, which is located on the first floor of the DMS Watson library. Staff at the security desk just inside the library entrance will be able to direct you to the museum (there are signs) and will give you a free visitor card providing access to the museum for the day. There is lift access to the museum on the first floor, and to the accessible toilet on the fourth floor. Inside, visitors must negotiate two steps to reach the second gallery: a wheelchair lift is available. Occasionally on Saturdays during academic vacations, or for evening events, lift access may not be possible; check in advance. Lighting within the museum is less than ideal, but torches are available to borrow. Seating is available.*

Royal Academy of Arts

Burlington House, W1J 0BD (7300 8000, www.royalacademy.org.uk). Green Park or Piccadilly Circus tube. **Open** 10am-6pm Mon-Thur, Sat, Sun; 10am-10pm Fri. **Admission** free. Special exhibitions vary; concessions for disabled visitors, carer free.

Britain's first art school was founded in 1768 and moved to the extravagantly

Palladian Burlington House a century later, but it's now best known not for education but exhibitions. Ticketed blockbusters are generally held in the Sackler Wing or the main galleries; shows in the John Madejski Fine Rooms are drawn from the RA's holdings, which range from Constable to Hockney, and are free. The Academy's biggest event is the Summer Exhibition, which for more than two centuries has drawn from works entered by the public. There's also a December arts programme, 'Contemporary', programming events, exhibitions and films nearby at 6 Burlington Gardens.

人占 人も よ P. ⇔ ↔ ↗ L ↗

Notes *Two designated free parking bays for Blue Badge holders, who should book at least a week in advance: call 7300 8028. The route from the car park to the entrance is accessible to a wheelchair user with assistance as the car park surface is cobbled. On-street marked Blue Badge bays are available on Sackville Street. There is a moderate ramp or steps to the entrance. There is a standard lift (accesses G -1) for public use located off the courtyard area; staff need to be notified for use of this lift. At reception there is an induction loop hearing assistance system, which staff are trained to use. Inside there is level access to the gallery. Motorised scooters are allowed in public parts of the venue (no re-charge facility). Floors G -1-2 accessed by lift located 30m from the entrance. The lift is staffed and visitors are assisted by a member of staff at all times. The exhibits can be audio described. Audio guides are available free of charge. A portable induction loop is available from the audio desk for use with the audio guides. Large-print gallery guides are available from the entrance to the exhibition. One-to-one descriptive tours and use of the thermoform images album can be arranged with advance notice. British Sign Language and Lipspeaking interpretation tours are also available. There is a wheelchair to borrow. Both café and restaurant have ample room for wheelchair users to manoeuvre. The accessible toilet is 12m from the main entrance.*

Science Museum
Exhibition Road, SW7 2DD (7942 4000 switchboard, 0870 870 4868 information, http://bit.ly/158LOs). South Kensington tube. **Open** 10am-6pm daily. **Admission** free; charges apply for special exhibitions.

Only marginally less popular with children than its natural historical neighbour (*see p108*), the Science Museum is a celebration of the wonders of technology in the service of our daily lives. On the ground floor, the shop – selling wacky toys and science-inspired gifts – is part of the 'Energy Hall', which introduces the museum's collections with impressive 18th-century steam engines.

In 'Exploring Space', rocket science and the lunar landings are illustrated by dramatically lit mock-ups and models, before the museum gears up for its core collection in 'Making the Modern World'. Introduced by Puffing Billy, the world's oldest steam locomotive (built in 1815), the gallery also contains Stephenson's Rocket. Also here are the Apollo 10 command module, classic cars and an absorbing collection of everyday technological marvels from 1750 to the present. Upstairs in the main body of the museum, the second floor holds displays on computing, marine engineering and mathematics; the third floor is dedicated to flight, among other things, including the hands-on Launchpad gallery, featuring levers, pulleys, explosions and all manner of experiments for children (and associated grown-ups).

On the fifth floor, you'll find an old-fashioned but intriguing display on the science and art of medicine. Beyond 'Making the Modern World', bathed in an eerie blue

Science Museum.

light, the three floors of the Wellcome Wing are where the museum makes sure it stays on the cutting edge of science.

On the ground floor, 'Antenna' is a web-savvy look at breaking science stories, displaying video interviews and Q&As with research scientists alongside the weird new objects they've been working on. Upstairs, the enjoyable and troubling 'Who Am I?' gallery was re-launched in summer 2010. The dozen silver pods that surround brightly lit cases of objects have engaging interactive displays – from a cartoon of ethical dilemmas designed to introduce you to your dorsolateral pre-frontal cortex to a chance to find out what gender your brain is.

Compelling objects include a jellyfish that's 'technically immortal', the statistically average British man (he's called Jose, by the way) and a pound of human fat, displayed alongside a gastric band. There's also contemporary art, including installations and Stephen Wiltshire's amazingly detailed drawing, from memory, of the Houses of Parliament. At the end of 2010, the museum opened a new permanent gallery on the second floor of the Wellcome Wing. 'Atmosphere: Exploring Climate Science' looks at how the climate works, greenhouse gases and what scientists predict will happen if the ambient temperature of the Earth's atmosphere continues to rise.

tours are available for some exhibitions. A loan wheelchair is available; call ahead to confirm. Large print versions of museum maps can be borrowed from the information desk. Braille information books are available for use in the Launchpad gallery. A BSL interpreter accompanies some free family events on the first Saturday of every month. Assistance dogs welcome.

Serpentine Gallery

Kensington Gardens, nr The Albert Memorial, W2 3XA (7402 6075, fax 7402 4103 www.serpentinegallery.org). Lancaster Gate, Knightsbridge or South Kensington tube. **Open** 10am-6pm daily. **Admission** free; donations appreciated.

The secluded location south-west of the Long Water and Serpentine makes this small and airy former tea house an attractive destination for lovers of adventurous contemporary art. The rolling two-monthly programme of temporary exhibitions features up-to-the-minute artists. Every spring, a renowned architect, who's never before built in the UK, is commissioned to build a new pavilion. It then opens to the public, running a hip programme of cultural events from June to September, thus providing welcome shelter from the inevitable summer rain. There's a tiny but rarely less than tempting bookshop as well.

Notes *On-street Blue Badge parking on Exhibition Road, outside the main entrance. Level access to the entrance with double-width push-open doors that are permanently held open. Both the information and ticket desks have an induction loop hearing assistance system. Every part of the museum is accessible by ramp or lift, except for the raised walkways in the Flight and Ships galleries, and simulators. Motorised scooters are allowed in public parts of the museum. Tactile signage and touch*

Notes *Car park 200m away. On-street Blue Badge bays available on West Carriage Drive behind the gallery. No designated drop-off point. An easy slope leads to the main entrance with level access to reception and throughout. Reception has hearing assistance system and staff receive disability awareness training. The accessible unisex toilet is 17m from main entrance. Motorised scooters allowed in public parts (no recharging facilities). Assistance dogs welcome.*

Sir John Soane's Museum

*13 Lincoln's Inn Fields, WC2A 3BP
(7405 2107, www.soane.org).
Holborn tube.* **Open** 10am-5pm
Tue-Sat; 6-9pm 1st Tue of mth. *Tours*
11am Sat. **Admission** free; donations
appreciated. *Tours* £5; free reductions.

When he wasn't designing notable buildings, among them the original Bank of England, Sir John Soane (1753-1837) obsessively collected art, furniture and architectural ornamentation. In the 19th century, he turned his house into a museum, to which, he said, 'amateurs and students' should have access. The result is this perfectly amazing place.

Much of the museum's appeal derives from the domestic setting. The modest rooms were modified by Soane with ingenious devices to channel and direct daylight, and to expand space, including walls that open out like cabinets to display some of his many paintings (by Canaletto, Watteau, Turner, Hogarth). The Breakfast Room has a beautiful domed ceiling, inset with convex mirrors. The extraordinary Monument Court contains a sarcophagus of alabaster, so fine that it's almost translucent, that was carved for the pharaoh Seti I (1291-78 BC) and discovered in his tomb in Egypt's Valley of the Kings. There are also numerous examples of Soane's eccentricity, not least the cell for his imaginary monk 'Padre Giovanni', and remnants salvaged from the original Houses of Parliament..

The museum has launched an appeal for funds that will go towards re-opening Soane's top-floor 'private apartments', recreated from contemporary watercolours, with Phase I due to be completed by 2012. No. 12 Lincoln's Inn Fields, including the Breakfast Room and Soane Gallery, are now closed. No.12 will reopen in summer 2012 on the completion of the first phase of Opening up the Soane. The main house and Museum collection in No. 13 will remain open as usual throughout the restoration project.

Notes *Nearest multi-storey car parks are in Drury Lane and Bloomsbury Square. Blue Badge holders can park in marked bays for up to four hours Mon-Fri 8.30am-6.30pm, and without time limit outside these hours. Eight steps at entrance (assistance available). Two narrow wheelchairs available for loan, making most of the Ground Floor and Basement accessible.*

Tate Britain

*Millbank, SW1P 4RG (7887 8888,
www.tate.org.uk). Pimlico tube.* **Open**
10am-6pm daily; 10am-10pm 1st Fri of
mth. *Tours* 11am, noon, 2pm, 3pm Mon-
Fri; noon, 3pm Sat, Sun. **Admission**
free. Special exhibitions vary.

Tate Modern gets the attention, but the original Tate Gallery, founded by sugar magnate and philanthropist Sir Henry Tate, has a broader brief. Housed in a stately building on the north bank of the Thames, Tate Britain is second only to the National Gallery when it comes to British art. The historical collection includes work by (among others) Hogarth, Gainsborough, Reynolds, Constable (who gets three rooms) and Turner (in the superb Clore Gallery). Many contemporary works were shifted to the other Tate when it opened in 2000, but Stanley Spencer, Lucian Freud and Francis Bacon are well represented here, and Art Now installations showcase up-and-coming British artists.

Temporary exhibitions include the controversy-courting Turner Prize exhibition (Oct-Jan). The gallery has a good restaurant and a well-stocked gift shop.

Notes *There is a car park at the rear of the gallery; parking is free for Blue Badge holders but should be booked in advance. The car park is accessed from John Islip Street. There is no designated*

Victoria & Albert Museum.
See p116.

drop-off point. The route from the car park to the entrance is accessible to a wheelchair user with assistance; the car park surface is tarmac and there is non-stepped access from car park to the building. Blue Badge parking bays available on Atterbury Street, close to the Manton Street entrance, and on Millbank close to the main entrance. The Manton Street entrance is the main accessible entrance with a moderate slope giving access to floor 1. The main galleries on floor 2 are accessible via the main lifts from here. The lift at the far end of the **Turner Wing** *accesses floors 1-2-3. The exhibits can be audio described and touch tours are available. An induction loop hearing assistance system is available, and staff are trained to use it. A loan wheelchair is available. Large-print gallery plans and a raised image gallery plan with Braille text are available from the information desks. Large-print captions are available in the exhibitions and displays at all four galleries. Large-print copies of the special exhibitions guides are available at the information desks.* **Films** *shown in the galleries and exhibitions have subtitles. A free multimedia guide in British Sign Language (BSL) that focuses on 15 works from the collection is available from the Information Desk. The audio guides are also available in BSL format. The gallery also offers BSL interpreted talks. These, and touch tours and visual description talks, should be booked in advance. The café and separate restaurant are both situated on floor 1 by the Manton Entrance and both have ample room for wheelchair users to manoeuvre. The accessible toilet is 54m from the Manton entrance up the ramp past the cloakroom. Staff receive disability awareness training. Assistance dogs welcome. Staff are Typetalk aware.*

Tate Modern

Bankside, SE1 9TG (7887 8888, minicom 7887 8687, www.tate.org.uk). Southwark tube or London Bridge tube/rail. **Open** 10am-6pm Sun-Thur, 10am-10pm Fri, Sat. *Tours* 11am, noon, 2pm, 3pm daily. **Admission** free; varies for special exhibitions.

Thanks to its industrial architecture, this powerhouse of modern art inspires awe even before you enter. Built after World War II as Bankside Power Station, it was designed by Sir Giles Gilbert Scott, architect of Battersea Power Station. The power station closed in 1981; nearly 20 years later, it opened as an art museum, and has enjoyed spectacular popularity ever since. The gallery attracts five million visitors a year to a building intended for half that number; work on the hugely ambitious, £215m TM2 extension began in 2010. You can see how far the workers have got in constructing the vast new origami structure, designed by Herzog & de Meuron who were behind the original conversion, by taking a peek through hoardings at the back of the power station. It is due for completion in 2012.

The original cavernous turbine hall is used to jaw-dropping effect as the home of large-scale, temporary installations. Beyond, the permanent collection draws from the Tate's collections of modern art (international works from 1900) and features such heavy hitters as Matisse, Rothko and Beuys. There are vertiginous views down inside the building from outside the galleries, which group artworks according to movement (Surrealism, Minimalism, Post-war abstraction) rather than theme. If you don't know where to start, take one of the tours.

Notes *Accessible parking is available but check in advance due to building works. The architects designed an* accessible building for around two million visitors a year; it receives five million so, at times, can feel very busy. The galleries are quieter on late night openings. The building has flat level access throughout, with the exception of the Turbine Hall ramp which can be avoided by entering the gallery at one of the three ground-level entrances rather than using the lower-ground main entrance. Throughout, doors are either automatic or held open with magnets (except toilet doors). Touch tours of the collections are available, as are British Sign Language (BSL) talks (first Friday of the month, 7pm). No booking required. A group of 70 deaf visitors have made First Friday at Tate Modern an unofficial Deaf Club.

Victoria & Albert Museum

Cromwell Road, SW7 2RL (7942 2000, www.vam.ac.uk). South Kensington tube. **Open** 10am-5.45pm Mon-Thur, Sat, Sun; 10am-10pm Fri. *Tours hourly, 10.30am-3.30pm daily.* **Admission** free; charges for special exhibitions, but free to visitors with access needs with up to two friends.

The V&A is one of the world's most magnificent museums, its foundation stone laid on this site by Queen Victoria in her last official public engagement in 1899. It is a superb showcase for applied arts from around the world, much calmer than its tearaway cousins on the other side of Exhibition Road. Some 150 grand galleries on seven floors contain countless pieces of furniture, ceramics, sculpture, paintings, posters, jewellery, metalwork, glass, textiles and dress, spanning several centuries. Items are grouped by theme, origin or age, but any attempt to comprehend the whole collection in one visit is doomed. For advice, tap the patient staff, who field a formidable combination of leaflets, floor plans, knowledge and polite concern.

Highlights include the seven Raphael Cartoons painted in 1515 as tapestry designs for the Sistine Chapel; the finest collection of Italian Renaissance sculpture outside Italy; Canova's *Three Graces*; the Ardabil carpet, the world's oldest and most splendid floor covering, in the Jameel Gallery of Islamic Art; Medici porcelain; and the Luck of Edenhall, a 13th-century glass beaker from Syria.

The Fashion galleries run from 18th-century court dress to contemporary chiffon numbers; the Architecture gallery has videos, models, plans and descriptions of various styles; and the famous Photography collection holds more than 500,000 images. The V&A's FuturePlan has been a revelation. The completely refurbished Medieval & Renaissance Galleries are stunning, but there are many other eye-catching new or redisplayed exhibits: the Gilbert Collection of silver, gold and gemmed ornaments has arrived from Somerset House; the Ceramics Galleries have been renovated and supplemented with an eye-catching bridge; there's lovely Buddhist sculpture in the Robert HN Ho Family Foundation Galleries; and the new Theatre & Performance Galleries take over where Covent Garden's defunct Theatre Museum left off. The 14th- to 17th-century sculpture rooms, just off the central John Madejski Garden, were recently jazzed up: restored mosaic floors and beautiful stained glass help to enhance the statues.

Notes *On-street Blue Badge parking on Exhibition Road outside the accessible entrance. Level access to main doors that open both ways. The reception has an induction loop hearing assistance system which staff are trained to use. The museum is spread over seven levels and a number of interconnecting buildings. A map shows which routes are inaccessible for wheelchair users; staff are happy to help. Access to upper* *galleries is by lift(s). There are designated spaces for wheelchair users. Both the* **Lecture Theatre** *(15m to the nearest accessible toilet) and* **Hochhauser Auditorium** *(22m to the nearest accessible toilet) have designated seating at the front. There is induction loop hearing assistance in both areas. Assistance dogs are allowed in the theatre and auditorium. The accessible toilet is located within the standard toilets on level 0, between the tunnel entrance and cloakroom. Staff receive disability awareness training. Documents available in Braille and large print. Assistance dogs welcome. A member of staff trained in BSL skills (BSL Level 1) is usually on duty.*

Wallace Collection

Hertford House, Manchester Square, W1U 3BN (7935 0687, www.wallacecollection.org).
Bond Street tube. **Open** 10am-5pm daily. **Admission** free.

Built in 1776, this handsome house contains an exceptional collection of 18th-century French furniture, painting and objets d'art, as well as an amazing array of medieval armour and weaponry. It all belonged to Sir Richard Wallace, who, as the illegitimate offspring of the fourth Marquess of Hertford, inherited in 1870 the treasures his father had amassed in the last 30 years of his life. A condition of the bequest was that no object should ever leave the collection, even for loan exhibitions.

Room after grand room contains Louis XIV and XV furnishings and Sèvres porcelain; the galleries are hung with paintings by Gainsborough, Velázquez, Van Dyck, Fragonard, Rembrandt, Titian and Reynolds; Franz Hals's *Laughing Cavalier* (neither laughing nor a cavalier) is one of the best known, along with Fragonard's *The Swing.* Since summer 2010, refurbished West Galleries have displayed the museum's 19th-century and Venetian works, including over 20 paintings by

Canaletto, and the collections of miniatures and gold boxes have been on show in the Boudoir Cabinet; new East Galleries should be complete by early 2012.

Notes *Limited parking at the front of the museum is available to disabled visitors. This should be booked in advance by calling the security desk on 7563 9524. There are two parking spaces for Blue Badge holders in Manchester Square and others in nearby streets. There is a sloped driveway up to the front entrance with ramp access to both the left and right. Both entrance double doors are automatic. There is wheelchair access to all public areas, including galleries, restaurant, library, education studio and lecture theatre. The* **lecture theatre** *has space for up to four wheelchair users. There is a lift to all three floors with voice announcer. Remote door openers are available from the security desk. Audio guides are available. 'Deaf Visions' is a quarterly programme introducing the Wallace Collection to the deaf community. Events are delivered in British Sign Language and/or sign-supported English with talks and art activities for children and adults. A BSL interpreter is available for hearing people, so both deaf and hearing people can enjoy the activities together. There is an audio guide (£4, including a large-print floor plan). Large-print labels are available for all temporary exhibitions in the Exhibition Galleries on the Lower Ground Floor. An arms and armour handling collection and wood marquetry handling material is available in the Conservation Gallery on the Lower Ground Floor. The accessible toilet is in the standard toilets on the lower ground floor. Assistance dogs welcome.*

NORTH LONDON

Attractions

British Library
*96 Euston Road, NW1 2DB (7412
7332, www.bl.uk). Euston or King's
Cross tube/rail.* **Open** *Galleries & Shop*
9.30am-6pm Mon, Wed-Sat; 9.30am-
8pm Tues; 9.30am-5pm Sat; 11am-5pm
Sun. *Reading Rooms* 10am-8pm Mon,
9.30am-8pm Tues-Thur; 9.30am-5pm
Fri, Sat. **Admission** free.
'One of the ugliest buildings in the world,'
opined a Parliamentary committee on the
opening of the new British Library in
1997. But don't judge a book by its cover:
the courtyard sets a welcoming tone of
openness for the venerable institution, and
the interior is a model of cool, spacious
functionality. The collection itself is
unmatched (150 million items and count-
ing), and the reading rooms (open only to
cardholders) have become so popular that
regular users now complain that they
can't find a seat. The focal point of the
building is the King's Library, a six-storey
glass-walled tower housing George III's
collection, but the library's main treasures
are displayed in the John Ritblat Gallery:
Magna Carta, the Lindisfarne Gospels,
original Beatles lyrics. There is also a
great programme of temporary exhibitions and events.

Notes *No designated drop-off point.
Access to the entrance is by easy
ramps/slope (or steps) to automatic
doors. Inside there is access to all areas
by lifts and ramps. There is an induction
loop hearing assistance system. There is
ample room for wheelchair users to
manoeuvre. There are accessible toilets.
Staff receive disability awareness
training. Documents can be requested in
Braille. A raised or tactile plan of the
building is available on request.
Assistance dogs welcome.*

Kenwood House/ Iveagh Bequest
*Hampstead Lane, NW3 7JR (8348
1286, www.english-heritage.org.uk).
Hampstead or Golders Green tube then
bus 210.* **Open** 11.30am-4pm daily.
Admission free. *Tours* (for groups by
appointment only) £5-£7.
Set in delightful grounds at the top of
Hampstead Heath, Kenwood House is
every inch the country manor house. Built
in 1616, the mansion was remodelled in
the 18th century for William Murray, who
made the pivotal court ruling in 1772 that
made it illegal to own slaves in England.
The house was purchased by brewing
magnate Edward Guinness, who donated
his art collection to the nation in 1927.
Highlights include Vermeer's *The Guitar
Player*, a panoramic view of old London
Bridge by Claude de Jongh (1630),
Gainsborough's Countess Howe, and one
of Rembrandt's finest self-portraits.

Notes *Free parking for Blue Badge
holders is available 500m from
entrance. Manual wheelchair users may
need assistance because of the car park
surface. Disabled visitors may be set
down in front of the house on request
via intercom at the East Lodge. Mobility
vehicle available on request via intercom
in West Lodge Park. Access is to the
ground floor, which is level, and toilet.
Wheelchairs and shooting sticks are
provided. Only step access to upstairs.
The polished wooden floors may be
slippery for assistance dogs.*

Lord's Tour & MCC Museum
*St John's Wood Road, NW8 8QN (7616
8595, www.lords.org). St John's Wood
tube.* **Open** *Tours* phone or see website
for details. **Admission** £15; £9
reductions; £40 family.
Lord's is more than just a famous cricket
ground. As the headquarters of the
Marylebone Cricket Club (MCC), it is the

British Library.

ZSL London Zoo. See p122.

official guardian of the rules – and self-appointed guardian of the elusive 'spirit' – of cricket. As well as staging Test matches and internationals, the ground is home to the Middlesex County Cricket Club (MCCC). Visitors can take an organised tour round the futuristic, pod-like NatWest Media Centre and the august, portrait-bedecked Long Room. Highlights of the museum include the tiny urn containing the Ashes (this coveted trophy never leaves Lord's, no matter how many times the Australians win it) and memorabilia celebrating the achievements of such legends of the game as WG Grace.

♿♿ ᵂᶜ ★★★ ♒ ⚲

Notes *The MCC Museum entrance is 120m from the Grace Gate, which is on St. John's Wood Road. There is a moderate slope at the Grace Gate into the ground, but there is level access via the North Gate, located off Wellington Place. Pathways around the ground have various easy and moderate slopes, and there is level access to the Lord's Shop. Information regarding car parking may be obtained from the MCC Club Facilities Department (7616 8653), and information about the Lord's Tour and MCC Museum from the MCC Museum and Tours Department (7616 8595).*

Madame Tussauds

Marylebone Road, NW1 5LR (0870 400 3000, www.madametussauds.com). Baker Street tube. **Open** 9.30am-6pm daily. **Admission** £28; £24 reductions; £99 family; free under-4s; 50 per cent discount for disabled visitors, and one carer admitted free.

Streams of humanity jostle excitedly here for the chance to take pictures planting a smacker on the waxen visage of fame and fortune. Madame Tussaud brought her show to London in 1802, 32 years after it was founded in Paris, and it's been expanding ever since, on these very premises since 1884. There are some 300 figures in the

collection now, under various themes: 'A-list Party' (Brad, Keira, Kate Moss, Will Smith), 'Première Night' (Monroe, Chaplin, Arnie as the Terminator), 'Sports Zone' (Tendulkar, Rooney, Muhammad Ali), 'By Royal Appointment' and so on. If you're not already overheating, your palms will be sweating by the time you descend into the Chamber of Horrors in 'Scream', where only teens claim to enjoy the floor drops and scary special effects.

Much more pleasant is the kitsch 'Spirit of London' ride, whisking you through 400 years of London life in a taxi-shaped pod. 'Spirit of London' is continuously moving and as such is not accessible to wheelchair users. Since summer 2010, Tussauds has also been host to Marvel Super Heroes 4D. Interactives and waxworks of Iron Man, Spiderman and an 18ft Hulk provide further photo opportunities, but the highlight is the nine-minute film in '4D' (as well as 3D projections, there are 'real' effects such as a shaking floor and smoke in the auditorium) in the dome that used to house the planetarium.

♿♿ ♿♿ ᵂᶜ ♒ ⚲ 🐾

Notes *No car park, on-street Blue Badge bays or designated drop-off point. Most areas are designed to be fully accessible. Staff receive disability awareness training and will ensure that disabled visitors are transported safely from floor to floor by specially designed lift. Only three wheelchair users are accepted in the building at any one time; booking is strongly advised on 0871 894 3000. Book online for discounted tickets. Admission for disabled visitors is discounted by 50 per cent and one carer is admitted without charge. Documentary proof of disability such as Blue Badge is required. Induction loop hearing system fitted at main till points. Accessible toilet on the tour and ample room for wheelchair users to manoeuvre in the café.*

Wembley Stadium

Stadium Way, Wembley, Middx HA9 0WS (8795 9000, www. wembleystadium.com). Wembley Park tube or Wembley Stadium rail.

Britain's most famous sports venue reopened in early 2007 after an expensive redevelopment. Designed by Norman Foster, the 90,000-capacity stadium is some sight, its futuristic steel arch now an imposing feature of the north London skyline. England football internationals and cup finals are played here, as are a number of one-off sporting events. Guided tours offer alternative access.

Notes *There are two car parks for the stadium (Red and Green) in which accessible parking spaces can be provided. The Green Car Park is an open air/surface car park with a large parking area that can be reserved for Blue Badge holders. The Red Car Park is a multi-storey in which standard parking bays can be reserved by Blue Badge holders. Blue Badge holders will need to book passes in advance, contact City and Suburban Parking at: www.csparking.com/ stadium. All areas are accessible by lift. The main reception desk has an induction loop hearing assistance system. Induction loop hearing facilities are provided on all information desks, kiosks, bars and merchandising counters. Headsets are available as part of an auditory enhancement system which provides event commentary, information and emergency announcements. The system covers the entire seating bowl and the public concourse areas within the stadium. A specific commentator is provided for sensory-impaired visitors. Headsets can be booked by email: accessforall@wembleystadium.com. There are 147 accessible toilets within the stadium; these require a RADAR key from a steward. Levels 1, 2, 3 and 5 each have an accessible toilet within 100m of accessible entrance. Assistance dogs are welcome. There are 16 standard manual wheelchairs available to borrow. Members of staff can also provide an escort service to those requiring assistance.*

ZSL London Zoo

Regent's Park, NW1 4RY (7722 3333, fax 7586 5743, www.zsl.org/london-zoo). Camden Town tube then 274 bus.
Open *summer* 10am-5.30pm daily, *winter* 10am-4.30pm daily.

London Zoo has been open in one form or another since 1826. Spread over 36 acres and containing more than 600 species, it cares for many of the endangered variety – part of the entry price (steep at nearly £20, in peak season and including the voluntary donation) goes towards the Zoological Society of London's projects around the world. The emphasis is on upbeat education. Regular events include 'animals in action' and keeper talks; explanations are simple, short and lively. Exhibits are entertaining: look out, in particular, for the re-creation of a kitchen overrun with large cockroaches. The relaunched 'Rainforest Life' biodome and the 'Meet the Monkeys' attractions allow visitors to walk through enclosures that recreate the natural habitat of, respectively, tree anteaters and sloths, and black-capped Bolivian squirrel monkeys, while personal encounters of the avian kind can be had in the Victorian Blackburn Pavilion. 'Gorilla Kingdom' is another highlight, and the reptile house delights and horrifies in equal measure. Bring a picnic basket and you could easily spend the entire day here.

Notes *The car park is at the front with five free designated parking bays for Blue Badge holders. The reception desk, 50m from the main entrance, has an induction loop, which staff are trained*

to use. Staff
are also Typetalk aware and receive
disability awareness training.
Information and maps are available
in large print. Assistance dogs are not
allowed within the zoo, kennels are
provided for dogs and a personal
escort is available if required. There are
many ramps and slopes of varying
gradients throughout the zoo.
Motorised scooters are allowed in public
areas. Six manual and two electric
wheelchairs are available to borrow at
the main entrance; a deposit is required,
refunded on return; to book in advance
call 7449 6576. An accessible toilet is
85m from the main entrance. Oasis
Café offers ample room for wheelchair
users to manoeuvre. There is an
accessible toilet, with level access, 7m
from the Oasis Café entrance.

Museums & galleries

Camden Arts Centre

Arkwright Road, Finchley, NW3 6DG
(7472 5500, www.
camdenartscentre.org). Finchley Road
tube or Finchley Road & Frognal rail.
Open 10am-6pm Tue, Thur-Sun; 10am-
9pm Wed. **Admission** free.
Under the directorship of Jenni Lomax,
Camden Arts Centre has consistently
eclipsed many of London's larger venues.
The annual artist-curated shows – by,
among others, Tacita Dean – have been
among the most memorable in recent history. The Centre also hosts a comprehensive programme of talks, events and
workshops (with a family-oriented one in
summer) and boasts a good bookshop and
a great café, which opens on to a surprisingly tranquil garden.

Notes *On-street parking available for*
Blue Badge holders. Level access
through alternative entrance with lift to
all floors. Call for information.

Freud Museum

20 Maresfield Gardens, NW3 5SX
(7435 2002, fax 7431 5452,
www.freud.org.uk). Finchley Road tube.
Open noon-5pm Wed-Sun. **Admission**
£6; £3-£4.50 reductions; free under-12s.
Driven from Vienna by the Nazis,
Sigmund Freud lived in this quiet house
in north London with his wife Martha and
daughter Anna until his death in 1939.
Now a museum with temporary exhibitions, the house displays Freud's antiques,
art and therapy tools, including his
famous couch. The building has two blue
plaques, one for Sigmund and another for
Anna, a pioneer in child psychiatry.

Notes *Parking on Maresfield Gardens*
is restricted to residents Mon-Fri 9am-
6.30pm and Sat 9.30am-1.30pm.
Pay and display parking is available at
the south end of Maresfield Gardens,
near South Hampstead High School
and also on Nutley Terrace. There is
no lift inside the museum. The step-
free front entrance gives access to
ground floor rooms: Hall, Freud's
Study, Dining Room, museum shop
and standard toilet. The side gate gives
level access to the garden. An audio
guide is available together with
induction loops for use with hearing
aids. Access to the garden is via a
shallow step from the shop. The garden
is open during fine weather only.

Jewish Museum

Raymond Burton House, 129-131
Albert Street, NW1 7NB (7284 7384,
7284 7385, fax 8291 5506, www.
jewishmuseum.org.uk). Camden Town
tube. **Open** 10am-5pm Mon-Wed, Sun;
10am-9pm Thur; 10am-2pm Fri.
Admission £7; £3-£6 reductions;
free under-5s.
Reopened in 2010, this expanded museum
is a fascinating exploration of Jewish life
in Britain since 1066. Access is free to the

downstairs café, located beside an ancient ritual bath, and the shop you enter past. There is an entry fee for the galleries upstairs, but they're well worth the money, combining fun interactives – you can wield the iron in a tailor's sweatshop, sniff chicken soup, pose for a wedding photo or take part in some Yiddish theatre – with serious history. There's a powerful Holocaust section, using the testimony of a single survivor, Leon Greenman, to bring tight focus to the horror of some of the darkest years of the 20th century in Europe. Opposite, a beautiful room of religious artefacts, including a 17th-century synagogue ark and centrepiece chandelier of Hanukkah lamps, does an elegant job of introducing Jewish ritual.

👩‍🦽 👨‍🦽 ♿ 🚻 L 🐕‍🦺

Notes *No on-street Blue Badge bays. Standard parking bays located on Albert Street. There is no designated drop-off point but a loading bay directly in front of the museum may be used by arrangement. There is a slope to the main entrance with a single-width door that opens outwards automatically; it can be made double-width manually. There is lift access to all floors and an induction loop system, which staff are trained to use. Most films shown in the museum have subtitles, except in the ground floor gallery, where transcripts of the films shown are available. Magnifying glasses are available from the information and ticket desk. Most displays are at an accessible height, including pull-out displays. The auditorium is located on the upper ground floor and does not have fixed seating. Assistance dogs are allowed in the auditorium. The café has ample room for wheelchair users to manoeuvre. The accessible toilet is 15m from the main lift on the upper ground floor. Large-print events brochures are available from the information and ticket desk..*

Wellcome Collection

183 Euston Road, NW1 2BE (7611 2222, fax 020 7611 8258, www.wellcomecollection.org). Euston Square tube or Euston tube/rail. **Open** 10am-6pm Tue, Wed, Fri, Sat; 10am-10pm Thur; 11am-6pm Sun. Sat. **Admission** free.

Sir Henry Wellcome, a pioneering 19th-century pharmacist, amassed a vast and idiosyncratic collection of implements and curios relating to the medical trade, now displayed here. In addition to these fascinating and often grisly items – ivory carvings of pregnant women, used guillotine blades, Napoleon's toothbrush – there are several serious works of modern art, most on display in a smaller room to one side of the main chamber of curiosities. The temporary exhibitions are imaginative and interesting ('Identity', 'Skin', 'Things'), and come with all manner of associated events, from lectures and walks to gigs and experimental food.

👩‍🦽 👨‍🦽 ♿ 🚻 🅿️★★★ 🛴 L ⠿ 🐕‍🦺

Notes *An underground car park has two designated parking bays for Blue Badge holders. Spaces should be booked in advance. There is no designated drop-off point. The route from the car park to the entrance is accessible to a wheelchair user only with assistance owing to slopes/ramps. The main doors open automatically and give access to floor L1. Visitors will be accompanied by a member of staff to the main lifts. The main entrance has both a slope and an 11-step access. Inside there is a platform lift to access a small level-change. Induction loop hearing assistance system. Motorised scooters are allowed in public parts of the venue. Inside access is by ramps with lift access to other floors. Exhibits can be audio described. Braille signage for exhibits is available. A loan wheelchair is available. Magnifying glasses and sheets are available to borrow from the ground*

Jewish Museum. *See p123.*

Wellcome Collection. *See p124*.

floor information point. Large-print guides are available for all exhibitions. Some of the exhibits in the Medicine Man Collection on the first floor have Braille labelling. BSL gallery tours are held on the last Thursday of the month. If the portable induction loop is required for a gallery tour, please call or email the venue. There are designated spaces for wheelchair users at the front of the auditorium. The nearest accessible toilet is 21m. Assistance dogs are allowed in the auditorium. The café has ample room for wheelchair users to manoeuvre. There is an accessible toilet 27m from the main entrance lift next to the cloakroom.

SOUTH LONDON

Attractions

Queen's House

Romney Road, SE10 9NF (8312 6565, fax 8312 6631, www.nmm.ac.uk). Cutty Sark DLR or Greenwich DLR/rail. **Open** 10am-5pm daily. Tours noon, 2.30pm daily. **Admission** free; occasional charge for temporary exhibitions. Tours free.

The art collection of the National Maritime Museum is displayed in what was formerly the summer villa of Charles I's queen, Henrietta Maria. Completed in 1638 by Inigo Jones, the house has an interior as impressive as the paintings on the walls. The house was given to the Royal Naval Asylum charity in 1805 by George III. Inside, as well as the stunning 1635 marble floor, look for Britain's first centrally unsupported spiral stair, and the fine painted woodwork and ceilings. The collection includes portraits of famous maritime figures and works by Hogarth and Gainsborough, as well as some wartime art from the 20th century and a room of amazing pictures of exotic tropical islands painted during Captain Cook's explorations. Oh, and there's a ghost, too.

ᏨᏏ ᏍᏓᏗ Ꮮ ᏔᎦ P★★★ 🔥 🐾 L 🐕

Notes There is a car park on Park Row at the administration building which is only open at weekends; six designated parking bays free for Blue Badge holders (pre-booking advised). The route from the car park to the entrance is accessible to a wheelchair user with assistance. There is no designated drop-off point. The main entrance has downward stairs but there is a level accessible entrance at the front of the building. The door is kept locked but there is a bell in a suitable position to allow wheelchair users to gain access. The main door pushes open. Motorised scooters are allowed in public parts of the venue (no re-charging facility). A loan wheelchair is available. The accessible toilet is 25m from the main entrance. Assistance dogs welcome.

Royal Observatory & Planetarium

Greenwich Park, SE10 9NF (8312 6565, fax 8312 6632, www.rog.nmm.ac.uk). Cutty Sark DLR or Greenwich DLR/rail. **Open** 10am-5pm daily. Tours phone for details. **Admission** Observatory free. Planetarium £6.50; £4.50 reductions; £17.50 family.

The northern section of this two-part attraction chronicles Greenwich's horological connection. Flamsteed House, the observatory that was built in 1675 on the orders of Charles II, contains the apartments of Sir John Flamsteed and other Astronomers Royal, as well as the instruments that have been used in timekeeping since the 14th century. An onion dome houses the UK's largest (28-inch) refracting telescope – it was completed in 1893.

The south site houses the Astronomy Centre, home to the Peter Harrison Planetarium and Weller Astronomy Galleries. The 120-seater planetarium's architecture cleverly reflects its astrological position: the semi-submerged cone tilts at 51.5 degrees, the latitude of Greenwich, pointing to the North Star, and its reflective disc is aligned with the celestial equator. Daily and weekend shows include 'Black Holes: The Other Side of Infinity' and 'Starlife', a show describing the birth and death of stars.

Notes *No parking or designated drop-off point. Access is by path and ramp via Meridian Garden to the reception area. The Astronomy Centre is fully accessible by lift. The Royal Observatory has more restricted access. Time Galleries accessible by lift. Motorised scooters are allowed in public parts of the venue. Standard toilets only, located outside the Flamsteed entrance.*

Thames Barrier Information & Learning Centre

1 Unity Way, Woolwich, SE18 5NJ (8305 4188, www.environment-agency.gov.uk/thamesbarrier). Charlton rail, or North Greenwich tube then bus 472. **Open** *Apr-Sept* 10.30am-5.30pm Thur-Sun. *Oct-Mar* 11am-3.30pm daily. **Admission** £3.50; £3 reductions; £2 disabled visitors; Children under 16 £2, disabled children £1.50; free under-5s.
This adjustable dam has been variously called a triumph of modern engineering and the Eighth Wonder of the World. The shiny silver fins, lined up across Woolwich Reach, are indeed an impressive sight. Built in 1982 at a cost of £535m, they've already saved London from flooding some 80 times. The barrier is regularly in action for maintenance purposes; check the website for a current timetable.

To learn more, visit the recently refurbished learning centre, where you'll find an account of the 1953 flood that led to the barrier's construction, as well as displays on wildlife in the Thames and how a flood would affect London. There's a pleasant café with picnic benches.

Notes *There is a car park with three designated parking bays for Blue Badge holders. The route from the car park to the entrance is accessible to wheelchair users only with assistance due to slopes/ ramps. There is a dropped kerb/non-stepped access from the car park. The dropped kerb has tactile paving. There is no designated drop off point. There is a portable induction loop, which staff are trained to use. Motorised scooters are allowed in public areas (no recharging facilities). There is a slope leading to the café but once inside there is level access and ample room for wheelchair users to manoeuvre. The platform lift is 19m from café entrance to access floors G -1. The accessible toilet is for the sole use of disabled people, situated 11m from the lift at the side of the building. Staff receive disability awareness training; documents can be requested in large print. A member of staff trained in BSL skills is not generally on duty, staff are Typetalk aware.*

Wimbledon Lawn Tennis Museum

Museum Building, All England Lawn Tennis Club, Church Road, SW19 5AE (8946 6131, www.wimbledon.org). Southfields tube, Wimbledon rail then bus 493 or black cab from outside station. Bus stop and drop-off point immediately outside museum. **Open** 10am-5pm daily; ticket holders only during championships. **Admission** (incl tour) £18; child £13; £15.75 reductions.
Highlights at this popular museum on the history of tennis include a 200° cinema that allows you to find out what it's like to play on Centre Court, and a re-creation of a 1980s men's dressing room, complete with a 'ghost' of John McEnroe. There's also a behind-the-scenes tour.

WWT Wetland Centre. *See p130.*

♿ 🚶 ♿ ᵂᶜ 🅿 ★★★

Notes *From Aug-May limited car parking is provided inside the grounds with entry through Gate 4. Provision is also made for Blue Badge parking close to the museum during this period. Automatic doors give access to the Wimbledon Shop where displays are within reach of all visitors, and a low level counter provides a service point for wheelchair users. Entry to the museum is via stairs or lift to the floor below. Seating is provided at various points around the museum, and displays are positioned for use by wheelchair users. The small cinema has dedicated spaces for wheelchairs. Accessible toilets are provided in the museum shop. The tour takes about 90 minutes. The route includes many steps. Several sections are fully accessible, while others are unsuitable for wheelchairs. Café Renshaw is separate from the museum building and is generally reached by external steps. Alternative ramped access is provided for wheelchairs, buggies and for those who find steps difficult. An accessible toilet is situated within the café.*

WWT Wetland Centre

Queen Elizabeth's Walk, Barnes, SW13 9WT (8409 4400, fax 8409 4401, www.wwt.org.uk). Hammersmith tube then bus 283, Barnes rail or bus 33, 72, 209. **Open** *Mar-Oct 9.30am-6pm daily. Nov-Feb 9.30am-5pm daily.*

Reclaimed from industrial reservoirs a decade ago, the 43-acre Wildfowl & Wetlands Trust Wetland Centre is four miles from central London, but feels a world away. Quiet ponds, rushes, rustling reeds and wildflower gardens all teem with bird life – some 150 species – as well as the now very rare water vole. Naturalists ponder its 27,000 trees and 300,000 aquatic plants and swoon over 300 varieties of butterfly, 20 types of dragonfly and four species of bat (now sleeping in a stylish new house designed by Turner Prize-winning artist Jeremy Deller). You can explore water-recycling initiatives in the new RBC Rain Garden or check out the new interactive section: pilot a submerged camera around a pond, learn about the life-cycle of a dragonfly or make waves in a digital pool. Traditionalists needn't be scared – binoculars can be hired to observe what's going on from one of seven hides. At weekends and during school holidays, there are regular programme of children's events. There's also a visitors' centre, a restaurant and a cinema, which screens a documentary telling the story of the centre.

🚶♿ 🚶 ♿ ᵂᶜ ★★★ 🛵 🦮 🚶

Notes *There is a car park at the front with 10+ Blue Badge-designated bays. Parking is free for all users. The route from the car park to the entrance does have slopes/ramps but is accessible to a wheelchair user with assistance. There is no designated drop-off point.* **Reception** *has fixed induction loop; all staff receive disability awareness training. There are moderate and easy slopes throughout. Main paths have a tarmac surface while minor paths are compacted gravel or wood. Motorised scooters are allowed in public parts; one is available at the* **Discovery Centre** *but needs to be booked in advance. There are steps and ramps in the* **Observatory Centre**, *a lift in the* **Visitors' Centre** *and* **Peacock Tower**. *The* **Water's Edge Café** *has ample room for wheelchair users to manoeuvre. The* **Theatre** *does not have designated wheelchair spaces but the front of the theatre is accessible, there is an induction loop, and assistance dogs are allowed in the auditorium. Accessible toilets can be found in the Car Park (53m from entrance), Visitors' Centre (6m from entrance) and in the Waterlife area next to the Explore adventure area.*

Museums & galleries

Fan Museum

12 Crooms Hill, SE10 8ER (8305 1441, www.fan-museum.org). Cutty Sark DLR or Greenwich DLR/rail. **Open** 11am-5pm Tue-Sat; noon-5pm Sun. **Admission** £4; free-£3 reductions; £10 family; free under-7s. Disabled visitors free Tue from 2pm (excludes groups).

The world's most important collection of hand-held fans is displayed in a pair of restored Georgian townhouses. There are about 3,500 fans, including some beauties in the Hélène Alexander collection, but not all are on display at any one time. For details of the regular fan-making workshops and temporary exhibitions, check the website.

Notes *Ramp at entrance. All floors are accessible by lift. There is an accessible toilet.*

Horniman Museum

100 London Road, Forest Hill, SE23 3PQ (8699 1872, fax 8291 5506, www.horniman.ac.uk). Forest Hill rail or bus 363, 122, 176, 185, P4, P13. **Open** 10.30am-5.30pm daily. **Admission** free; donations appreciated. Temporary exhibitions prices vary.

South-east London's premier free family attraction, the Horniman was once the home of tea trader Frederick J Horniman. It's an eccentric-looking art nouveau building (check out the clocktower, which starts as a circle and ends as a square), with a main entrance that looks out on to extensive gardens that are currently being remodelled and renovated..

The oldest section is the Natural History gallery, dominated by an ancient walrus (mistakenly overstuffed by Victorian taxidermists), and now ringed by glass cabinets containing pickled animals, stuffed birds and insect models. Other galleries include the Nature Base, African Worlds and the Centenary Gallery, which focuses on world cultures. Downstairs, the Music Gallery contains hundreds of instruments: their sounds can be unleashed via touchscreen tables, while hardier instruments (flip-flop drums, thumb pianos) can be bashed with impunity.

The most popular part of the museum is its showpiece Aquarium, where a series of tanks and rockpools cover seven distinct aquatic ecosystems. There are mesmerising moon jellyfish, strangely large British seahorses, starfish, tropical fish and creatures from the mangroves. It forms a key part of the Evolution project, which is bringing together the natural history collection, aquarium and gardens to explore biodiversity and the story of how life has evolved on Earth.

Notes *No car park. Wheelchair access to the main entrance is by an easy slope to automatic doors. A lift connects all gallery areas, plus the shop and café which has ample room for wheelchair users to manoeuvre. The reception and museum areas have a fixed induction loop, which staff are trained to use. Tactile signage for exhibits is available. A loan wheelchair is available. The accessible toilet is 10m from the accessible entrance. Assistance dogs welcome. A member of staff trained in BSL skills is generally on duty. Staff are Typetalk aware.*

Imperial War Museum

Lambeth Road, Elephant & Castle, SE1 6HZ (7416 5320, fax 7416 5374 www.iwm.org.uk). Lambeth North tube or Elephant & Castle tube/rail. **Open** 10am-6pm daily. **Admission** free. Prices for special exhibitions vary.

Antique guns, tanks, aircraft and artillery are parked in the main hall of this imposing edifice, built in 1814 as a lunatic asylum (the Bethlehem Royal Hospital, aka Bedlam). After the inmates were relocated in 1930, the central block became the war museum, only to be damaged by World War II air raids. Today, the museum gives the history of armed conflict, especially involving Britain and the Commonwealth, from World War I to today.

Moving on from the more gung-ho exhibits on the ground floor, there are extensive galleries devoted to the two World Wars. The museum's tone darkens as you ascend. On the third floor, the Holocaust Exhibition (not recommended for under-14s) traces the history of European anti-Semitism and its nadir in the concentration camps. Upstairs, Crimes Against Humanity (unsuitable for under-16s) is a minimalist space in which a film exploring contemporary genocide and ethnic violence rolls relentlessly.

There is also the world's largest collection of Victoria Crosses and excellent, long-running temporary exhibitions that are suitable for children: 'Children's War', exploring the Home Front from a child's viewpoint using letters, recordings and a reconstructed 1940s house, will be here until 29 Feb 2012, after which 'Once Upon a Wartime: Classic War Stories for Children' will run until 2 September 2012.

♿ ♿ ♿ ♿ ♿ ♿ ♿ ♿

Notes *There is a car park at the rear of the museum. Parking for Blue Badge holders is free but should be booked in advance; there are two designated bays. The route from the car park to the entrance is accessible to a wheelchair user with assistance. There is no designated drop-off point. The main entrance has 10 stairs; wheelchair access is by the Park Entrance at the side of the museum. All areas of the museum are accessible to wheelchair users except the upstairs of the 1940s house in The Children's War exhibition. Lifts serve all floors. Exhibits can be audio described. There is a portable*

induction loop, which staff are trained to use. A wheelchair is available; ask at the information desk or call 7416 5000. There is a special audio guide for The Holocaust Exhibition. This tour includes extracts from the museum's sound archive and access to boxes containing replica exhibits for handling. Visually impaired visitors are also permitted to touch the exhibits in the Large Exhibits Gallery on the ground floor and first-floor balcony. Magnifying sheets are available to aid reading captions or documents. Some special exhibitions have large-print captions produced for exhibits. Video clips played in special exhibitions are often subtitled. The cinema has level access. There is an infrared hearing system, subtitles are not available. Assistance dogs are allowed in the cinema. The café has ample room for wheelchair users to manoeuvre. The accessible toilet is 25m from the Park entrance and located within the standard toilets next to the Park entrance. There is level access to the accessible toilet.

National Maritime Museum

Romney Road, SE10 9NF (8858 4422, 8312 6565, fax 8312 6632, www.nmm.ac.uk). Cutty Sark DLR or Greenwich DLR/rail. **Open** 10am-5pm daily. *Tours* phone for details.

Admission free; donations welcome. The world's largest maritime museum contains a huge store of creatively organised maritime art, cartography, models and regalia. Ground-level galleries include Explorers, which covers great sea expeditions back to medieval times, and Maritime London, which concentrates on the city as a port and currently contains Nelson's uniform, complete with fatal bullet-hole; it will move to the new Sammy Ofer Wing on completion in 2013.

Upstairs are Your Ocean, which reveals our dependence on the health of the world's oceans. Level two holds the interactives:

the Bridge has a ship simulator, and All Hands lets children load cargo or try their hand as a gunner. Oceans of Discovery commemorates world exploration and the Atlantic World gallery examines the complex relationship between Britain, Africa and the Americas.

Notes *The car park on Park Row at the administration building is only open at weekends; there are six designated bays free for Blue Badge holders (booking advised). The route from the car park to the entrance is accessible to wheelchair users with assistance. There is no designated drop-off point. There is level access to the entrance, which has two sets of automatic doors. All floors are accessible by lifts. Touch tours are available. Loan wheelchair can be reserved. The accessible toilet is 23m from the main entrance within the Stanhope entrance and on the upper ground level 100m from the main entrance. There is ample room for wheelchair users to manoeuvre in both cafés. Staff receive disability awareness training. Documents can be requested in Braille and large print. A member of staff trained in BSL skills is usually on duty.*

EAST LONDON

Museums & galleries

Geffrye Museum
136 Kingsland Road, E2 8EA (7739 9893, www.geffrye-museum.org.uk). Hoxton rail. **Open** 10am-5pm Tue-Sat; noon-5pm Sun. *Almshouse tours timed entries Sat, Wed, Thur each month.* **Admission** free; donations appreciated. *Almshouse tours £2; free disabled visitors and under-16s.*

Housed in a set of 18th-century almshouses, the Geffrye Museum offers a vivid physical history of the English interior. Displaying original furniture, paintings, textiles and decorative arts, the museum recreates a sequence of typical middle-class living rooms from 1600 to the present. It's an oddly interesting way to take in domestic history, with any number of intriguing details to catch your eye – from a bell jar of stuffed birds to a particular decorative flourish on an armchair. There's an airy wheelchair-user accessible restaurant overlooking the lovely gardens, which include a walled plot for herbs and a chronological series in different historical styles.

Notes *Limited number of designated parking bays in front of the museum available for up to three hours between 10am-4pm. Entrance and gardens are ramped and accessible for wheelchair users. There is an accessible toilet. All main displays located on the ground floor. Note that the Restored Historic Almshouse is not accessible for wheelchair users. There is a programme of BSL-interpreted talks plus talks and handling sessions for blind and visually impaired visitors. Neck loop and transcript of audio guide available.*

Museum of London Docklands
No.1 Warehouse, West India Quay, Hertsmere Road, E14 4AL (7001 9844, fax 7001 9801, www.museumindocklands.org.uk). Canary Wharf tube or West India Quay DLR. **Open** 10am-6pm daily. **Admission** free.

Housed in a 19th-century warehouse (itself a Grade I-listed building), this huge museum explores the complex history of London's docklands and the river over two millennia. Displays spreading over three storeys take you from the arrival of the Romans all the way to the docks' 1980s closure and the area's subsequent redevelopment. The Docklands at War section is very affecting, while a haunting new per-

Geffrye Museum. *See p133.*

manent exhibition sheds light on the dark side of London's rise as a centre for finance and commerce, exploring the city's heavy involvement in the transatlantic slave trade. You can also walk through full-scale mock-ups of a quayside and a dingy riverfront alley. Temporary exhibitions are frequently set up on the ground floor, where you'll also find a café and a docks-themed play area for children. Just like its elder sibling, the Museum of London, the MoLD has a great programme of screenings and special events.

Notes *The museum has designated parking spaces for Blue and Orange Badge holders; drive to the barrier at the front of the Museum. There is also a public car park directly behind the museum, in Hertsmere Road. Lift access to all floors with accessible toilets. Wheelchairs and disability scooters are available to borrow from the information desk. Spaces are available for wheelchair users in the theatre and learning rooms. Folding seats available. Theatre has an induction loop. Large-print events brochure and floor plan available from the information desk. Assistance dogs welcome. Touch Tours are available.*

Museum of St Bartholomew's Hospital

St Bartholomew's Hospital, North Wing, West Smithfield, EC1A 7BE (3456 5798, bit.ly/qLB720). Barbican tube or Farringdon tube/rail. **Open** 10am-4pm Tue-Fri. **Admission** free; donations welcome. **No credit cards**.

Be glad you're living in the 21st century. Many of the displays in this small museum inside St Bart's Hospital relate to the days before anaesthetics, when surgery and carpentry were kindred occupations. Every Friday at 2pm, visitors are invited on a guided tour of the museum (£5; for information, call 7837 0546) that

takes in the Hogarth paintings in the Great Hall, the little church of St Bartholomew-the-Less, neighbouring St Bartholomew-the-Great and Smithfield.

Notes *Wheelchair access is by prior arrangement only. A hearing induction loop is available. Assistance dogs welcome.*

Whitechapel Gallery

80-82 Whitechapel High Street, E1 7QX (7522 7888, fax 7377 7887, www.whitechapelgallery.org). Aldgate East tube. **Open** 11am-6pm Tue, Wed, Fri-Sun; 11am-9pm Thur. **Admission** free. Prices for temporary exhibitions vary.

This East End stalwart reopened in 2009, following a major redesign that saw the Grade II-listed building expand into the similarly historic former library next door. Rather brilliantly, the architects left the two buildings stylistically distinct rather than trying to smooth out their differences. As well as nearly tripling its available exhibition space, the Whitechapel gave itself a research centre and archives room, as well as a proper restaurant and café. It looks set to improve a stellar reputation as a contemporary art pioneer built on shows of Picasso – *Guernica* was shown here in 1939 – Jackson Pollock, Mark Rothko and Frida Kahlo. The museum lacks a permanent collection, but has a strong programme of temporary shows.

Notes *Entrance is at street level and all the galleries are accessible to wheelchair users. The accessible toilet is located on the ground floor by the entrance. A lift services all levels. Brochures are available in large print, British Sign Language events are held on the first Thursday of the month at 7pm.*

William Morris Gallery
*Lloyd Park, Forest Road, E17 4PP
(8496 4390, http://bit.ly/2356Cg).
15min walk from Walthamstow Central
tube/rail or bus 34, 97, 215, 275.*
Open 10am-5pm Wed-Sun. *Tours*
phone for details. **Admission** free;
donations appreciated.

Artist, socialist and source of much flowery wallpaper, William Morris lived here between 1848 and 1856. There are plenty of designs in fabric, stained glass and ceramic on show, produced by Morris and his acolytes. The gallery – which in 2010 was awarded a £1.5m grant for improvements by the Heritage Lottery Fund – features the medieval-style helmet and sword the designer used as props for some of his murals, but there are also plenty of equally fascinating and humble domestic objects: his coffee cup, for instance.

Notes *A car park is located next to
the Forest Road entrance to
Lloyd Park. The ground floor of
the Gallery is accessible for wheelchair
users. A portable ramp is available.
Please ring the doorbell on arrival.
The Gallery is a member of the
Community Toilet Scheme.
No access to first floor galleries
for wheelchair users.*

V&A Museum of Childhood
*Cambridge Heath Road, E2 9PA (8983
5235, www.museumofchildhood.org.uk).
Bethnal Green or Cambridge Heath rail.*
Open 10am-5.45pm daily. **Admission**
free; donations appreciated.

Home to one of the world's finest collections of children's toys, dolls' houses, games and costumes, the Museum of Childhood shines brighter than ever after extensive refurbishment, which has given it an impressive entrance. Part of the Victoria & Albert Museum (*see p116*), the museum has been amassing childhood-related objects since 1872 and continues to

do so, with Incredibles figures complementing 1970s puppets, Barbie Dolls, Thunderbirds costumes and Victorian praxinoscopes. The museum has lots of hands-on stuff for children dotted about the many cases of historic artefacts. Regular exhibitions are held upstairs, while the café in the centre of the main hall helps to revive flagging grown-ups.

Notes *Parking for visitors with
access needs can be reserved.
By prior arrangement there is lift
access from the car park at the rear
entrance of the museum; call 9983
5200. The museum is accessible to
wheelchair users, with a gently
sloped approach to the front entrance
and interior lift and ramp access to
all public areas. The museum is
equipped with an induction loop on
audio visual displays. Arrangements
for BSL interpreters can be made for
performances. Requests for this
service must be made at least two weeks
in advance. Accessible toilets are located
at the front and rear of the museum,
on the lower ground floor. Assistance
dogs welcome.*

WEST LONDON
Attractions

BBC Television Centre
*TV Centre, Wood Lane, W12 7RJ
(0370 603 0304, www.bbc.co.uk/tours).*
White City or Wood Lane tube. **Open**
by appointment only Mon-Sat.
Admission £9.95; £7.75-£9.25
reductions; £30 family. No under-9s.

Catch it while you can. The BBC's main production centre, now more than 60 years old, is up for sale. By 2013 most staff will have relocated north to Salford, and by 2015 the BBC hopes to begin redevelopment in collaboration with a private partner. For now, if you book in advance, you

V&A Museum of Childhood.

can experience a fascinating snoop around the temple of British televisual history. Tours include visits to the news desk, the TV studios and the Weather Centre, though children and Dr Who fans might be most excited about the TARDIS on display.

♿ 🦻 ♿ ★★★ 🤚 👂 🐕

Notes *Parking can be arranged for Blue Badge holders – ask when booking. The tours cover some distance and visitors with access needs are advised to call the booking line on 0370 901 1227 or textphone for hearing impaired callers 0370 010 0212. A wheelchair is available, but must be booked. There is wheelchair access, plus lifts and accessible toilets. Assistance dogs welcome. A sign language interpreter can be booked to accompany tours.*

Chelsea Physic Garden

66 Royal Hospital Road, SW3 4HS (7352 6458, www.chelseaphysicgarden.co.uk). Sloane Square tube or bus 11, 19, 239. **Open** *Apr-Oct* noon-5pm Wed-Fri; noon-6pm Sun. *Tours* times vary; phone to check. **Admission** £8; £5 reductions (carers free); free under-5s. *Tours* free.

The sprawling grounds of this gorgeous botanic garden are filled with healing herbs and vegetables, rare trees and dye plants. The garden was founded in 1673 by Sir Hans Sloane with the purpose of cultivating and studying plants for medical purposes. The first plant specimens were brought to England and planted here in 1676, with the famous Cedars of Lebanon (the first to be grown in England) arriving a little later. The garden opened to the public in 1893.

♿ 🦻 ★★ 🐕

Notes *There is a non-reservable designated parking bay outside 66 Royal Hospital Road with dropped kerb access to the pavement, and another by the West Gate. The entrance at 66 Royal*

Hospital Road is the most accessible. There are no steps in the garden and access is via gravel or grass paths. A loan wheelchair is available, but should be booked in advance.

Chiswick House

Burlington Lane, W4 2RP (8995 0508, www.chgt.org.uk). Hammersmith tube then bus 190, or Chiswick rail. **Open** *Apr-Oct* 10am-5pm Mon-Wed, Sun. **Admission** £5; £2.50-£4.30 reductions; free under-5s.

Richard Boyle, third Earl of Burlington, designed this lovely Palladian villa in 1725 as a place to entertain the artistic and philosophical luminaries of the day. The Chiswick House & Gardens Trust has been restoring the gardens to Burlington's original design, with much now reopened to the public. The restoration will be helped by details from the newly acquired painting *A View of Chiswick House from the South-west* by Dutch landscape artist Pieter Andreas Rysbrack (c1685-1748).

♿ 🧑 ♿ ★★★ 🚻 👂 🐕

Notes *There are designated parking bays in the public car park off the westbound A4. The house and café can be reached via a 5min walk along level gravel paths. If you require disabled parking closer to the house contact staff on 8995 0508 to book a parking space within the gardens. Spaces are limited and booking is required. The house is reached via a gravel courtyard. There is one step at the entrance and a ramp is available if required. All areas of the ground floor can be accessed and contain some seating. The first floor is reached via a narrow spiral staircase. If you find this staircase difficult, staff can provide access via the external portico steps. Weather permitting, a stair climber is available to the first floor via the portico steps. If you require the stair climber or wish to book a wheelchair, contact staff in advance on 8995 0508.*

Chelsea Physic Garden.

Leighton House. *See p142.*

The **café** *and* **conservatory** *are fully accessible. The accessible toilet is situated beside the café. An audio tour is included in the admission price. Visitors to the cellars should be accompanied as there are steep steps and low ceilings. Barrels in the cellars may be touched. An audio tour with portable induction loop is included in the admission price.*

Ham House

Ham Street, Richmond, Surrey TW10 7RS (8940 1950, www.nationaltrust. org.uk/hamhouse). Richmond tube/rail then bus 371. **Open** *Gardens* Jan, Nov, Dec 11am-4pm Mon-Sun; Feb-Oct 11am-5pm Mon-Sun. *House* Feb, Mar 11.30am-3.30pm Mon-Thur, Sat, Sun; Apr-Oct 12am-4pm Mon-Thur, Sat, Sun; Nov 11.30am-3pm Mon, Tue, Sat, Sun. **Admission** prices vary; check website for details.

Built in 1610 for one of James I's courtiers, Thomas Vavasour, this lavish red-brick mansion is full of period furnishings, rococo mirrors and ornate tapestries. Detailing is exquisite, down to a table in the dairy with sculpted cow's legs. The restored formal grounds also attract attention: there's a lovely trellised Cherry Garden and some lavender parterres. The tearoom in the old orangery turns out historic dishes (lavender syllabub, for instance) using ingredients from the Kitchen Gardens.

♿ ♿ 🚻 ★★★ 🐾

Notes *There is designated parking. six steps to entrance, ramp available, no handrails. Three manual wheelchairs are available. Ground floor has steps, narrow doorways, small rooms – ramp available. Stairs with handrail to other floors – lift available. Audio visual/film. Accessible toilet in courtyard opposite gift shop. The grounds are fully accessible, loose gravel paths, cobbles. Map of accessible route. Two single-seat, powered mobility vehicles are available, but reservation is essential.*

Hampton Court Palace

East Molesey, Surrey KT8 9AU (0844 482 7777, www.hrp.org.uk). Hampton Court rail, or riverboat from Westminster or Richmond to Hampton Court Pier (Apr-Oct). **Open** *Palace* Apr-Oct 10am-6pm daily; Nov-Mar 10am-4.30pm daily. *Park* dawn-dusk daily. **Admission** *Palace, courtyard, cloister & maze* £14; £7-£11.50 reductions; £38 family; free under-5s. *Maze only* £3.50; £2.50 reductions. *Gardens only* Apr-Oct £4.60; £4 reductions; Nov-Mar free.

It is a half-hour train ride from central London, but this spectacular palace, once owned by Henry VIII, is worth the trek. It was built in 1514 by Cardinal Wolsey, the high-flying Lord Chancellor, but Henry liked it so much he seized it for himself in 1528. For the next 200 years it was a focal point of English history: Elizabeth I was imprisoned in a tower by her jealous and fearful elder sister Mary; Shakespeare gave his first performance to James I in 1604; and, after the Civil War, Oliver Cromwell was so besotted by the building that he ditched his puritanical principles and moved in to enjoy its luxuries.

Centuries later, the rosy walls of the palace still dazzle. Its vast size can be daunting, so it's a good idea to take advantage of the guided tours. If you do decide to go it alone, start with Henry VIII's State Apartments, which include the Great Hall, noted for its beautiful stained-glass windows and elaborate religious tapestries; in the Haunted Gallery, the ghost of Catherine Howard – Henry's fifth wife, executed for adultery in 1542 – can reputedly still be heard shrieking. The King's Apartments, added in 1689 by Wren, are notable for a splendid mural of Alexander the Great, painted by Antonio Verrio. The Queen's Apartments and Georgian Rooms feature similarly elaborate paintings, chandeliers and tapestries. The Tudor Kitchens are great fun, with their giant cauldrons, fake pies and blood-spattered walls.

More spectacular sights await outside, where the exquisitely landscaped gardens contain superb topiary, peaceful Thames views, a reconstruction of a 16th-century heraldic garden and the famous Hampton Court maze. In summer, there's a music festival and a flower show that rivals the more celebrated one at Chelsea; every winter, an ice-skating rink is installed.

Notes *There is a car park beside the welcome centre with nine designated Blue Badge bays. The route from the car park to the entrance is accessible to a wheelchair user with assistance. The welcome centre contains the ticket office and a gift shop. There is a ramp or slope to access this area. There is a moderate ramp with a level landing at the top. There are also steps to access this area. Inside access is by ramps and slopes with lift access to other floors.* **Young Henry VIII's Story** *is step-access only; visitors who cannot manage these steps can view a video in the information centre on the ground floor.* **Henry VIII's Wine Cellar** *and the* **Tudor Kitchen Shop** *are accessed by eight deep steps with a handrail on the right hand side going up. The* **Henry Shop** *is also accessed by steps only. Exhibits can be audio described. A loan wheelchair and mobility scooters are available, for use in the* **Gardens** *only. General audio tours for visitors with visual impairments are available for* **William III's Apartments**, *the* **Georgian Rooms**, *the* **Tudor Kitchens** *and the Young Henry VIII Story. There are also escorted description tours for visually impaired visitors on the 9th of the month. These must be booked at least 14 days in advance. Braille and large-print guidebooks are available to borrow free from the information centre. Braille and large-print folders are available in Young Henry VIII's Story. A BSL interpreter is available from 10.30am on the 2nd weekend of the month to interpret scheduled tours. Copies of the guidebook are available to borrow from the information centre for people with hearing difficulties. The scripts of the audio tours are also available. Accessible toilets are 58m from the East Gate on the south side of* **Base Court** *and in the toilet block in the Gardens to the north of the Palace. Staff receive disability awareness training and are Typetalk aware. Assistance dogs welcome. The* **Maze** *is accessible to wheelchair users, although some of the turning areas are tight so may be unsuitable for mobility scooters.*

Leighton House

12 Holland Park Road, W14 8LZ (7602 3316 www.rbkc.gov.uk). High Street Kensington tube. **Open** 10am-5.30pm Mon, Wed-Sun. *Closed Christmas week.* Free tour 3pm Wed (other times by appointment only). **Admission** £5; £1 reductions.

Behind its stern Victorian red-brick façade, Leighton House has received an impressive £1.6m refurbishment. In the 1860s, the painter Frederic Leighton commissioned a showpiece house, which he filled with classical treasures from all over the world, as well as his own works and those of his contemporaries. Every inch is decorated in high style: magnificent downstairs reception rooms designed for lavish entertaining; a dramatic staircase leading to a light-filled studio that takes up most of the first floor; and the 'Arab Hall', which showcases Leighton's extensive collection of 16th-century Middle Eastern tiles. The only private space in the entire building is a tiny single bedroom.

Notes *No wheelchair access.*

Royal Botanic Gardens at Kew.
See p144.

Marble Hill House

Richmond Road, Twickenham, Middx TW1 2NL (8892 5115, www.english-heritage.org.uk). Richmond tube/rail, St Margaret's rail or bus 33, 90, 490, H22, R70. **Open** *Apr-Oct* 10am-2pm Sat; 10am-5pm Sun & Bank Holidays; *group visits Nov-Mar by request.*
Admission £5.00; £4.30 reductions; £13.80 family (prices may change). Free for English Heritage members.

King George II spared no expense to win the favour of his mistress, Henrietta Howard. Not only did he build this perfect Palladian house (1724), he almost dragged Britain into a war in doing so: by using Honduran mahogany for the grand staircase, he managed to spark a row with Spain. It was worth it. Picnickers welcome in the grounds, as are sporty types (there are tennis, putting and cricket facilities).

👫🧎‍♂️♿🚻 **P** ⭐⭐⭐ L 🐕

Notes *Disabled visitors may be set down outside the entrance by arrangement. Level floors throughout the ground floor. There is an introductory film with subtitles and albums available on the ground floor. Limited access to the second floor via a staircase. Large-print text is available for rooms/ collections on the upper floors. Accessible toilet on the ground floor. The shop has level access. Dogs on leads only in restricted areas.*

Royal Botanic Gardens (Kew Gardens)

Kew, Richmond, Surrey TW9 3AB (8332 5655, www.kew.org). Kew Gardens tube/rail, Kew Bridge rail or riverboat to Kew Pier. **Open** *Apr-Aug* 9.30am-6.30pm Mon-Fri; 9.30am-7.30pm Sat, Sun. *Sept, Oct* 9.30am-6pm daily. *Late Oct-early Feb* 9.30am-4.15pm daily. *Early Feb-Mar* 9.30am-5.30pm daily.
Admission £13.90; £11.90 reductions; free under-17s.

Kew's lush, landscaped beauty represents the pinnacle of our national gardening obsession. From the early 1700s until 1840, when the gardens were given to the nation, these were the grounds for two fine royal residences – the White House and Richmond Lodge. Early resident Queen Caroline, wife of George II, was fond of the exotic plants brought back to Britain by voyaging botanists. In 1759, the renowned 'Capability' Brown was employed by George III to improve on the work of his predecessors, William Kent and Charles Bridgeman. Thus took shape the extraordinary garden that now attracts hundreds of thousands of visitors each year.

Covering more than 300 acres, Kew feels surprisingly big – pick up a map at the ticket office and follow the handy signs. Head straight for the 19th-century greenhouses, filled to the roof with plants – some of which have been here as long as the huge glass structures themselves. The sultry Palm House holds tropical plants: palms, bamboo, tamarind, mango and fig trees, not to mention fragrant hibiscus and frangipani. The Temperate House features *Pendiculata sanderina*, the Holy Grail for orchid hunters, with petals some 90cm long. Also worth seeking out are the Princess of Wales Conservatory, divided into ten climate zones; the Marine Display, downstairs from the Palm House (it isn't always open, but when it is you can see the seahorses); the lovely, quiet indoor pond of the Waterlily House (closed in winter); and the Victorian botanical drawings of the impressive Marianne North Gallery. The Xstrata Treetop Walkway has been a hugely popular addition to the gardens, allowing you to walk in the leaf canopy 18m up.

♿🧎‍♂️🧎♿🚻 🐕

Notes *There are three dedicated parking bays for disabled drivers near the Main Gate. There are also several spaces in the car park next to the Brentford Gate, which are free for disabled drivers. If these are full, disabled drivers are welcome to park* elsewhere in the car park. On-street parking is also usually available on Kew Road (A307) providing easy access to Victoria Gate (restricted before 10am). Note that on busy days the spaces on the Kew Road can fill up quickly so parking here is not guaranteed. Note if taking the District line to Kew Gardens station from central London, there is no wheelchair-accessible exit to Kew Gardens from the westbound platform. Instead you will need to travel one stop further to Richmond station where the train terminates, and wait until it travels back to Kew Gardens station, when it will stop at the eastbound platform. The eastbound platform has a level exit leading to the Kew village area which is a short distance (400m) from the Gardens. If you require assistance to alight from the train, please contact TFL in advance on 0845 330 9880. Kew Gardens covers over 300 acres and there are four entrance gates. The closest entrance to the Kew Gardens Underground station (400m) is **Victoria Gate**. Adjacent to this entrance is the Victoria Plaza which has a shop, café and accessible toilet facilities. There is no drop-off area or designated parking spaces outside this gate. The **Main Gate** is the closest entrance to the Kew Bridge mainline rail station (800m) with a drop-off area right outside and designated parking spaces only a short distance away. **Brentford Gate** is adjacent to Kew's Ferry Lane car park. Designated parking spaces are available. **Lion Gate** is the only gate in the southern part of the Gardens, and is therefore much further from the popular attractions such as the Palm House, Princess of Wales Conservatory and the Climbers and Creepers children's play area, it is closest to Kew's Pagoda (200m from the gate) and the Pavilion Restaurant (400m). This area of the Gardens is consequently much quieter

with fewer visitors. The nearest toilets are about 300m from the gate, at the **Pavilion Restaurant**. Kew's land train, the **Kew Explorer** (additional charge) is a great introduction to the gardens and an easy way to explore all the main attractions. The trip lasts approximately 40min and stops at eight points including the Temperate House, the Palm House and the Pagoda. There is space for one wheelchair in the last carriage of the vehicle, and ample room for storage of folded-up wheelchairs. The footpaths and the majority of buildings are suitable for wheelchairs. The terrain is generally flat, with tarmac paths in most places. There is, however, **no wheelchair access to the following areas:** Marine Display in the Palm House basement; the galleries levels at the top of the Palm House and Temperate House; the upper levels inside the Princess of Wales Conservatory (accessed by gentle slope which includes some small steps). For information about access to the **Xstrata Treetop Walkway**, see the website. Wheelchairs can be borrowed free of charge at any entrance gate. Eight **mobility scooters** can be borrowed free of charge, but must be booked in advance, on 8332 5121. Scooters can be made available at either Brentford Gate, Victoria Gate or Main Gate. Pavement-use mobility scooters are allowed on footpaths only. A large-print map is available at ticket offices and at the Victoria Plaza information desk. Registered disability assistance dogs are allowed within the gardens. Water is available upon request. Accessible toilets are within easy reach of all main attractions and gates: these are marked on the 'Welcome to Kew Map' (provided on arrival). All restaurants, cafés and shops are accessible to wheelchair users. There are also accessible toilets adjacent to all cafés and restaurants.

Royal Hospital Chelsea

Royal Hospital Road, SW3 4SR (7881 5200, www.chelsea-pensioners.org.uk). Sloane Square tube or bus 11, 19, 22, 137, 170, 239. **Open** *Apr-Sept* 10am-noon, 2-4pm Mon-Sat; 2-4pm Sun. *Oct-Mar* 10am-noon, 2-4pm Mon-Sat. **Admission** free.

Roughly 350 Chelsea Pensioners (retired soldiers) live in quarters at the Royal Hospital, founded in 1682 by Charles II and designed by Sir Christopher Wren (with later adjustments by Robert Adam and Sir John Soane). Retired soldiers are still eligible to apply for a final posting here if they're over 65 and in receipt of an Army or War Disability Pension for Army Service. The pensioners have their own club room, bowling green and gardens, and get tickets to Chelsea FC home games – the club's home strip for the 2010/11 season added a flash of red at the collar, sleeve and shorts in their honour. The museum, open at the same times as the Hospital, has more about their lives.

Notes *Wheelchair access to some public areas. Assistance dogs welcome.*

Syon House

Syon Park, Brentford, Middx TW8 8JF (8560 0882, www.syonpark.co.uk). Gunnersbury tube/rail then bus 237, 267. **Open** *House* (mid Mar-Oct only) 11am-5pm Wed, Thur, Sun. *Gardens* (all year) 10.30am-dusk daily. *Tours* by arrangement. **Admission** *House & gardens* £20; £4-£8 reductions; £22 family. *Gardens only* £5; £2.50-£3.50 reductions; £11 family. *Tours* free.

The Percys, Dukes of Northumberland, were once known as 'the Kings of the North'. Their old house is on the site of a Bridgettine convent, suppressed by Henry VIII in 1534. The building was converted into a house in 1547 for the Duke of Northumberland. Its neoclassical interior, created by Robert Adam in 1761, has made

the house a favourite with TV and film producers: everything from *Poirot* to *The Madness of King George III* has been shot here. Inside, there's an outstanding range of Regency portraits. The gardens, by 'Capability' Brown, are enhanced by the splendid Great Conservatory and in winter you can take an evening walk through illuminated woodland.

Notes *There is a free car park at the front of the house which has six designated bays close to the visitor centre entrance. The front entrance does not have level access, with seven steps to heavy push-open doors. Inside there are six steps from the foyer into the house. There is another set of four steps on the other side of the foyer. Floors LG-G (Syon Abbey exhibition) are also accessed by 15+ steps. Exhibits can be audio described. A loan wheelchair is available. There is no accessible toilet but standard toilets are available. Assistance dogs welcome.*

Museums & galleries

Kew Bridge Steam Museum

Green Dragon Lane, Brentford, Middx TW8 0EN (8568 4757, www.kbsm.org). Gunnersbury tube/rail or Kew Bridge rail. **Open** 11am-4pm Tue-Sun. **Admission** £9.50; £8.50 reductions; under-16s £3.50.

One of London's most engaging small museums, this impressive pumping station is a reminder that steam wasn't just used for powering trains, but also for supplying fresh water to the citizens of a rapidly expanding London. Built in 1838 by the Grand Junction Waterworks Company, the building is now home to a huge collection of steam-driven pumping engines. The 250-ton Grand Junction 90 engine is the world's largest surviving Cornish beam engine, and is still steamed once a month. There are hands-on exhibits

Royal Hospital Chelsea.

Syon House. *See p146.*

for children, a dressing-up box and a miniature steam train.

Notes *Free car park for 50 cars, one designated space Blue Badge holder. Reserve space in advance. Level access from the car park to the museum shop and reception area. Approximately 85 per cent of the museum is accessible to wheelchair users via ramped flooring or a lift. Access to the Boulton & Watt, Maudslay & Bull engines is via ramp or rising platform lift. Access to the 90in engine is via stair-climbing lift and temporary ramp. Access to the railway and waterwheel is via ramp or rising platform lift. Access to the Babcock café is via ramp or rising platform lift. There is an accessible toilet adjacent to the museum car park, which requires the RADAR key held at the museum reception. Two manual wheelchairs are available for loan. These can be pre-booked. A large-print guide to the museum is available for 50p. Assistance dogs welcome. Touch tours can be arranged but require at least two weeks' notice.*

Museum of Brands, Packaging & Advertising

Colville Mews, Lonsdale Road, W11 2AR (7908 0880, www.museumofbrands.com). Notting Hill Gate tube. **Open** 10am-6pm Tue-Sat; 11am-5pm Sun. **Admission** £6.50; £2.25-£4 reductions; free under-7s.

Robert Opie began collecting the things others throw away when he was 16. His collection now includes anything from milk bottles to vacuum cleaners and cereal packets. The emphasis is on the last century of British consumerism, design and domestic life, but there are older items, such as an ancient Egyptian doll.

Notes *The museum has full access for wheelchair users to all public areas.*

National Army Museum

Royal Hospital Road, SW3 4HT (7730 0717, www.national-army-museum. ac.uk). Sloane Square tube or bus 11, 137, 170. **Open** 10am-5.30pm daily. **Admission** free.

Far more entertaining than its modern exterior suggests, this museum dedicated to the history of the British Army begins with 'Redcoats', a gallery that starts at Agincourt in 1415 and ends with the American War of Independence. Upstairs, 'The Road to Waterloo' marches through 20 years of struggle against the French, featuring 70,000 model soldiers. Also on display is the kit of the Olympic medal winner Kelly Holmes (an ex-army athlete), while Major Michael 'Bronco' Lane, a conqueror of Everest, has donated his frostbitten fingertips.

Notes *On-street designated Blue Badge parking bays in Royal Hospital Road. There is a ramp or three shallow steps to the entrance. The museum is accessible and there is a fixed induction loop. A loan wheelchair is available. All other floors are accessed by lift. The café has level access and ample room for wheelchair users to manoeuvre. The accessible toilet is 22m from the accessible entrance next to the museum shop. Staff receive disability awareness training. Assistance dogs welcome.*

Orleans House Gallery

Riverside, Twickenham, Middx TW1 3DJ (8831 6000, fax 8744 0501 www.richmond.gov.uk/orleans_house _gallery). Richmond tube then bus 33, 490, H22, R68, R70, or St Margaret's or Twickenham rail. **Open** *Apr-Sept* 1-5.30pm Tue-Sat; 2-5.30pm Sun. *Oct-Mar* 1-4.30pm Tue-Sat; 2-4.30pm Sun. **Admission** free.

Secluded in pretty gardens, this Grade I-listed riverside house was constructed in

1710 for James Johnson, Secretary of State for Scotland. It was later named after the Duke of Orleans, Louis-Philippe, who lived in exile here from 1800 to 1817. Though partially demolished in 1926, the building retains James Gibbs's neoclassical Octagon Room. There are also regularly changing temporary exhibitions here and in the nearby Stables Gallery.

Notes *Wheelchair access to the ground floor of Orleans House Gallery, Octagon Room, the Coach House, the Stables Gallery, the Stables Café and the artist in residence studio. Limited free car parking space is available within the grounds; call in advance to check availability. Vehicle access is via Orleans Road only. Assistance dogs welcome.*

Saatchi Gallery

Duke of York's HQ, off King's Road, SW3 4SQ (7823 2363, www.saatchi-gallery.co.uk). Sloane Square tube.
Open 10am-6pm daily.
Admission free.

Charles Saatchi's gallery offers 50,000 square feet of space for temporary exhibitions. Given his fame as a promoter in the 1990s of what became known as the Young British Artists – Damien Hirst, Tracey Emin, Gavin Turk, Sarah Lucas – it was a surprise to many that the opening exhibition a few years ago was of new Chinese art. More recent shows have continued the international feel. The details of a plan to donate the gallery to the public, as a renamed Museum of Contemporary Art London, by 2012 are being worked out.

Notes *There are two Blue Badge parking bays to the rear of the gallery which can be accessed via Turk's Row off Lower Sloane Street. Book a parking bay well in advance, or a wheelchair on 7811 3085. Assisted or ramp access is available at the main entrance. All floors have lifts and there is level access between the galleries on each floor. Note that you will need to check in large rucksacks and bags with the cloakroom on arrival. Assistance dogs welcome.*

World Rugby Museum/Twickenham Stadium

Twickenham Rugby Stadium, Rugby Road, Twickenham, Middx TW1 1DZ (8892 8877, www.rfu.com).
Hounslow East tube then bus 281, or Twickenham rail. **Open** *Museum* 10am-5pm Tue-Sat; 11am-5pm Sun. *Tours* 10.30am, noon, 1.30pm, 3pm Tue-Sat; 1pm, 3pm Sun. **Admission** £14; £8 reductions; £40 family. *No stadium tours on match days.*

The impressive Twickenham Stadium is the home of English rugby union. Despite the capacity of 82,000, tickets for international matches are extremely hard to come by, but the Museum of Rugby is also on the site to provide some measure of compensation for fans of the oval ball game. The informative guided tours take in the England dressing room, the players' tunnel and the Royal Box. Memorabilia (a jersey from 1871, the Calcutta Cup) charts the game's development from the late 19th century, and there's a scrum machine which allows you to pit your strength against the pros'. *See also p201.*

Notes *There is free parking for visitors to the World Rugby Museum in the Stadium's main car park. Groups are requested to park in the north car park. The museum and stadium tour routes are fully accessible to wheelchair users. There are accessible toilets. Assistance dogs welcome. Call 8892 8877 for copies of the Access Guide, which is available in large print; specify font size when ordering.*

Accessible tours

London Taxi Tour
Broadwall, SE1 9QE (07957 272179, londontaxitour.com).
Small company offers a selection of bespoke themed tours of London, with qualified tour guide. Taxis with built-in ramps for wheelchair users can be reserved.

The Original London Sightseeing Tour
17-19 Cockspur Street, SW1Y 5BL (7389 5040, www.theoriginaltour.com). **Open** *daily 8.30am-7pm. Tickets £26; £13 children.*
One in three of the fleet of buses run by London's leading bus tour company is accessible to wheelchair users. The company is committed to increasing this proportion as ageing buses are replaced. Customers can alight, then get back on, and a river cruise and walking tours are included in some tickets. Concessions available for disabled customers, but book in advance on 8877 2120, or by email: info@theoriginaltour.com.

The Original London Walks
PO Box 1708, NW6 4LW (switchboard 7624 3978; recorded tour schedule 7624 9255, www.walks.com).
London's leading walking tour company offers a bewildering variety of expertly guided tours, some of which can be tailored for individual customer needs or special requirements.

For more guided tours, see p28.

The Original London Sightseeing Tour.

Eating & drinking

From fine dining to feeding the family, or a perfect pie and a pint.

RESTAURANTS

Banana Tree Canteen
412-416 St John Street, EC1V 4NJ (7278 7565, bit.ly/qcwgT7). Angel tube. **Open** noon-11pm Mon-Sat; noon-10.30pm Sun. **Main courses** £5.45-£9.85. **Set lunch** (noon-5pm) £5.45-£6.85.

This expanding Wagamama-style chain serves up superb-value Thai, Malaysian, Indonesian and Vietnamese food in a modishly spartan, semi-communal environment. The varied menu offers very good set-price deals for stir-fries that you can make up yourself, and for set meals in which you choose your preferred main course to accompany rice, glass-noodle salad, prawn crackers and thai-style corn fritters. Warned about long queues, we went early in the evening and found one whole side of the large room all but empty. As a result, service was prompt and attentive. Starters of pork and prawn dumplings and lamb and lettuce wrap were both very tasty. We were sorely tempted by the Singapore laksa but went instead for blackened chilli pork, and ginger chicken with mushrooms, the latter accompanied by a good bowl of jasmine rice. Both were nicely flavoured and satisfying. With two beers and some fizzy water, our meal for two came to an equally satisfying £42, including service. In an area lacking good budget options, Banana Tree Canteen is welcome.

Notes *Assistance dogs welcome. Staff receive disability awareness training. N1 Centre Car Park is approx 300m away, on Berners Road. A ramp/slope gives access to main single-width door which is permanently held open. The second single-width, heavy door pulls open. Level access inside and motorised scooters allowed in public parts of the restaurant. All tables and seats (bench-style) are permanently fixed but there is room for wheelchair users to manoeuvre. The accessible toilet is at the rear, on the right. Children welcome.*

Botanist. *See p155.*

High Timber. *See p156*.

Botanist

7 Sloane Square, SW1W 8EE
(7730 0077, bit.ly/7lSsxa). Sloane
Square tube. **Breakfast** 8-11.30am
Mon-Fri; 9-11.30am Sat, Sun. **Lunch**
noon-3.30pm Mon-Fri; noon-4pm Sat,
Sun. **Tea** 3.30-5.30pm, **dinner** 6-
10.30pm daily. **Main courses** £14-
£19. **Set meal** (lunch, 5.30-6.30pm)
£20 2 courses, £25 3 courses.

There's not much in the way of biodiversity in the creatures native to the Botanist. Such a prime patch of Sloane Square was always going to be the habitat of the horse and hound brigade, and this venture from gastropub magnates Ed and Tom Martin leaves no stone unturned in cultivating their approval. The front bar is all cream surfaces and gleaming metal fixtures, with a few stools. But it's the rear room that steals the show (there is a medium step from the bar but a moveable ramp is available), with large windows flooding the place with light by day, and a mix of artful spot lighting, modern chandeliers and a backlit glass mural of botanical specimens lending the feel of a science fiction ark by night. Food is nothing if not artful: a mackerel fillet starter came cubed and arranged with studs of lemon confit on a smear of olive tapenade; a main of chicken breast with mushroom stuffing was cut into thirds and balanced on a bed of spinach and morels. A great deal of thought has gone into presentation and flavour combinations, but portions seem shy given the prices. The wine list is lengthy, the service attentive and knowledgeable.

Notes *Registered assistance dogs welcome. Blue Badge parking available in nearby Sedding Street; the approach is level except for one shallow step to double push doors. The accessible unisex toilet is past the bar and accessed by a key obtained from the bar. Babies and children welcome: high chairs. Booking advisable. Four table outdoors.*

Carluccio's

305-307 Upper Street, N1 2TU (7359
8167, www.carluccios.com). Angel tube.
Meals served 8am-11pm Mon-Fri;
9am-11pm Sat; 9am-10.30pm Sun. **Main**
courses £7.50-£14.95. **Set meal** (Mon-
Fri) £9.95 2 courses, £12.95 3 courses.

North London branch of reliable and reasonably priced chain of Italian restaurants and delicatessens. Branches all over London.

Notes *This branch does not have its own car park. There is an easy ramp to main entrance. Ample room for wheelchair users to manoeuvre inside. Staff receive disability awareness training. Babies and children welcome. Assistance dogs welcome.*

Frederick's

Camden Passage, N1 8EG
(7359 2888, www.fredericks. co.uk).
Angel tube. **Lunch** noon-2.30pm, 5.45-
10.30pm Mon-Sat. **Main courses**
£12.50-£26. **Set meal** (lunch; dinner
Mon, Tue; 5.45-7pm Wed-Sat) £14 2
courses, £17 3 courses.

There's a palpable sense of occasion at Frederick's, especially if you dine in the large rear conservatory, where picture windows overlook a garden. There's also a popular bar at the front. The restaurant has been here for years, but still feels fresh: smart, spacious, with white walls and grey slate floors – a place for pleasure rather than business. Both our starters were winners: luscious, buttery scallops with tiny cubes of pancetta were matched with a small portion of risotto, whose creaminess and dense flavour verged on perfection; and a dome of tuna tartare with avocado, which melded fresh, smooth textures and flavours with a dash of hot wasabi. A main course of duck with pak choi and oyster mushrooms was also a success, the oriental twist of the vegetables (with a trace of soy sauce) blending well with rare, juicy, chunky pieces of duck. No such luck with our other main – grouper fillet with a distinctly odd taste and texture – but this was immediately and politely replaced. Chocolate pot was another mini flavour bomb, the dark, dense chocolate contrasting with white chocolate ice-cream.

Notes *Parking 200m away in N1 Centre, Upper Street. One shallow step to main doors that push open. Intercom out of reach for most wheelchair users. A second heavy, single-width door accesses the level dining area. There are steps to the upper dining area. The private dining area is also accessed by stairs. Standard toilets at basement level (no accessible toilet). Babies and children welcome: children's menu; high chairs. Booking advisable weekends. Separate rooms for parties, seating 16 and 30. Tables outdoors (12, garden).*

High Timber
8 High Timber Street, EC4V 3PA (7248 1777, www.hightimber.com). Mansion House tube. **Open** noon-3pm, 6.30-10pm Mon-Fri. **Main courses** £13-£29. **Set lunch** £16.50 2 courses, £20 3 courses.

Smart, with an air of classy simplicity (slate floor, wooden tables, picture windows with amazing views of the Globe, the Millennium Bridge and Tate Modern), High Timber has an equally unfussy menu, akin to that of a superior steakhouse. Starters – pan-fried foie gras with apricots and fig galette; terrine of pressed ham hock with parsley, onion marmalade and gherkins – are standard Modern European. However, it's the grill that counts here, and the Lake District beef. Sold in two weights and according to cut, it's pricey (rump and ribeye are £19/250g, £27/350g), but geared to the expense-account clientele. Quality is assured, and meat is cooked exactly as requested. Sauces (including a luxury

truffle butter) cost extra, but all steaks come with braised mushrooms, onion rings and chips. There are other options too: roast gnocchi with wild mushrooms and truffles, perhaps; Gloucester Old Spot sausages and mash; rack of lamb, or fish. Prestige suppliers are name-checked (Denham Estates venison, Label Anglais chicken, Forman's smoked salmon). In summer, desserts of Kentish strawberries with shortbread and strawberry and lemon thyme soup, and apple and elderflower jelly with raspberries and vanilla ice-cream, hit just the right light note.

Notes *Lift access from the Millennium Bridge with level access into the restaurant. Accessible toilet on ground floor. Assistance dogs welcome.*

Inn The Park
St James's Park, SW1A 2BJ (7451 9999, www.innthepark.com). St James's Park tube. **Breakfast** 8-11am Mon-Fri; 9-11am Sat, Sun. **Lunch** noon-3pm Mon-Fri; noon-4pm Sat, Sun. **Tea** 3-5pm Mon-Fri; 4-5pm Sat, Sun. **Dinner** 6-8.30pm daily. **Main courses** £10.50-£18.50.

After several years of so-so meals at this beautifully appointed and designed café-restaurant, we weren't expecting much. We were, however, expecting hot food.

A Herdwick beef burger with glazed goat's cheese and chips suffered most from being served cold, while a still-tasty lemon sole with squid came off best, but this was a lacklustre performance, especially as prices aren't cheap.

Disappointment was compounded by various ingredients being unavailable. Intentionally cold dishes – mackerel tartare, and pressed ham hock with piccalilli (starters), and British cheeses (to finish) – were by far the most successful choices, though crab salad was watery.

On the plus side, staff are lovely (and on a cool evening, happy to cope with diners

Kensington Wine Rooms. *See p159*.

Lutyens. *See p160.*

dithering about whether to sit inside or out), and the setting (overlooking the duck lake, with trees all around and the London Eye lit up in the distance) is wonderful.

Inn The Park has to cater for all-comers, and the strain of offering everything from summer barbecues to formal sit-down three-course meals, and being open all day (breakfast includes a build-your-own option) is showing. Our recommendation? Wait for warm weather, grab a takeaway, and picnic on the grass.

Notes *No parking or designated drop-off point. Level access, motorised scooters permitted. Adapted toilet. Baby changing facilities. Babies and children welcome. Assistance dogs welcome.*

J Sheekey

28-32 St Martin's Court, WC2N 4AL (7240 2565, www.j-sheekey.co.uk). Leicester Square tube. **Lunch** noon-3pm Mon-Sat; noon-3.30pm Sun. **Dinner** 5.30pm-midnight Mon-Sat; 6-11pm Sun. **Main courses** £13.50-£39.50. **Set lunch** (Sat, Sun) £25.50 3 courses.

This is the consummate theatreland restaurant. The walls are lined with acting greats, as often are its tables (along with those who aspire to be), and the buzz is as thrilling as an opening night. Many diners opt for the fondly remembered salmon fish cake or spectacular fruits de mer. Nevertheless, it's worth casting your net wider: perhaps a starter of pickled Arctic herring with potato salad and dill sauce, followed by a fillet of organic salmon with Suffolk bacon and razor clams. Don't forget to check the weekly specials for the likes of grilled turbot with béarnaise for two, or a lobster salad featuring new-season potatoes and asparagus. British cheeses, Welsh rarebit and herring roes on toast provide appealing savoury alternatives to the lengthy list of puds. Staff don't always perform at their best, at times giving the impression they're too cool for school, but on the whole Sheekey's is a slick show and still one of the hottest tickets in town. Enjoy it for a fraction of the price at weekend lunchtimes when the mood is relaxed and friendly and a £25.50 set menu takes centre stage.

Notes *Level access to the single pull-open door. Small cosy dining rooms with some moveable chairs, offer a degree of manoeuvrability for wheelchair users. Accessible toilet. Babies and children welcome: colouring books; high chairs. Booking essential. Vegan dishes. Vegetarian menu. Assistance dogs welcome.*

Kensington Wine Rooms

127-129 Kensington Church Street, W8 7LP (7727 8142, www.greatwinesbytheglass.com). Notting Hill Gate tube. **Open** noon-11pm Mon-Sat; noon-10.30pm Sun. **Main courses** £13.50-£39. **House wine** £18.20 bottle, £4.30 glass.

It took plenty of courage to launch a serious restaurant within a minute's walk of two real Modern European luminaries, Kensington Place and Clarke's, but this 2009 opening has hit on a sound approach. In a low-slung room with a sleek metal bar and stylish decor of burgundy, dark wood and exposed brickwork, KWR is a wine merchant's, wine bar and restaurant all in one – and it does some things very well. Above all, there's an outstanding list including 40 wines served by the glass from Enomatic machines that keep the wine impeccably fresh. The food, which includes both à la carte and authentic Spanish tapas, complements the wine well, but a quick lunch displayed contrasts in quality. Spicy gazpacho was a marvel: thick, chewy and deeply flavourful. But tuna tartare with green apple, tzatziki and peashoot salad was a let-down: the poorly trimmed fish chunks were overpowered by sun-dried tomatoes. Sometimes the kitchen tries too hard to be original. Much else on the menu is more straightforward, and some careful ordering will allow you to enjoy the excellent wine.

Notes *Uneven access to main door which pushes open (usually held open) to second set of heavy doors that open both ways. Inside, level access with ample room for wheelchair users to manoeuvre, though some tables and chairs are permanently fixed. Standard toilets (no accessible toilet). Babies and children welcome: high chairs. Booking advisable evenings. Assistance dogs welcome.*

Lutyens

85 Fleet Street, EC4Y 1AE (7583 8385, www.lutyens-restaurant.co.uk). City Thameslink or Blackfriars rail, or 4, 11, 15, 23, 26 bus. **Bar** Open noon-midnight, breakfast 7.30-10.30am, meals served noon-9pm Mon-Fri. **Main courses** £12.50-£18. Set lunch £17.50 2 courses. **Restaurant** Lunch noon-3.30pm, dinner 5.30-10pm Mon-Fri. **Main courses** £12.50-£33. **Set meal** (5.30-10pm) £39.50 3 courses incl half bottle of wine.

Sir Terence Conran's latest restaurant venture occupies Fleet Street's venerable Reuters/AP building, designed by Edwin Lutyens in the 1930s. It's an iconic spot, next door to St Bride's Church, opposite the gorgeous, art deco, ex-Daily Express building and down the road from Goldman Sachs. Lutyens is a typical Conran operation, with a buzzy bar in stylish, masculine tones of white, maroon and dark wood, and a separate, more formal ground floor dining room. Service is warm and polished; the maître d' greeted the stream of mainly male diners with practised first-name bonhomie. In the restaurant you can feast on the likes of lobster mousse or steak tartare, followed by Landaise chicken,

braised lamb or dover sole; crustacea loom large too, of course. Eating in the bar is a simpler affair (though oysters and a petit plateau de fruits de mer are also available here). The set lunch was a mixed blessing, yielding creamy, tangy mackerel pâté and a juicy beef burger with crispy chips, but also crab hash that was more like a fish cake, squishily textured and with a distinctly odd-tasting basil mayo. A problem with the gas supply meant a half-hour wait for our mains, but the staff were most apologetic, offering complimentary glasses of champagne (and knocking a chunk off the bill).

Notes *Wheelchair access via side entrance (the doorman will direct you). Some moveable chairs make way for wheelchair access. Accessible toilet in basement accessed by lift. Babies and children welcome: high chairs. Booking advisable. Separate rooms for parties seat 6-20. Assistance dogs welcome.*

Maghreb

189 Upper Street, N1 1RQ (7226 2305, bit.ly/roqgeK). Highbury & Islington tube/rail. **Open** 6-11.30pm Mon-Thur; 5-11.30pm Fri-Sun. **Main courses** £9.50-£14.50. **Set dinner** £12.95 2 courses, £15.95 3 courses.

Chef-patron Mohamed Faraji's restaurant feels welcoming even on a quiet night. Warm ochre walls and red silk lanterns spread their rosy glow over the narrow room, and a fine soundtrack of urban rai and more traditional North African music helps enhance the relaxed atmosphere. Faraji's mission to innovate, combining Modern European style with Moroccan staples, can backfire. Starters of marinated squid with capers had a strangely dense, meaty texture; crab börek was a touch stodgy; and coriander-infused zaalouk was served too cold (serving it at room temperature instead would have

Maze. *See p163.*

Masala Zone.

emphasised the complexity of the spicing). The traditional Moroccan mains tend to score more highly than the fusion-style dishes. A portion of lamb tagine with prunes was enough for two. The meat was extremely tender if slightly overcooked, and the sauce tasty, although it needed reducing further to produce an intense, sweet richness of flavour. Tagines are served with couscous, but Turkish-style bread is on hand to mop up the juices in a more authentic manner. To drink, we usually refrain from the small, expensive cocktails and head straight for the impressive Moroccan wine list instead. This contains several bottles that are rarely found in London, such as the oaky, vanilla-toned red L'Excellence de Bonassia.

Notes *There is a shallow step up to the heavy, single-width main door which pushes open. Inside there is level access in the dining area although some seats are permanently fixed and there are steps up to additional seating area. Standard toilets (no accessible toilet) on first floor (15+ steps). Babies and children welcome: high chairs. Booking advisable. Separate rooms for parties seat 38 and 40. Takeaway service. Assistance dogs welcome.*

Masala Zone

30 Upper Street, N1 0NU (7359 3399, www.realindianfood.com). Highbury & Islington tube/rail. **Open** *12.30-3pm, 5.30-11pm Mon-Fri; 12.30-11pm Sat; 12.30-10.30pm Sun.* **Main courses** *£10-£15.*

Branches of this smart, clever chain are popping up faster than mustard seeds in a pan of hot ghee. Each outlet is decorated with a different theme – on Parkway it's advertising posters of the 1930s and '40s; at Covent Garden Rajasthani puppets hang from the ceiling; in Soho, Islington and Earl's Court the walls feature striking work by tribal artists.

The mood is both vibrant and relaxed - as cheering to singletons having a thali for supper, as it is to family groups and couples. Conceived by the Panjabi sisters of Chutney Mary and Amaya fame, Masala Zone is not expensive, yet even so there's a high rotation of attractive discount offers.

The menu takes in street-food snacks (springy, grease-free onion bhaji; dahi poori), wraps, grills, curried noodles, curry and rice plates. There are also two sizes of thali; well-trained, multicultural staff describe the daily veg, dahl and raita on your arrival, and you choose which of the curries you would like included – clove-scented lamb roghan gosht, say, or a tomatoey tilapia masala.

To drink, try the cola with mint and spices, or the bright Portuguese rosé created specially to match the fiery dishes.

Notes *No car park. Ramp to main entrance. Children welcome. There is ample room for wheelchair users to manoeuvre. Adapted toilet. Staff receive disability awareness training. Assistance dogs welcome.*

Maze

13-15 Grosvenor Square, W1K 6JP (7107 0000, www.gordonramsay.com). Bond Street tube. **Lunch** *noon-2.30pm, dinner 6-10.30pm daily.* **Main courses** *£15-£29.50.* **Set lunch** *£28.50 4 courses, £35.50 5 courses, £42.50 6 courses.*

Once a beacon in the Gordon Ramsay group, Maze has witnessed the departure of Jason Atherton, followed by its recently appointed executive chef, James Durrant. Despite such changes, service remains reassuringly smooth, knowledgeable and friendly. The glamorous bar provides a classy line in cocktails for the monied customers. It's a spacious venue furnished in shades of coffee and cream, and fronted by large windows looking on to leafy Grosvenor Square.

Maze has earned its culinary spurs for serving sophisticated, European-style morsels, some containing pan-Asian ingredients – though, on our visit, the set menu consisted of Modern British choices. Chilled lobster cream was notable for its full-flavoured shellfish stock mellowed with cream. Poured around a mound of flaked crayfish, the soup unleashed surprise hits of lovely lemony avocado purée. Two-hour cooked duck egg wasn't as triumphant; we weren't convinced by the mushroom purée base, which detracted from the smoky character of juicy mussels and tender asparagus spears. A parade of indulgent dishes followed; our favourite was a meltingly tender morsel of boneless rabbit, served with a fresh-tasting minted risotto studded with broad beans. Most desserts didn't make the grade, except for an outstanding creamy rice pudding, streaked with warm orange-and-thyme marmalade and molten chocolate.

Notes *Located on the ground floor of the Marriott Grosvenor Square Hotel. Wheelchair access is via the main hotel entrance, and the spacious restaurant has ample room for manoeuvre. Accessible toilet. Babies and children admitted. Booking essential. Dress: smart casual; no trainers. Separate rooms for parties, seating 15 and 36. Assistance dogs welcome.*

Morgan M

*489 Liverpool Road, N7 8NS
(7609 3560, www.morganm.com).
Highbury & Islington tube/rail.*
Lunch noon-1.30pm Wed-Fri, Sun.
Dinner 7-8.45pm Tue-Sat. **Set lunch** (Wed-Fri) £23.50 2 courses, £27.50 3 courses, £39-£45 tasting menu.
Set dinner £39 3 courses, £43-£48 tasting menu.
From the smell of an uncovered cheeseboard and the complex, classical menu, to the old world wine list and thickly accented staff – Morgan M is unreservedly French. The restaurant consists of an intimate dining room with immaculately dressed, well-spaced tables and smart decor (including chef-patron Morgan Meunier's own paintings). Ensure you arrive hungry, as dinner is either three courses from the carte or a five-course tasting menu, both featuring amuse-bouches and entremets.

We chose the tasting menu, which is only marginally more expensive, though we passed on the option of wine pairings. A cucumber gazpacho with mint sorbet primed the taste buds nicely for an almost overpowering salad of aubergine caviar, confit tomatoes and French beans, with basil pesto, whole roasted garlic and red pepper sorbet. A simpler dish of steamed gnocchi in asparagus cream with summer truffles and girolles was an altogether more balanced dish.

Desserts hit the high notes; a raspberry soufflé was served with light pistachio custard poured inside, while a pastry-perfect rhubarb confit tarte came with gorgeous, sweet white wine ice-cream. On our visit, Monsieur M took the time to tour the floor. Speaking to each table during the evening, he laughed off the suggestion that he'd just bought himself a new ice-cream maker.

Notes *The accessible entrance is located on Sherringham Road and has an easy ramp/slope from the pavement to the main double-width doors which pull open. Inside there is level access with ample room for wheelchair users to manoeuvre. Standard toilets (no accessible toilet) on first floor (15+ steps). Babies and children admitted (lunch, Sun). Booking essential weekends. Dress: smart casual. Separate room for parties seats 12. Vegetarian menu. Assistance dogs welcome.*

Pasha (Gloucester Road). *See p167.*

Roast. *See p168.*

Pasha

*301 Upper Street, N1 2TU
(7226 1454, fax 7359 1155,
www.pasharestaurant.co.uk). Angel tube
or Highbury & Islington tube/rail.*
Open 11am-11.30pm Mon-Sat;
11am-11pm Sun. **Main courses**
£7.95-£14.95. **Set meal** £16.95 2
courses, £19.95 3 courses.

Pasha's contemporary feel makes a
refreshing change from the London norm of
hectic, wipe-down Turkish caffs or
restaurants decked with extravagant
Ottoman opulence. One step up to the main
entrance and the heavy door pushes open
to reveal large windows opening on to a chic
stretch of Upper Street and, inside level
access; shiny banquettes, chandeliers and
sparkling candles complement a stylish
room. It's a place for impressing your dining
companions, rather than a BYO party stop-
off. The well-trained and personable staff
reflect this, and the wine list and cocktail
menu complete the effect. Appropriately,
dishes are more sophisticated than you'll
find elsewhere, with a lot of thought going
into presentation – although critics might
say the edges that make this cooking style
so vital have been somewhat smoothed off.
Also, the extensive menu has made
concessions to those who might think of
Turkish cuisine as unreconstructed dude
food; the appearance of Moroccan spiced
salmon or rocket and parmesan salad is
unusual. However, ingredients are of a high
quality and cooking is consistently
excellent. Portions are up to the usual
generous Turkish standards too, so take
advantage and veer from the standard
meze-kebab route.

Notes *Ample room for a wheelchair
user to manoeuvre. Available for hire.
Standard toilets (no accessible toilet).
Babies and children admitted. Booking
advisable. Tables outdoors (2
pavement). Takeaway service.
Assistance dogs welcome.*

Pasha

*1 Gloucester Road, SW7 4PP (7589
7969, www.pasha-restaurant.co.uk).
Gloucester Road tube.* **Open** noon-11pm
Mon-Wed, Sun; noon-midnight Thur-
Sat. **Main courses** £13-£26. **Set meal**
£30-£40 per person (minimum 2).

For voluptuous glamour, the Arabian
Nights decor here (no relation to Pasha,
left) is incomparable. The heavy carved
wooden door pushes open on to a vista of
swishing beaded lamps, intricate North
African-style tiles, intimate recesses with
harem-like wooden trellises, pink and
orange silk cushions and hammered brass
tables – all scattered with rose petals.

On our most recent visit, something had
gone awry. For a start, no tap water was
available due to a murmured excuse about
plumbing problems. Initially only pricey
set ' feast' menus were proffered, the à la
carte appearing only when we asked.
Beetroot salad had little sign of its
promised cinnamon, orange and honey
dressing; over-salty but nicely crisp
courgette and cheese fritters were short on
courgette; our usual favourite, deep-fried
baby squid with coconut and chilli dipping
sauce, had the texture of rubber bands. To
follow, s'csou darna (couscous with lamb
shank, chicken and merguez), often one of
London's best, was bland and watery. A
delicate Volubilia Gris rosé from Meknes
partially saved the evening, but we left
disappointed. We've had better meals here,
so hope Pasha returns to form soon.

Notes *No level access, stairs to
access different levels (G-LG 15+ steps),
ramps not available. Staff receive
disability awareness training and are
Typetalk aware. Standard toilets (no
accessible toilet). Babies and children
welcome: high chairs. Booking advisable.
Separate room for parties, seats 20.
Tables outdoors (2, pavement).
Takeaway service. Assistance
dogs welcome.*

Roast

The Floral Hall, Borough Market, Stoney Street, SE1 1TL (7940 1300, www.roast-restaurant.com). London Bridge tube/rail. **Breakfast** 7-11am Mon-Fri; 8-11.30am Sat. **Lunch** noon-3pm Mon, Tue; noon-4pm Wed-Sat; 11.30am-6pm Sun. **Dinner** 5.30-11pm Mon-Fri; 6-11pm Sat. **Main courses** £14.50-£24.50. **Set lunch** (Sun) £22 2 courses, £26 3 courses.

Roast is one hard-working establishment. Set on the first floor above the hugely popular foodie paradise of Borough Market, the restaurant offers lift access to the expansive views of the retail action taking place below. It's busy from breakfast (tattie scone with smoked streaky bacon, field mushrooms and fried egg, for instance) through to classy bar bites (who could resist the fish fingers with tartare sauce or cocktail chipolatas in Worcestershire sauce?).

At lunch and dinner, the choice can feel overwhelming: not only whether to have Wye Valley asparagus with minted butter sauce or potted salt beef with gherkins and Hoxton rye bread, followed by slow-roast Wicks Manor pork belly with mash and bramley apple sauce, or beetroot pan haggerty with pea shoots and poached egg – but also which of the ten-plus side dishes to order.

After this, there are the likes of toffee apple sundae or gooseberry queen of puddings, or a fine selection of English cheeses. On the plus side, quality rarely seems to suffer, despite the many options. The drinks list is similarly wide-ranging, with a strong suit in teas, rums, whiskies and cocktails. Roast is equally popular for business or pleasure, and deservedly so.

♿ ♿ 🐕

Notes *Available for hire. Lift; accessible toilet. Babies and children welcome: children's menu; high chairs. Booking advisable. Dress: smart casual. Assistance dogs welcome.*

Saké No Hana

23 St James's Street, SW1A 1HA (7925 8988, www.sakenohana.com). Green Park tube. **Lunch** noon-3pm Mon-Fri. **Dinner** 6-11.30pm Mon-Sat. **Main courses** £4-£40. **Set meal** £45-£65.

Always something of a looker, this Japanese restaurant has recently been remodelled, the bar swapping places with its sushi counterpart. From the dimly lit reception, ascend escalators to a first-floor dining room with huge windows and swathes of cedar wood, much of it suspended from the ceiling. Friendly staff sashay around dressed in black, looking after their customers very well.

The menu too has been overhauled; now raw fish is available alongside robata dishes, as well as noodles and that Japanese winter favourite shabu shabu. The cooking may not be as ground-breaking as originally, but there are still innovative dishes.

Some of the most intriguing recipes contain little or no meat; we were blown away by the delicate flavours of the agedashidofu, which was served with three coatings (bonito, seaweed and rice cracker), and deep-fried mashed taro with shiitake mushrooms and rocket. Braised aubergine was also thoroughly delicious, though we were less convinced by the accompanying scraps of duck meat. Sushi can be ordered singly, and our fatty tuna and eel were faultless.

We ended with a boozy sakura saké jelly with mixed berries, which arrived with a separate shot of the rice wine.

As you might expect, noble sakés from across Japan head the drinks list, augmented by cocktails and wines, but any far-reaching exploration would require a very fat wallet.

🧑 ♿ 🧑 ♿ 🐕

Notes *Babies and children welcome. Adapted toilet. Access for wheelchair users via lift. Assistance dogs welcome.*

Saké No Hana.

Sedap.

Scott's

20 Mount Street, W1K 2HE (7495 7309, fax 7647 6326, www.scotts-restaurant.com). Bond Street or Green Park tube. **Open** *noon-10.30pm Mon-Sat; noon-10pm Sun.* **Main courses** *£15-£39.50.* **Cover** *£2.*

The menus of Scott's and J Sheekey aren't identical, and the decors are vastly different, but there's an undeniable sense of formula to these Caprice Holdings operations. Scott's is the flashier, wealthier younger sibling – a hedge-fund manager to Sheekey's theatrical sophisticate – but the moment the corporate bread basket lands on the table you know you're visiting a blood brother. Scott's pricing may suggest a desire to keep out hoi polloi, yet it attracts a diverse crowd, particularly at weekends when family groups sit alongside sports-casual celebs, couples of all ages, and friends who've come up west for posh fish and chips.

Tables are laid around a large central bar and a space-age-style crustacea altar laden with oysters, caviar and other goodies. Such seafood and a clutch of asparagus dishes could make the list of starters redundant, but there's a further dozen or so offered, including a lovely heritage vegetable salad with goat's cheese to keep many a waist-watching WAG happy. The cooking is mostly accurate – we enjoyed wonderfully tender razor clams sautéed with seashore vegetables and cured ham, and moist, herb-roasted monkfish – though rhubarb and custard trifle easily outclassed a bland chocolate tart for dessert.

Notes *On street Blue Badge parking on South Audley Street. Level access from the street into dining room, where some chairs are fixed but there is room for wheelchair users to manoeuvre. Accessible toilet at rear of restaurant. Babies and children welcome: high chairs. Booking essential. Separate room for parties seats 40. Tables outdoors (7, pavement). Vegan dishes. Vegetarian menu. Assistance dogs welcome.*

Sedap

102 Old Street, EC1V 9AY (7490 0200, www.sedap.co.uk). Old Street tube/rail. **Lunch** 11.30am-3pm Mon-Fri. **Dinner** 5-11pm daily. **Main courses** *£5.70-£7.50.* **Set lunch** *£5.95-£6.95 2 courses.*

The Yeohs have settled well since moving here from their former outfit, Nyonya in Notting Hill. Two generations of the family run the restaurant, and service is welcoming. a spick and span venue, where black furnishings are set against a backdrop of olive green.

Nyonya or Peranakan food is a fusion of Chinese and Malay cuisines, and the menu encapsulates this cooking style. Chicken satay came with a sauce that had just the right balance of peanuts and spices. The char kway teow is renowned, but we have mixed feelings about the seafood char mee (yellow noodles in a thick soya sauce) – even though the freshly made blachan (hot shrimp paste) is fabulous. Perhaps the restaurant could buy higher quality ingredients in some instances, but we've nothing but praise for the curry tumis: fleshy pieces of sea bream and okra served in a hot and sour sauce. To finish, don't miss the Nyonya kueh (coconut cakes in a variety of bright colours, including blue). The set lunch menus are a steal.

Notes *One shallow step up to entrance and single push open door. Level access inside, no chairs or tables are permanently fixed and there is ample room for wheelchair users to manoeuvre. Standard toilet (no accessible toilet). Babies and children welcome. Booking advisable evenings. Separate room for parties seats 14. Takeaway service. Assistance dogs welcome.*

Tapas Brindisa

18-20 Southwark Street, SE1 1TJ
(7357 8880, www.brindisa.com).
London Bridge tube/rail. **Open** 11am-
11pm Mon-Sat. **Tapas** £3.20-£22.

Top-quality ingredients have always been
the mainstay at Brindisa, whose genius
lies in assembling them into eminently
tempting tapas: a cup of green pea soup
with manchego, say, or pan-fried fillet
steak with caramelised onion and torta de
barros cheese on toast.

The set-up is equally simple, with a bar
area at one end dotted with high tables,
and a close-packed, concrete-floored
dining room at the other. Both are
generally thronged; no bookings are
taken, and the waiting list is invariably
long. Behind the bar is a hatch into the
kitchen, from which chefs in immaculate
whites produce a succession of
deceptively simple dishes.

The flavours shine through. A hearty
wedge of tortilla, crammed with peppers,
potato and chorizo, was served with a
dollop of pungent aïoli, while a dish of
pan-fried squid and green beans was
studded with sweet, slow-roasted garlic
cloves. Cheese remains a strength, and the
charcuterie is also superb.

Notes *Children and families welcome.
Level access from street, though crowds
mean booking advisable.*

Tom's Kitchen

*27 Cale Street, SW3 3QP (7349 0202,
www.tomskitchen.co.uk). Sloane Square
or South Kensington tube.* **Breakfast**
8-11am Mon-Fri. **Lunch** noon-3pm
Mon-Fri. **Brunch** 10am-4pm Sat, Sun.
Dinner 6-11pm daily. **Main courses**
£14.50-£29.50.

Tom Aikens' joint venture with Compass
Catering at Somerset House (replacing the
Admiralty restaurant) has grabbed the
headlines, but you only have to spend five
minutes in the Chelsea Green original to

wish there were more like it. A shallow
step to heavy double-width pull-open
doors reveal the semi-communal dining
room which has level access and includes
places at the long marble bar, where solo
diners can watch the chefs in action. Wear
a pink striped shirt to feel most at home,
though staff are friendly to all.

Breakfast is our favourite time to visit:
the pancakes and waffles are superb, the
ingredients for the full English sourced
carefully, the coffee just-so. At other times
Tom's Kitchen usually hits the mark:
Devon crab salad needed more crab
to match the fennel and orange
accompaniments, but an open steak
sandwich was both perfect and pretty.
Comfort-food dishes are thrilling: cod and
salmon fish pie sings with fresh herbs.
Our copper saucepan of baked Alaska
(one of a few dishes for sharing) was
theatrically flamed at table: a shame the
meringue was too burnt, but a good idea
to use panettone and vanilla ice-cream.
Wines start at £20.50 a bottle, though
there's a good selection under £25. The
bar upstairs is accessed by 15 deep stairs.

Notes *Disability awareness trained
staff. Good access for wheelchair users
and motorised scooters (charging
facilities available). Accessible unisex
toilet near main entrance. Babies and
children welcome: high chairs; nappy-
changing facilities. Booking advisable
dinner and weekends. Separate rooms
for parties, seating 22 and 40.
Assistance dogs welcome.*

Wagamama

*1 Ropemaker Street, EC2Y 9AW
(7588 2688, www.wagamama.com).
Moorgate tube/rail.* **Open** 11.30am-
10pm Mon-Fri (branches vary with
location). **Main courses** £6.35-£11.

Wagamama was the first – and is still one
of the best – canteen-style pan-Asian
diners, zooming out udon and soba

Tom's Kitchen.

Chain reactions

In recent years, London has experienced an explosion in mid-level restaurant chains, all offering consistently good food at reasonable prices (typically around £10-£15 for a main course). Here is our pick of the chains, and their best branches for disabled access. All of these restaurant chains welcome families with babies and children.

Belgo

50 Earlham St, WC2H 9LJ (7813 2233, www.belgo-restaurants.co.uk). Covent Garden tube.

The reliable Belgian beer, mussels and sausages specialist has five branches in London. Along with the similarly superior chains Bella Italia, Café Rouge and Strada (*all below*), it is part of the Targus restaurant group. The flagship Covent Garden branch (*details above*) has access for solo wheelchair users, disabled toilet facilities and a low-level counter. Assistance dogs welcome. Very little access info on the website.

Bella Italia

55-57 Queensway, W2 4QH (7792 2880, www.bellaitalia.co.uk). Queensway tube.

Fast-growing Italian trattoria chain offers a tasty selection of pizza, pasta and panini. Over 80 branches all over the UK, and the website has a dedicated accessible information page (bit.ly/mxOckR). The company claims this Queensway branch is its most accessible in London, with step-free access for wheelchair users, accessible toilet and large-print and Braille menus. Assistance dogs welcome. Good basic access info for individual branches on the website. High chairs can be provided.

noodles, grilled or in broth, for diligent slurping. It's now a worldwide phenomenon, with branches as far afield as the States and Australia.

Notes *Menus available in Braille and large print. This City location offers level approach to heavy, double pull-open doors leading to ground floor dining space. All tables permanently fixed with some moveable chairs; ample room for wheelchair users to manoeuvre. Access-trained staff will help. Accessible unisex toilet 20m from entrance. Children welcome. Assistance dogs welcome.*

Wahaca

Westfield London Shopping Centre, Ariel Way, W12 7GB (8749 4517, www.wahaca.co.uk). Shepherd's Bush tube/rail. **Open** 9am-midnight Mon-Sat; 11am-11pm Sun (branches vary with location). **Main courses** £3.25-£9.95.

Eating street food in Mexico is a laid-back, chatty, cheap, wholesome experience. Going to Wahaca – which sells itself as a street-food purveyor – is the opposite. By not taking reservations, Wahaca aims to generate excitement.

Does it deliver? Only partially, we reckon. The classic quesadillas, burritos and platos fuertes (mains, including a slow-roasted pork pibil and enchiladas) are fair value. Two can share four to five items, drink a bottle of acceptable wine, and have change from £40.

But the real test is the food, and the cooking rarely rises above the complexity of a burrito bar. The meat in some of our dishes was dry; fillings are sometimes mean-spirited too. As snacks, the antojitos are OK, but there's little to savour. Owner Thomasina Miers drew her inspiration from Oaxaca's amazing Casa Oaxaca restaurant; unfortunately, London has nothing similar. Other branches in Covent Garden and Canary Wharf.

&.&. ᵂᶜ

Notes *Level access from Westfield shopping mall (see p196). Babies and children welcome. No booking.*

The Wolseley

160 Piccadilly, W1J 9EB (7499 6996, www.thewolseley.com). Green Park tube.
Breakfast 7-11.30am Mon-Fri;
8-11.30am Sat, Sun. **Lunch** noon-3pm
Mon-Fri; noon-3.30pm Sat, Sun.
Tea 3-6.30pm Mon-Fri; 3.30-5.30pm
Sat; 3.30-6.30pm Sun. **Dinner** 5.30pm-
midnight Mon-Sat; 5.30-11pm Sun.
All-day menu 11.30am-midnight
daily. **Main courses** £6.75-£28.75.
Set tea £9.75-£21. **Cover** £2.
On a good day, the Wolseley makes you feel as glamorous as the celeb and media regulars you'll probably spot here. On a bad day – peak hour during a particularly bustling lunch, perhaps – you could be perched on small tables near the front door and made to feel inadequate for not ordering a sufficiently sumptuous meal.

At first, the idea was that customers could pop into the café for cake and coffee, yet this has become impractical as demand for the main dining room has grown. Still, better eating in the café, or the fun bar opposite, than in the foyer. Some great chefs have passed through the Wolseley's kitchens (Chris Galvin, Claire Clark), but the cooking generally punches below its weight.

Reliable dishes include the omelette Arnold Bennett, ice-cream coupes and no-brainers like a dozen Islay rock oysters or the fruits de mer. Plats du jour are suitably diverse: faschierter braten (a traditional Austrian dish of minced meat, potatoes and onions) on Wednesday; chicken, ham and leek pie on Thursday; seven-hour lamb on Saturday.

The attitude of staff ranges from charming to authentic French brasserie-style (brusque, indifferent), but let's face it, you're not here for the service.

Café Rouge

*2 Lancer Square, W8 4EH
(7938 4200, www.caferouge.co.uk).
High Street Kensington tube.*
French bistro style on a budget is the hallmark of this fast-growing chain, which has branches all over London. This branch has access for wheelchair users, accessible toilet and large-print and Braille menus. Assistance dogs welcome. Website gives basic access information on individual cafés.

Fine Burger Company

*02 Centre, 255 Finchley Road,
NW3 6LU (7433 0700,
www.fineburger.co.uk).
Finchley Road tube.*
Hand-made burgers from free-range East Anglian cattle, plus all the trimmings. This branch (one of four in London) has step-free access, accessible toilet and disability-aware staff. Assistance dogs welcome.

Giraffe

*Behind the Royal Festival Hall,
Riverside Level 1, SE1 8XX (7928
2004, www.giraffe.net). Waterloo
tube/rail.*
The flagship branch of this reliable all-day diner chain has step-free access and an accessible toilet, as well as great views over the Thames (*see pp208-216*). Assistance dogs welcome. Website gives basic access information on individual branches.

Gourmet Burger Kitchen

*102 Baker Street, W1U 6TL
(7486 8516, www.gbk.co.uk). Baker
Street tube.*
This branch of the posh burger joint has a ramp for access via two steps (intercom outside). Once inside, main dining area and accessible toilets are step-free. Large-print menu available. Assistance dogs welcome. Website has access info on every branch.

Nando's

66-68 Chandos Place Covent Garden, WC2N 4HG (7836 4719, www.nandos.co.uk). Leicester Square tube or Charing Cross tube/rail.
This basement branch of the piri-piri chicken empire has a lift for wheelchair users (call to check it's working), a disabled toilet and large-print menus. Assistance dogs welcome. Website gives basic access information on individual branches.

Pizza Express

215-227 Great Portland Street, W1W 5PN (7580 2272, www.pizzaexpress.com). Great Portland Street tube.
This branch of the pizza chain has unassisted access for wheelchair users, a customer lift, an accessible toilet and a hearing-loop induction system. Assistance dogs welcome. No access information on website.

YO! Sushi

Unit 3, Royal Festival Hall, Southbank Centre, SE1 8XX (3130 1997, yosushi.com). Waterloo tube/rail.
This branch of the conveyor belt sushi chain features its first outdoor belt, with dedicated seating for disabled customers (call to reserve). The restaurant is accessible, with accessible toilet. Website gives basic access information on branches.

Zizzi

Ivory House, St Katharine Docks, E1W 1AT (7488 0130, www.zizzi.co.uk). Tower Hill tube or Tower Gateway DLR.
Wheelchair users who brave the cobbles of this historic waterfront area by Tower Bridge will be rewarded by pleasant surroundings with ramped access, an accessible toilet and an al fresco dining area. Booking is essential at weekends. Website has no access information.

Wagamama. *See p172.*

Notes *One step to main entrance. Advance booking advised. Make special requirements clear at time of booking as some seating is fixed. Babies and children welcome. High chair and nappy-changing facilities available.*

Zaika

1 Kensington High Street, W8 5NP (7795 6533, www.zaika-restaurant.co.uk). High Street Kensington tube. **Lunch** noon-2.45pm Tue-Sun. **Dinner** 6.30-10.45pm Mon-Sat; 6.30-9.45pm Sun. **Main courses** £15-£19.50. **Set lunch** £20 2 courses incl glass of wine and coffee, £25 3 courses incl glass of wine and coffee. **Set meal** £58 tasting menu.
A former bank with step up to heavy double wooden doors that push open to reveal a smart clubby atmosphere, the interior notable for its high ceiling,

sweeping drapes and stone deities. Dark wood panelling and rich maroon and chocolate-brown colours lend warmth to the bar and expansive dining area.

The modern Indian cooking is elaborate, sometimes too much so, but it's always creative, drawing upon global flavours for inspiration. A first course of griddled potato cake, sandwiched with sweet yoghurt and fried gram-flour batter strands, was rather fussy for our taste. Surrounded by a ring of tamarind dots, it needed more tanginess. A substantial main course of masala duck was given a modern European spin; the tender sautéed breast, surrounded by a dark, sticky moat of meaty jus, was further enriched by buttery parsnip and celeriac mash, finished with a tangle of deep-fried okra. Imaginative, yes, but there was too much unrelenting richness on one plate. A no-messing lamb biriani brought things back on track; aromatic cardamom and cumin, cut through with ginger, gave us the full flavour. Sadly, it wasn't helped by overcooked rice. Service is smooth and attentive, and the wine list contains some choice selections.

Notes *Tables and chairs moveable with plenty of space for wheelchair users to manoeuvre. Staff receive disability awareness training. Standard toilets (no accessible toilet). Babies and children welcome: high chair. Booking advisable; essential weekends. Vegetarian menu. Assistance dogs welcome.*

Zucca
184 Bermondsey Street, SE1 3TQ (7378 6809, www.zuccalondon.com). London Bridge tube/rail or Bermondsey tube. **Open** *noon-3pm, 6.30-10pm Tue-Sat; noon-3pm Sun.* **Main courses** *£8.50-£13.95.*
If only more restaurants had Zucca's approach: good food at great prices, served by interested staff with a genuine

Pub chains

London also has several flourishing pub chains, making up with good food and keen prices for what they may lack in individual atmosphere. Children generally welcome until 6pm.

All Bar One
108 New Oxford Street, WC1A 1HD (7307 7980, www.allbarone.co.uk). Tottenham Court Road tube.
Level access for wheelchair users and an accessible toilet at this branch of the pub and food chain. No access information on the website.

JD Wetherspoon
Penderel's Oak, 283-288 High Holborn, WC1V 7HP (7242 5669, www.jdwetherspoon.co.uk). Chancery Lane or Holborn tube.
This branch of the pub chain that prides itself on its beer and prices, has level access from the street, an accessible toilet and a Braille menu. No access information on the website.

Pitcher and Piano
28 Cornhill, EC3V 3ND (7929 3989, www.pitcherandpiano.com). Bank tube/DLR.
City branch of upmarket chain with four pubs in central London. Sloped access via Change Alley entrance. Steps to main entrance. Level access on ground floor, but no accessible toilet. No access information on the website.

Slug and Lettuce
19/20 Hanover Street, W1S 1YR (7499 0077, www.slugandlettuce.co.uk). Oxford Circus tube.
Entrance is up one shallow step, and there's an accessible toilet. No access information on the website.

regard for diners. Sounds simple, but it's becoming increasingly rare on London's crowded restaurant scene. The only complaints we have are that the tables are very close together – a problem when you have a loved-up couple murmuring sweet nothings on one side, and two, too-loud geezers bellowing away on the other – and that a couple of the dishes were a tiny bit on the salty side.

That's it; otherwise the evening was a pleasing progression of plus-size, flavour-packed dishes, from starters of irresistible zucca fritti (battered pumpkin slices), delicate pea ravioli and punchy vitello tonnato, to a finale of dreamy panna cotta with roast peach.

Mains of quail with lentils, speck and salsa verde, and grilled squid with borlotti beans, chilli and samphire were top-notch, though the samphire got rather lost under the chilli heat. A huge mixed salad, slightly overdressed, easily fed two, as did the glorious focaccia.

This modern Italian menu is partnered by an all-Italian wine list; staff are happy to help or enlarge upon both.

Decor is open-plan, with the kitchen completely exposed to view, and lots of shiny white surfaces with the occasional splash of intense orange. We liked it a lot, though the chairs may prove unforgiving over a whole evening.

More new restaurants like this, please.

Notes *Union Car Parks within 200m on St Thomas Street. Marked on-street Blue Badge bays on Bermondsey Street in front of the restaurant. One small step to main entrance. There is ample room for wheelchair users to manoeuvre. The adapted toilet is 5m from the main entrance, on the right as you enter. Staff receive disability awareness training. Babies and children welcome. Assistance dogs welcome.*

Meals on wheels

Sometimes, you just want to stay inside and be fed and watered. If room service is too pricey, these websites will arrange delivery with a local restaurant or takeaway.

Hungry House
www.hungryhouse.co.uk
Search near you for restaurants or takeaways that deliver to your door, and order online.

Just Eat
www.just-eat.co.uk
Find which of the 8,000 eateries listed nationwide will deliver to you, place your order and wait.

Urbanbite
www.urbanbite.com
In business since 1999 and offering a great choice of local delivery options in London.

All Star Lanes.

PUBS AND BARS

All Star Lanes
95 Brick Lane, E1 6QL (7426 9200, www.allstarlanes.co.uk).
Shoreditch High Street rail. **Open** 4pm-midnight Mon-Thur; noon-1am Fri; 11am-1am Sat; 11am-midnight Sun.
Bowling £8.75 per person per game after 6pm; £6.75 before 6pm (shoe hire included).
Styling itself on stateside 'boutique' bowling alleys, this retro-themed venue has six lanes (plus two private lanes upstairs), diner-style booths, and a glamorous side bar with red leather banquettes, subdued lighting, an extensive cocktail menu. Food is good old American diner fare – ribs, steaks, Texas chilli con carne – or just have a peanut butter and banana shake, which constitutes a meal in itself. Branches in Holborn and Bayswater.

Notes *Children welcome until 6pm, and special menu available. Public car park off Brick Lane. Level access to front doors. Motorised scooters allowed in public parts, but no charging facilities. Nine steps to foyer; platform lift available to rear of the restaurant. Staff must be notified before lift can be used. Restaurant has ample space for wheelchair users to manoeuvre. Accessible toilet has baby changing facilities. Assistance dogs welcome.*

Alma
499 Old York Road, SW18 1TF (8870 2537, www.thealma.co.uk).
Wandsworth Town rail. **Open** 11am-midnight Mon-Sat; noon-11pm Sun.
Food served noon-4pm, 6-10.30pm Mon-Sat; noon-9.30pm Sun.
A landmark Young's pub and rightly so, the large, Victorian-era Alma serves punters of all stripes gathered around a low, island bar. Some perch on barstools, others at tables nearer the windows: most

will be gawping at the large, pull-down screen for big matches. Outside of these magic 90 minutes – plus stoppages, the Alma attracts ale fans eager to sample Sambrook's Wandle, Wells Bombardier or something from the regular Young's range. Bar food is another plus: deli boards of cured meats, honey-and-mustard chipolatas, burgers with brie and bacon. For finer dining, head to the adjoining restaurant for honey-glazed Gressingham duck breast and more; 23 hotel rooms were added in 2011, and double rooms start at £119 per night.

🧏 👪 🐕 🚻

Notes *Babies and children welcome. Function room (80 capacity). Wireless internet. No parking or designated drop-off point. There is a level approach to the main entrance located on Old York Road. The main heavy double-width doors push open to a second heavy single (86cm) door. Inside there is level access with ample room for wheelchair users to manoeuvre. Motorised scooters are allowed in public parts of the venue (recharging facility available). There is no accessible toilet. The standard male and female and male toilets are in the basement 5m from the stairs. Staff receive disability awareness training. Assistance dogs welcome.*

Beaufort House
354 King's Road, SW3 5UZ (7352 2828, bit.ly/bIY9us). Fulham Broadway or South Kensington tube. **Open** *9am-midnight daily.* **Food served** *10am-3.30pm, 6.30-10.30pm daily.*

The grand Beaufort House comprises a public bar at the front, of slightly continental appearance, and a back room where members may withdraw after midnight. A large horseshoe bar counter is lined with stylish, turquoise-topped bar stools and surrounded by wooden, window-view tables; each is centrepieced by large menus detailing drinks, wines and food. Cocktails, around £8, make ample use of Tanqueray gin, and Finlandia and Ketel One vodkas; note, in particular, the Beaufort Garden of Tanqueray, fresh cucumber and home-made camomile syrup. The wine list runs to almost 100 labels; a humbler dozen by the glass include a sauvignon blanc Caliterra from Chile and a Stellenbosch Eikendal merlot. The food menu is just as smart.

🧏 👪 🚻 🐕

Notes *Babies and children admitted. Booking advisable Fri, Sat. Entertainment (DJs 9.30pm Fri, Sat). Function room (60 capacity). Wireless internet. No car parking or designated on street Blue Badge parking bays nearby. Small slope to entrance with double-width doors that pull open. Inside there is level access with ample room for a wheelchair user to manoeuvre. The accessible toilet is on the ground floor opposite the main entrance. Staff receive disability awareness training. Assistance dogs welcome.*

The Bedford
77 Bedford Hill, SW12 9HD (8682 8940, www.thebedford.co.uk). Balham tube/rail. **Open** 3pm-midnight Mon-Thur; 2pm-2am Fri; 11am-2am Sat; noon-midnight Sun. **Food served** 6.30-10pm Mon-Fri; noon-10pm Sat, Sun.

As busy and prominent as any local can be, this corner pub in Balham attracts all-comers, who sit and commune in a nondescript interior or at outdoor tables by busy traffic. No, that doesn't sound attractive, but the Bedford succeeds because they've got the knack of making people feel comfortable. After all the developments in pub culture over the last decade, mates, dates and strangers still make that easy text-message invitation of an afternoon: 'Bedford?' By then, the place is pretty full, the day's suggestions of steak sandwiches and pies wiped from the board behind the bar, but the likes of Adnams Explorer, O'Hanlon's Yellowhammer and Sharp's Doom Bar should still be on, and roughly ten wines should be available. The calendar takes in cabaret, comedy, music, dance classes, quiz nights (*see below*)… It's still all happening at the Bedford.

Notes *Assistance dogs welcome. Babies and children admitted until 7pm. Entertainment (line-dancing 7.30pm Mon; swing dancing 8pm Tue; comedy 9pm Tue; salsa 7.45pm Wed; quiz 8.30pm Wed; tango 7.15pm Thur, alt Sun; nightclub 11pm-2am Fri, Sat). Function rooms (75, 200 capacity). Tables outdoors (4, pavement; 5, garden). Wireless internet. Sainsbury's pay and display parking within 200m (check restrictions) on Bedford Hill. No on-street Blue Badge bays or designated drop-off point. Main and side entrance have one step to double-width doors. Once inside, the bar has level access. Food or drinks are ordered from the service counter, but can be brought to the table. No tables permanently fixed but some chairs are. There is ample room for wheelchair users to manoeuvre. There are 15+ steps between G-1-2 floors to access additional seating and standard toilets. There is a female accessible toilet (within the standard female toilets) 27m from the main entrance. Standard male toilets are 27m from the main entrance.*

Big Chill Bar

Old Truman Brewery, E1 6QL (7392 9180, www.bigchill.net). Liverpool Street tube/rail or Shoreditch High Street rail. **Open** noon-midnight Mon-Thur; noon-1am Fri, Sat; 11am-midnight Sun. **Food served** noon-8pm daily.

This music-oriented venue, which had a minor refurbishment in March 2010, is an essential part of the Truman Brewery complex. Italian squat renegades and Japanese voyeurs join dog-on-string types and pot-bellied ex-longhairs to partake in pints of Heineken, Amstel and Budvar, or bottles of Namibian Windhoek, Iberian Sagres and Scottish Innis & Gunn, while DJs spin several nights a week and all day Sunday. There's plenty of room to stretch out in the main lounge and on the front terrace for smokers. Cocktails come by the glass or the four-measure pitcher: the Big Chill Punch of vodka, champagne, passion fruit and white peach purées, for example. Food includes a £5 lunch menu and house-made burgers.

Notes *Babies and children admitted until 6pm. Entertainment (DJs 7pm Wed & Thur, 8pm Fri & Sat, 2pm Sun). Tables outdoors (7, terrace). Wireless internet. No parking nearby. Easy ramp/slope to left to access main entrance. Once inside there is level access. Some tables and chairs are permanently fixed but there is ample room for wheelchair users to manoeuvre. Accessible toilet. Assistance dogs welcome.*

Chelsea Potter

119 King's Road, SW3 4PL (7352 9479). Sloane Square tube then bus 11, 22. **Open** 11am-11pm Mon-Thur; 11am-midnight Fri, Sat; noon-10.30pm Sun. **Food served** 11am-9pm Mon-Sat; noon-9pm Sun.

Right on the King's Road, this cabin has seen its share of action down the years: the Rolling Stones, it's said, were once regulars. Old light fittings hint at the pub's pedigree, while the music emanating from the CD jukebox is set to 1968. Today, though, you're more likely to be mingling with local ladies, a handful of should-know-better spiky-haired gents and Italian tourists with truculent offspring in tow. The resulting bonhomie takes place in a classic, one-room pub interior and a few tables on Radnor Street, fuelled by

Sharp's Doom Bar, London Pride and assorted bottled beers (Budvar and San Miguel among them). Considering the location, the wines are well priced, although the eight choices by the glass won't get anyone over-excited.

Notes *Babies and children admitted until 9pm. Tables outdoors (5, pavement). On street marked Blue Badge bays in Radnor Walk. Level access in King's Road to heavy single-width door that pushes open. There is a second set of doors. Inside there is level access. Full table service is not available; food is ordered from the service counter but can be brought to the table. Some tables and chairs are permanently fixed but there is ample room for a wheelchair user to manoeuvre. No accessible toilet. Male and female standard toilets are on the lower ground floor. Assistance dogs welcome.*

The Driver

2-4 Wharfdale Road, N1 9RY (7278 8827, www.driverlondon.co.uk). King's Cross tube/rail. **Open** noon-midnight Mon-Fri; 5pm-midnight Sat; noon-6pm Sun.

Since opening in 2009, this Swiss Army Knife of a venue has helped with the gentrification of the formerly sleazy area around the back of King's Cross station.

Within, there's a good gastropub-ish restaurant, a small roof terrace, a members' bar (which resembles the set of *Dragons' Den*), a la-di-da lounge and a dining room that, later on, transforms into a dancefloor.

The wine list is filled with familiar names, as is the range of lagers, but in a poor show for a pub, there's just the one real ale (Landlord). The grub is standard smart pub food: steak and chips, burgers, seared scallops. Nothing too fancy, and all served with frightening briskness. For the best seats, head to the roof.

Notes *Two steps to entrance. Level access inside, with room for wheelchair users to manoeuvre. Seating also available outside on Killick Street. Accessible toilet. Staff receive disability awareness training. Assistance dogs welcome.*

Earl Spencer

260-262 Merton Road, SW18 5JL (8870 9244, www.theearlspencer.co.uk). Southfields tube. **Open** 11am-11pm Mon-Thur; 11am-midnight Fri, Sat; noon-10.30pm Sun. **Food served** 12.30-2.30pm, 7-10pm Mon-Sat; 12.30-3pm, 7-9.30pm Sun.

Although the blue frontage and blue-painted terrace tables are somehow at odds with the humdrum surroundings, this is a very smart joint. Both food and drink are worth a trip. Sought-after ales (Hook Norton's Old Hooky, Sharp's Doom Bar, Theakston's Old Peculier, Fuller's London Pride) and standard lagers line the long, low bar that joins two spacious areas of a large, high-ceilinged interior. Wines and bar food are also superior: a choice of almost 30 wines (with a handful by the glass) can be matched with nibbles such as Normandy oysters and deep-fried whitebait. A photocopied daily menu might list chargrilled sardines or lamb shoulder goulash with steamed rice; children are treated to small portions of old-school favourites. Little wonder punters are beating a path to SW18.

Notes *Babies and children admitted. Function room (100 capacity). Tables outdoors (10 patio). Wireless internet. No parking or designated drop-off point nearby. The main entrance on Merton Road is accessed by a moderate ramp/slope from the pavement up to the entrance. The main single-width door (78cm) is heavy and pulls open to*

Earl Spencer.

another single-width door that also pulls open. Ground floor has level access. Food and drinks ordered from the bar can be brought to the table. No tables or chairs are permanently fixed. Ample room for wheelchair users to manoeuvre. Motorised scooters allowed in public parts, recharging facilities available. There is no accessible toilet. Standard male and female toilets are located at the rear of the restaurant 15m from the main entrance. Assistance dogs welcome.

Fox & Anchor

115 Charterhouse Street, EC1M 6AA (7250 1300, www.foxandanchor.com). Barbican tube or Farringdon tube/rail. **Open** 7am-11pm Mon-Thur; 7am-1am Fri; 8.30am-1am Sat; 8.30am-10pm Sun. **Food served** 7-11am, noon-9.45pm Mon-Fri; 8.30-11am, noon-9.45pm Sat; 8.30-11am, noon-4pm, 6-9pm Sun. Pristine mosaic tiling and etched glass scream 'sensitive refurbishment' from the moment you arrive at this stalwart. Inside,

the dark wood bar is lined with pewter tankards (don't expect to be given one if you want to drink outside); to the back is the Fox's Den, a series of intimate booths used for both drinking and dining.

Local sourcing is a priority and a pleasure here: in addition to the pub's own-label ale, the cask beers might include rarely found offerings from Suffolk's Nethergate brewery or Purity's Mad Goose from Warwickshire.

The bar food is really outstanding, uncomplicated British cuisine rendered in perfect and generous portions; the bar snacks range from pork scratchings, pickled eggs and cockles to generous mains (roasts, pies, burgers, accompanied by excellent chips cooked in goose fat).

Even if you don't stay overnight in the seductively masculine bedrooms upstairs, you can always drop by for one of their huge breakfasts, accompanied by various hair-of-the-dog concoctions. In fact, only the excruciating slogan – 'Hops and chops, cuvées and duvets' – strikes a false note at this Smithfield treasure.

ᛆᛢ ᚫ ᛒ **Notes** *Smithfield car park around 200m away. Step to entrance. Motorised scooters permitted inside. Adapted toilet 14m from entrance. Staff receive disability awareness training. Children welcome. Assistance dogs welcome.*

Lamb and Flag
33 Rose Street, WC2E 9EB (7497 9504). Covent Garden tube.
Open 11am-11pm Mon-Sat; 11am-10.30pm Sun.

Rose Street wasn't always the domain of puzzled tourists sipping pints of Bombardier on the cobbled stones outside this famous boozer. Squeezed between Garrick Street and the old Covent Garden market, this dog-leg alleyway was once the haunt of whores and bare-knuckle fighters, the latter hosted at this low-ceilinged tavern when it was called the Bucket of Blood (the poet Dryden was beaten up here in 1679). Today's regulars are now honoured with a photo and a plaque by the bar; Robert 'Bob' Townley even has his flat cap framed.

Estrella and Peroni make welcome appearances as draught beer options, though most customers seem to stick to bottled Corona or Beck's. Food consists of ploughman's lunches and huge doorstep sandwiches; heartier meals (sausages, roasts) can be taken upstairs or in the often crowded back room.

Two centuries of mounted cuttings and caricatures amplify the sense of character and continuity, although not everyone gets to see them: space is always at a premium, hence the pavement cluster on summer nights.

ᛁᛏ **wc**

Notes *No parking nearby. No adapted toilet, though there is level access to ground floor and room (crowds permitting) for wheelchair users to manoeuvre. No assistance dogs.*

Morgan Arms
43 Morgan Street, E3 5AA (8980 6389, www.geronimo-inns.co.uk/themorgan).
Mile End tube. **Open** noon-11pm Mon-Thur, Sun; noon-midnight Fri, Sat. **Food served** noon-3pm, 7-10pm Mon-Sat; noon-4pm, 6-9pm Sun.

A large corner pub on a quiet residential street, the Morgan has a country kitchen vibe. Its gastropub status is signalled by a large triptych of garlic and fresh produce on the wall of the main bar area and the separate dining area with a chalked-up daily menu. Food doesn't disappoint: diners may find spiced chicken liver and devilled whitebait for starters, and grilled sea bass fillet and the Morgan's classic fish cakes, with wilted spinach, poached eggs and cream sauce, for mains. But, this being a Geronimo Inns venue, drinkers are not forgotten: Sharp's Doom Bar, Adnams and Bitburger are served from a small bar counter, and there'll be about three dozen wine choices on the regularly updated list.

ᛆᛢ ᚫ ᛒ **Notes** *Babies and children welcome. Function room (40 capacity). Tables outdoors (4, pavement; 3, garden). Wireless internet. Drop-off point outside the entrance. Morgan Street is residents' only parking 8.30am-5.30pm Mon-Fri. Pay and display parking, free to Blue Badge holders, on Tredegar Square, 120 metres away. The most accessible entrance is in Morgan Road, accessed via a gate, 119cm wide, which slides open. Gate is locked and must be opened by staff. Moderate ramp/slope between the gate and the pub entrance. Once inside there is level access. No tables are permanently fixed, though some chairs are. Ample room for wheelchair users to manoeuvre. Waitress service evenings and on Sundays. The accessible toilet is 20m from the accessible entrance. Staff receive disability awareness training. Assistance dogs welcome.*

North London Tavern

375 Kilburn High Road,
NW6 7QB (7625 6634,
www.northlondontavern.co.uk).
Kilburn tube. **Open** noon-11.30pm Mon-Wed; noon-midnight Thur; noon-1am Fri, Sat; noon-11pm Sun. **Food served** 6.30-10.30pm Mon; noon-3.30pm, 6.30-10.30pm Tue-Fri; noon-4.30pm, 6.30-10.30pm Sat; noon-9.30pm Sun.

Despite a substantial and sympathetic refit in spring 2010 by the fast-growing Realpubs group, this remains at heart a tiled-exterior local boozer, where the impressive culinary offerings need not dissuade the drinker from strolling in for a quiet pint. In expansive, high-ceilinged, wood-panelled surroundings, pull up a bar stool and sup on such lagers as Sagres, Bitburger and Moretti, or ales including Brains Milkwood and Deuchars IPA, with Vedett, Duvel, Budvar and Chimay (of both colours) brightening the fridge behind. Wines include a dozen choices by the glass, rising to include the likes of a Tremblay Chablis at around £25-£30 a bottle. The superior food menu might include pan-fried Cornish sardines, Lancashire hotpot and poached haddock, with occasional forays into continental variety (seafood, chicken and smoked sausage paella). Music and monthly movie screenings should bring customers from further afield than NW6; they'll find the place 120m closer to Brondesbury rail station than Kilburn tube.

Notes *Babies and children admitted until 6pm. Booking advisable Fri-Sun. Entertainment (jazz 8.30pm Mon, 6.30pm Sun; musicians 8pm Tue, Wed). Function room (80 capacity). Tables outdoors (8, pavement). Wireless internet. No nearby parking. The most accessible entrance is in Cavendish Road, which has one shallow step up to heavy double-width doors that push open to a second heavy single-width door that also pushes open. Once inside there is level access. No tables or chairs are permanently fixed and there is ample room for wheelchair users to manoeuvre. Table service available. Accessible toilet is 30m from accessible entrance at rear of bar. Assistance dogs welcome.*

Prospect of Whitby

57 Wapping Wall, E1W 3SH (7481 1095). Wapping rail. **Open** noon-11pm Mon-Wed; noon-midnight Thur, Fri; 11am-midnight Sat; 11am-10.30pm Sun. **Food served** noon-10pm Mon-Sat; noon-9pm Sun.

Dwarfed by new residential housing on either side, the Prospect proclaims its history from the off. ' Built c.1520', offers the sign at the front; inside, signs on the walls suggest that the pub was a regular haunt of everyone from Captain Kidd to Samuel Pepys, Richard Burton to Princess Margaret. Even the bar is over 200 years old. Behind the Prospect's bowed, boiled-sweet windows is a solid, barrel-studded, black wooden bar that now offers draught Erdinger, Leffe and Staropramen alongside such real ales as Greene King's toothsome Suffolk Swift. Steak and ale pie and Sunday roasts echo the beams-galore tradition of the decor. For those who prefer a good vista with their food and drink, excellent views of the Thames can be had from the raised eating section just to the left of the bar or outside on the terrace.

Notes *Babies and children welcome until 5.30pm. Function rooms (up to 150 capacity). Tables outdoors (6, balcony; 7, garden). No nearby parking. There is a traffic island directly outside that can be used as a drop-off point. Also, the driveway for the flats next door can also be used, if advance notice is given. There is level access to the entrance though the pavement is uneven. The heavy double-width doors* *push open (these are normally kept open) to a second set of heavy pull-open double-width doors. 15 stairs to the first floor function room. Staff are can assist with access if required. Accessible toilet 22m from accessible entrance next to entrance to beer garden, where seating is also available. Table service not normally available, food or drinks usually ordered from the service counter but assisted table service is available. No tables or chairs are permanently fixed and there is ample room for wheelchair users to manoeuvre. Menus available in Braille and large print. Staff receive disability awareness training. Assistance dogs welcome.*

Putney Station

94-98 Upper Richmond Road, SW15 2SP (8780 0242, www.brinkleys.com). East Putney tube. **Open** *noon-midnight Mon-Thur, Sun; noon-1am Fri, Sat.* **Food served** *noon-11pm daily.*

This outpost of the Brinkley's group is a vision of 1980s styling, all big plate-glass windows, venetian blinds and pot plants. It's very much a neighbourhood joint, with a food menu consisting mostly of a populist collection of pizzas, burgers and salads, but it's one with an unusually well constructed wine list, which has a revolutionary pricing policy that does away with conventional restaurant mark-ups and sticks closer to shop-retail prices. No one country or region dominates the 60-bottle list, which takes in a spread of varieties from France, Italy, Spain, Australia, New Zealand, South Africa, South America and beyond. Bottles start around £11 and run to about £40; given the extremely decent prices, it's easy to forgive the limited choice of wine by the glass.

Notes *Babies and children admitted. Tables outdoors (4, pavement; 10, garden). Wireless internet. No parking*

nearby, and no stopping on the Red Route outside between 7am-7pm. The main entrance (on Richmond Road) has one step up to heavy double-width doors that push open to a second set of double-width doors that pull open (usually permanently held open). Inside no tables are permanently fixed but some seats are. There is ample room for wheelchair users to manoeuvre. Full table service is available. Motorised scooters are allowed in public parts of the venue (no facility to recharge). The accessible toilet is 11m from the main entrance located off the dining area. Assistance dogs welcome.

Roebuck

130 Richmond Hill, Richmond, Surrey, TW10 6RN (8948 2329). Richmond tube/rail. **Open** *noon-11pm Mon-Fri; 10.30am-midnight Sat; noon-10.30pm Sun.* **Food served** *noon-3pm, 6-10pm Mon-Fri; noon-10pm Sat, Sun.*

This pub's appeal isn't quite all about location, location, location. But by the same token, the views from here, a hike up Richmond Hill, are beautiful – take your drink outside to one of the benches and you'll be looking out towards rural Petersham and across the Thames, with only the odd passing plane to disturb you. Inside, the Roebuck is a straightforward local, untouched by current trends in pub culture: so-so beers, line-the-stomach food, uncomplicated decor, efficient staff. So far, so so – but it's the views from outside that make it worth the walk.

Notes *Assistance dogs welcome. Babies and children admitted until 9pm. Function room (80 capacity). Games (board games). Tables outdoors (30, terrace). No parking available. The main doors push open away from you. There are two shallow steps to the entrance, which has a heavy single door. Inside there is level access. Food or*

drink ordered from service counter but can be brought to table. No tables are permanently fixed though some chairs are; ample room for wheelchair users to manoeuvre. No accessible toilet. Standard male and female toilets are located at rear of bar area, 25m from accessible entrance.

Spencer Arms

237 Lower Richmond Road, SW15 1HJ (8788 0640, www.thespencerarms.co.uk). Putney Bridge tube or 22, 265, 485 bus. **Open** 11am-midnight Mon-Sat; 11am-11pm Sun. **Lunch** noon-3pm Mon-Sat. **Dinner** 6-10pm Mon-Sat. **Meals served** noon-9pm Sun. **Main courses** £8.95-£17.95.

The Spencer Arms is one of those fine, easy-going neighbourhood pubs that has sprung up around London in recent years. There's a TV in one corner and a broad sweep of bar glittering with bottles and pumps, but this being Putney/Barnes borders (with Putney Heath spread out appealingly beyond a cluster of pavement tables), the signs are to 'the loos' and the flowers in the vases are fresh and dainty. A muted, costume-drama paint job lends a wholesome atmosphere, no doubt helped by the fact that the place is rarely rammed with baying punters. The chefs at work behind their hatch take the cooking well beyond the commonplace. In the past, we've tested their ambition and have never been disappointed with the likes of crab linguine with chilli and garlic, and sardines with salsa verde. But visit on a Sunday and you can tuck into exquisite roasts (Suffolk lamb, Norfolk chicken, Yorkshire pudding plus mounded extras, for about £15), or spot-on burgers for a tenner. There's no attitude to the Spencer – although we'd like it if they put as much thought into their beers as they do their weighty wine list – and they deserve local support.

Notes *Staff receive disability awareness training. One deep step up to the heavy, push open door reveals level access with ample room for wheelchair users to manoeuvre. Key is required for the accessible toilet (not RADAR) ask behind the bar. Babies and children welcome until 9pm: high chairs; nappy-changing facilities. Tables outdoors (11, pavement). Assistance dogs welcome.*

The White Horse

1-3 Parsons Green, SW6 4UL (7736 2115, www.whitehorsesw6.com). Parsons Green tube. **Open** 9.30am-11.30pm Mon-Wed, Sun; 9.30am-midnight Thur-Sat. **Food served** 10am-10.30pm daily.

Only the lack of ceiling fans stop the main bar of this renowned hostelry from feeling like something from the days of the Raj. The Victorian ceilings are airily high, and wide windows with wooden venetian blinds let plenty of light into the bar. Chesterfield-style sofas surround huge tables, ideal for families and groups of friends, though the umbrella-covered outdoor tables are most coveted.

You can expect plenty of turned-up collars and rugby shirts (which once gave this pub the nickname 'The Sloaney Pony'), but the spread of customers is wider than you might imagine. Beer is the great leveller: there are eight ales on offer at the mahogany bar, among them Harveys Sussex Best and Jaipur IPA from the Thornbridge Brewery in Derbyshire, while the glorious list of bottled brews is particularly strong on Belgian and American beers.

Regular beer festivals usually come with a tight focus, with May's London Beer Festival and November's Old Ale Festival well worth marking in the calendar.

Notes *Off-street parking, wheelchair access and disabled toilets. Babies and children welcome.*

Shopping & entertainment

If world-famous shops and theatre don't grab you, how about a film?

Useful contacts

Artsline
(7388 2227, www.artsline.org.uk)
General access information to arts and entertainments. Online database not the clearest or most accurate, though.

DisabledGo
(www.disabledgo.com)
Free, detailed access information about a range of venues across the UK, from shops to hotels, cinema and theatres.

Shape Arts
(0845 521 3457, www.tickets.shapearts.org.uk)

Members pay £10 per year, for which they benefit from the right to request tickets for shows in London and the option to book a free access assistant if they have trouble getting to a venue.

Shopmobility
(www.shopmobilityuk.org)
A nationwide scheme that lends manual and powered wheelchairs, and powered scooters to enable members of the public with limited mobility to visit shops and places of entertainment. Details of individual schemes vary by location or London borough. Consult the website for details and search facility.

Fortnum & Mason. *See p191*.

Society of London Theatres

(7557 6700,
www.officiallondontheatre.co.uk/access).
The best source of access information
for theatres, sensibly organised by
production. Choose the show you want
to see from the comprehensive list
then click through for access
information on the venue, plus details
of any special captioned, audio-
described or signed performances.

SHOPPING

Below is a small selection of London's
thousands of top-class shops and stores.
For a fuller picture, we recommend the
Time Out Guide to London's Best Shops.

Canary Wharf

Canary Wharf, E14 5AB (7477 1477,
www.mycanarywharf.com). Canary
Wharf tube/DLR. **Shops open** 9am-
7pm Mon-Wed; 9am-8pm Thur, Fri;
10am-6pm Sat; noon-6pm Sun.
The three linked shopping malls in
London's growing high-rise City in the
east have a plethora of high-street fashion
stores and chain food retailers, including
Marks & Spencer, Waitrose and the oblig-
atory Starbucks. At weekends, when the
hordes of local office workers are relaxing
at home, it's one of the quietest shopping
experiences in the capital.

Notes *Three hours parking free at*
weekends and bank holidays. All three
malls are accessible to wheelchair users,
with step-free access throughout. Access
at individual retailers may vary.
Designated Blue Badge parking
available, as is a free loan wheelchair
service. This service is subject to an ID
check on collection: valid passport or
driving licence and a recent utility bill in
the same name required. For
information on access and wheelchair
availability, call 7418 2675.

Fortnum & Mason

181 Piccadilly, W1A 1ER (7734 8040,
www.fortnumandmason.co.uk). Green
Park or Piccadilly Circus tube. **Open**
10am-8pm Mon-Sat; noon-6pm Sun.
Revamped and repainted in signature eau
de nil blue and gold in 2007 for its 300th
anniversary, this is one of London's most
inspiring department stores. A sweeping
spiral staircase soars through the four-
storey building, while light floods down
from a central glass dome. The five restaurants, all redesigned by David Collins (of
Wolseley fame), are equally impressive.
The food hall in the basement has a huge
range of fresh produce, and the honey
comes from beehives on the roof. This
shop gives luxury a good name.

Notes *Step-free access to the store*
via the entrance on Piccadilly.
Lift access to all floors, with accessible
toilets located on second and fourth
floors. Step-free access to St James's
Restaurant, staff can guide wheelchair
users to alternative entrances for
Fountain and Patio restaurants.
Assistance available upon request.
Loan wheelchair available by prior
arrangement. Induction loops in most
departments. Assistance dogs welcome.

Foyles

113-119 Charing Cross Road, WC2H
0EB (7437 5660, www.foyles.co.uk).
Tottenham Court Road tube. **Open**
9.30am-9pm Mon-Sat; noon-6pm Sun.
Probably the single most impressive independent bookshop in London, Foyles built
its reputation on the volume and breadth
of its stock: there are 56 specialist subjects
covered here in the flagship store. The
shop's five storeys accommodate several
concessions, too, including one for
Unsworth's antiquarian booksellers and
one for Ray's Jazz. Foyles has branches in
the Royal Festival Hall, St Pancras
International and Westfield. *(cont. p195)*

Major venues

Apollo Victoria Theatre
*17 Wilton Road, SW1V 1LL
(0844 826 8000,
apollovictorialondon.org.uk).
Victoria tube/rail.*

Barbican Centre
*Silk Street, EC2Y 8DS
(7638 8891, www.
barbican.org.uk). Barbican tube
or Moorgate tube/rail.*

Donmar Theatre
*41 Earlham Street, WC2H 9LX
(8544 7424, bit.ly/V5KOy).
Covent Garden or
Leicester Square tube.*

Hammersmith Apollo
*45 Queen Caroline Street,
W6 9QH (8563 3800,
venues.meanfiddler.com).
Hammersmith tube.*

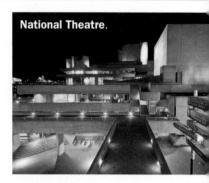

National Theatre.

National Theatre
*South Bank, SE1 9PX
(7452 3000, www.
nationaltheatre.org.uk). Waterloo
tube/rail.*

New London Theatre
*Drury Lane, WC2B 5PW
(7087 7960, bit.ly/d0DoBo).
Covent Garden or Holborn tube.*

Barbican Centre.

Royal Albert Hall.

The O2 Arena
*Greenwich Peninsula, SE10 0BB
(8463 3359, www.theo2.co.uk).
North Greenwich tube.*

Open Air Theatre
*Regent's Park, NW1 4NR
(7486 4966, openairtheatre.org).
Regent's Park tube.*

Piccadilly Theatre
*16 Denman Street, W1D 7DY
(8544 7432, www.
piccadillytheatre.co.uk).
Piccadilly Circus tube.*

Royal Albert Hall
*Kensington Gore, SW7 2AP
(0845 401 5045, bit.ly/9vWAU0).
South Kensington tube or bus 9,
10, 52, 452.*

Royal Opera House
Covent Garden, WC2E 9DD

*(7304 4000, www.roh.org.uk).
Covent Garden tube.*

Shakespeare's Globe
*Bankside, SE1 9DT (7401
9919, www.shakespeares-
globe.org). Southwark tube or
London Bridge tube/rail.*

Southbank Centre
*Belvedere Road, SE1 8XX
(0844 875 0073, www.
southbankcentre.co.uk).
Waterloo tube/rail.*

Royal Opera House.

Notes *The Foyles building is accessible throughout and there is a toilet accessible to wheelchair users. Help available on request. Assistance dogs welcome.*

Hamley's

188-196 Regent Street, W1B 5BT (7479 7317, www.hamleys.com). Oxford Circus tube. **Open** 10am-8pm Mon-Fri; 9am-8pm Sat; noon-6pm Sun.

The world's largest toyshop spreads over seven floors, all of which are accessible by lift or escalator.

Notes *Accessible toilet located on the fifth floor. Assistance is available on request. The shop also offers assistance for customers with hearing or visual impairments.*

Harrods

87-135 Brompton Road, SW1X 7XL (7730 1234, www.harrods.com). Knightsbridge tube. **Open** 10am-8pm Mon-Sat; noon-6pm Sun.

All the glitz and marble can be a bit much, but in the store that boasts of selling everything, it's hard not to leave with at least one thing you'll like. The fashion floors are crammed with designer names, including a Chanel boutique. The legendary food halls and restaurants on the ground floor have added a branch of Venetian coffee bar Caffè Florian and the 5J ham and tapas bar from Spain's oldest Jabugo ham-producing company.

Notes *Blue Badge parking on Lowndes Square, approximately 500 metres away. Valet parking available (minimum charge £10); call ahead to arrange assistance. As Harrods is organised around a series of concessions, limited assistance to the whole store is available. Most of the store has step-free access,* and accessible toilets are dotted throughout the building. Detailed store guides are available at the main entrance. Loan wheelchairs are available. Call ahead to arrange.

HMV

150 Oxford Street, W1D 1DJ (7631 3423, http://hmv.com). Oxford Circus tube. **Open** 9am-8.30pm Mon-Sat; 9am-9pm Thur; 11.30am-6pm Sun.

Times are tough for the UK's largest emporium for DVD, CD and video games, but for the time being, this offers London's largest selection.

Notes *Step-free access throughout with assistance available on request. No accessible toilets.*

John Lewis

300 Oxford Street, W1A 1EX (7629 7711, www.johnlewis.com). Oxford Circus tube. **Open** 9.30am-8pm Mon-Sat; 9.30am-9pm Thur; noon-6pm Sun.

Even in these internet-savvy times, the John Lewis mantra, 'Never knowingly undersold', still holds true. Over seven floors, there's everything from bedding to curtains to stationery, fashion and the latest technology, all competitively priced. Come with proof of a lower price elsewhere and they'll come down to beat it. There's also a branch of Waitrose in the basement. Branches at Brent Cross and Sloane Square (as Peter Jones).

Notes *Assistance available for disabled customers, and free delivery on all UK mainland orders over £30. Wide lift access to all floors. Typetalk available via main number. Accessible toilets located on fourth floor, next to coffee shop, and accessible fitting rooms in all fashion and menswear departments. Loan wheelchairs available, as are large-print and audio store guides. Mobile induction loops.*

Selfridges

400 Oxford Street, W1A 1AB (0800 123 400). Bond Street or Marble Arch tube. **Open** *9.30am-9pm Mon-Sat; noon-6pm Sun.*

Now well into its second century, the giant store founded by Henry Gordon Selfridge has consistently and successfully re-invented itself to make shopping an experience. The best destination for fashion addicts, but a great food hall too.

Notes *Wheelchair access with automatic doors is available on Edward Mews and with manual doors at the Spirit entrance on Duke Street. In-store, there are ramps to ease access around split-level floors. Wheelchair lifts are available between the Foodhall and stationery levels on the ground floor, as well as from wines and spirits to the Wonder Bar. Car parking is available on Level 1 with a lift to all floors. Accessible toilets on third floor. Limited central assistance available. Loan wheelchair available; reserve via main switchboard.*

Westfield London

Ariel Way, W12 7GF (7333 8118, uk.westfield.com). White City or Wood Lane tube, or Shepherd's Bush tube/rail. **Open** *10am-10pm Mon-Wed, Fri; 10am-10pm Thur; 9am-9pm Sat; noon-6pm Sun.*

Occupying 46 acres, its 265 shops and 50 restaurants covering nine different postcodes, this became Europe's biggest inner-city shopping centre when it opened in 2008. If all goes according to plan, the new Westfield Stratford City near the Olympic Park (*see p54*) will take over the mantle of the largest shopping centre in Europe when it opens in late 2011.

Notes *Loan wheelchairs and motorised scooters available by prior arrangement. Call 3371 2402 for details. Blue Badge*

drivers get four hours free parking Mon-Fri, with validation at Shopmobility desk. Shopmobility is signposted from the car park entrance next to the Ariel Way roundabout. Proof of ID required for scooter loan. The mall has level access and lifts, though individual store access may vary.

MARKETS

Camden Market

Camden Lock *Camden Lock Place, off Chalk Farm Road, NW18AF (www.camdenlockmarket.com).* **Open** 10am-6pm daily. **Note** *fewer stalls Mon-Fri.*
Camden Lock Village *east of Chalk Farm Road, NW1 (www.camdenlock.net).* **Open** 10am-8.30pm daily.
Camden Market *Camden High Street, at Buck Street, NW1 (www.camdenmarkets.org).* **Open** 9.30am-5.30pm daily.
Inverness Street Market *Inverness Street, NW1 (www.camdenlock.net).* **Open** 8.30am-5pm daily.
Stables Market *off Chalk Farm Road, opposite Hartland Road, NW1 8AH (7485 551, www.stablesmarket.com).* **Open** 10.30am6pm Mon-Fri (reduced stalls); 10am-6pm Sat, Sun.
All *Camden Town or Chalk Farm tube.*

Camden Market is in fact a collection of smaller markets that proliferate in the north Camden area. The Camden Market is the place for neon sunglasses and be-sloganed T-shirts. Inverness Street Market sells similar garb, and a steadily decreasing amount of fruit and vegetables. North, near the railway bridge, you'll find crafts, clothes, trinkets and curiosities at Camden Lock and Camden Lock Village. North again is the Stables market, best for vintage clothing. Finally, the Horse Hospital market is good for old clothing and vintage furniture.

Selfridges.

Notes *There is one accessible parking place in Arlington Road, (between Jamestown Road and Inverness Street). Blue Badge holders can park on yellow lines as long as they follow the applicable regulations.* **Stables Market:** *Easy access to all retail outlets via any of the four entrances. There is an accessible toilet within Unit 23.* **Camden Lock Market:** *This is fully accessible on all floors. A lift is situated in the north west corner of the Market Hall, accessible from Camden Lock Place, and there is an accessible toilet on the first floor.*

Portobello Road

Portobello Road, Notting Hill, W10 (www.portobelloroad.co.uk). Ladbroke Grove or Notting Hill Gate tube. **Open** General 8am-6.30pm Mon-Wed, Fri, Sat; 8am-1pm Thur. Antiques 4am-4pm Fri, Sat. **No credit cards**.

Best known for antiques and collectables, this is actually several markets rolled into one: antiques start at the Notting Hill end; further up are food stalls; under the Westway and along the walkway to Ladbroke Grove are emerging designer and vintage clothes on Fridays (usually slightly less busy) and Saturdays (invariably manic). The market runs for 2 miles from where Goldborne Road meets Portobello Road, to where Westbourne Grove meets Portobello Road.

Notes *There is on street parking surrounding the market but this can be limited, particularly on Saturday. Three streets have designated Blue Badge bays: two on Lancaster Road where it meets Portobello Road, one on Westbourne Park Road where it meets Portobello Road and one on Oxford Gardens where it meets Portobello Road. There is mostly level access on the paths and roads throughout. There are some easy to moderate slopes located at both ends of the market with level access in between. There are dropped kerbs on the paths where they meet the roads off Portobello Road. The road through the middle of the market can be used to access the market. There are two unisex accessible toilets: one where Tavistock Road meets Portobello Road, the other where Lonsdale Road meets Portobello Road. The toilet doors are automatic and slide open.*

CINEMA, THEATRE & MUSIC

For contact details of major venues not listed below, see p192, or artsline.org.uk.

BFI Southbank

Southbank, SE1 8XT (7928 3535, 7928 3232 tickets, www.bfi.org.uk). Embankment tube or Waterloo tube/rail. **Tickets** £9; £5-£6.25 reductions; £5 Tue. **Screens** 4.

In 2007, the expanded, former National Film Theatre gained a new name, a destination bar-restaurant (from museum-caterers Benugo) and the truly superb Mediatheque. Since then the perennially popular promenade-facing café-bar has also been improved by Benugo, but the BFI's success is still built on its core function: providing thought-provoking seasons that give film-hungry cinephiles the chance to enjoy rare and significant British and foreign films.

Notes *Nearest car park 200m. Cars can access Charlie Chaplin Walk to drop off outside entrance, but not to park. On-street Blue Badge parking available outside the rear of the Royal Festival Hall. There is level access to the entrance on Charlie Chaplin Walk. The main double doors open automatically to a second single width door which also opens automatically. Access to Charlie Chaplin Walk from the* (cont. p203)

Camden Market. *See p196.*

Spectator sports

Chelsea Football Club.

Most of London's major sporting venues offer access and facilities for disabled people, though spaces for wheelchair users may be limited. Induction loops and live commentary can be provided for spectators with visual or hearing difficulties. Assistance dogs are welcome at all venues.

Every venue below is accessible to wheelchair users and offers facilities for hearing and visually impaired spectators. Most also have Blue Badge parking spaces available, though reservation is always necessary.

Arsenal Football Club
Highbury House, 75 Drayton Park, N5 1BU (7619 5003 switchboard; 7619 5000 tours; 7619 5050 disability helpline, www.arsenal. com). Arsenal tube or Finsbury Park tube/rail.

The Oval.

Ascot Racecourse
*Ascot, Berkshire SL5 7JX
(01344 878500,
www.ascot.co.uk). Ascot rail.*

Chelsea Football Club
*Stamford Bridge, Fulham Road,
SW6 1HS (7386 9373,
www.chelseafc.com).
Fulham Broadway tube.*

Lord's Cricket Ground
*Lord's Cricket Ground NW8 8QN
(7616 8500, www.lords.org).
St John's Wood tube.*

The O2 Arena
*The O2, Peninsula Square,
SE10 0DX (8463 3359;
Typetalk 18001 020 8463
3359, www.theo2.co.uk).*

The Oval
*The Oval Cricket Ground SE1 5SS
(7820 5700, www.kiaoval.com).
Oval tube.*

Tottenham Hotspur Football Club
*748 High Road, N17 0AP
(8365 5161, www.
tottenhamhotspur.com). White
Hart Lane rail.*

Wembley Stadium
*Wembley Stadium, HA9
0WS (8795 9000, www.
wembleystadium.com).
Wembley Central or Wembley
Park tube*

Wimbledon Tennis
*All England Lawn Tennis and
Croquet Club, Church Road,
SW19 5AE (8971 2473,
www.wimbledon.com).
Wimbledon tube/rail.*

**The World Rugby Museum
at Twickenham**
*Twickenham Stadium, Rugby
Road, TW1 1DS (8892 8877,
www.rfu.com/museum).
Twickenham rail.*

Wimbledon.

Portobello Road. *See p198.*

(from p198) South Bank and Waterloo is via steps and ramps of varying gradients. The Film Café entrance has level access to pull-open double-width doors. The reception desk is 12m from the main entrance. There is level access. Motorised scooters are allowed in public parts of the venue, (recharging available next to the larger lift on the ground floor). Floors G-1-4 accessed by a standard lift 20m from the main entrance. The controls for the lift are within reach for a wheelchair user. There is a similar lift located on the right of the foyer. The cinema has one screen with two permanently designated spaces for wheelchair users (back row in either corner). The seats in this area can be removed to create up to six further spaces for wheelchair users. The seats next to the designated spaces have movable arms, allowing wheelchair users to transfer into the seat if preferred. The wheelchair is then stored in a room at the rear of he auditorium. Assistance dogs will be looked after by staff. There is an induction loop assistance system. Staff are trained to use the hearing system and are Typetalk aware. Subtitles are available. Level access to the Film Café located at the rear of the ground floor. Food or drinks are ordered from the service counter, but can be brought to the table. There is ample room for wheelchair users to manoeuvre. The accessible toilet is 25m from the main entrance, next to the Film Café, at the rear of the ground floor.

The Comedy Store

1a Oxendon Street, SW1Y 4EE (7930 2949, 8544 7424 box office, www.thecomedystore.co.uk). **Open** 6.30-11pm Mon-Thur; 6.30pm-1am Fri, Sat. **Box office** 9am-10pm Mon-Sat; 10am-8pm Sun. **Admission** varies. 'The greatest and most influential comedy club on the planet,' says *Time Out London*, and we are highly unlikely to disagree. The

400-capacity venue mixes special nights with open-mic try-out sessions and even impromptu sets by such big-name comedians as Chris Rock or Robin Williams. See website for the current schedule and details of pricing for individual shows. Late shows start 11pm on Fridays and Saturdays.

Notes *Blue Badge parking on Whitcomb Street and St Martin's Street, around 100m away. Access to wheelchair users via stairlift only. Wheelchair users should be capable of getting out of their wheelchairs to use lift. No scooters. Accessible toilet facilities, and special seating by prior arrangement. Induction loop installed in the raised section of the auditorium and bar. Assistance dogs welcome.*

Kings Place

90 York Way, King's Cross, N1 9AG (0844 264 0321, www.kingsplace.co.uk). King's Cross tube/rail. **Box office** noon-8pm Mon-Sat; noon-7pm Sun (performance days only). **Tickets** £6.50-£34.50. This is the most exciting of all the new projects currently springing up in the formerly down-at-heel King's Cross area. The building, designed by the architectural firm Dixon Jones, is tidily integrated with the adjacent canal basin. Above the airy lobby, the top seven floors of the building are given over to offices; the *Guardian* newspaper is the most high-profile resident. There's a gallery, a restaurant and a café on the ground floor. But the real appeal lies in the basement, where you'll find one of the city's most exciting music venues.

With just over 400 seats, the main hall is a beauty, dominated by wood carved from a single, 500-year-old Black Forest oak tree and ringed by invisible rubber pads that kill unwanted noise. Whether for amplified jazz or small-scale chamber music, the sound is immaculate. Each week, the selection of concerts takes a different theme:

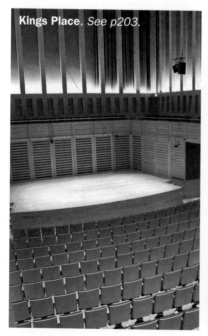

Kings Place. *See p203.*

anything from baroque opera to Norwegian jazz, 21st-century classical music to English folk. Some series are built around the London Sinfonietta and the Orchestra of the Age of Enlightenment, the two resident ensembles. These weekly themes are supplemented by other strands (chamber music on Sundays, experimental music on Mondays) and one-offs, as well as the annual Kings Place Festival in September: 100 events in just four days. It's all part of an ethos that dares to be different.

Notes *300m from King's Cross Station. King's Cross St Pancras underground has step-free access from platform to street. Blue Badge holders can park anywhere on nearby Crinan Street. The entrance on York Way has a slope down to an automatic door giving step-free access to the ground-floor foyer. Kings Place is fully accessible for wheelchair users. There are accessible toilets on each floor. Wheelchair and carer spaces are available in both auditoria. Infrared hearing assistance in Hall One. Hall Two and the Box Office are equipped with induction loops. Assistance dogs welcome. For details contact Box Office or download access guide from website.*

Roundhouse

Chalk Farm Road, NW1 8EH (7424 9991 information, 0844 482 8008 tickets, www.roundhouse.org.uk). Chalk Farm tube. **Box office** In person 11am-6pm Mon-Sat. By phone 9am-7pm Mon-Sat; 9am-4pm Sun.
Tickets £5-£50.
The main auditorium's supporting pillars are a reminder of the building's origins as a railway turntable shed, and mean there are some poor sightlines, but this intriguing venue has been a fine addition to London's music venues since its reopening in 2006. As befits its history as a home of hippie happenings in the 1960s (there is a

Cinema chains

Artsline and DisabledGo (see p188) have full accessibility details for many London cinemas. Further information is on the sites below.
Cineworld *www.cineworld.co.uk*
Empire *www.empirecinemas.co.uk*
Odeon *www.odeon.co.uk*
Picturehouse Cinemas
www.picturehouses.co.uk
Vue *www.myvue.com*

celebrated film of The Doors playing here in 1968) and punk rock gigs for the likes of The Clash a decade later, the bills here favour alternative fare. Expect a mixture of experimental rock gigs, dance performances, theatre and multimedia events.

Notes *There are 22 steps up to the entrance with handrails on both sides. Accessible entrance available in car park at the rear of the building. All areas accessible (except the merchandise centre, down steps near the main entrance). Floor is bumpy and uneven. Some events have no seating, though seating can be arranged in advance by phone. Infrared hearing system in the main auditorium. Induction loop in the box office. Staff receive disability awareness training. Bars are on a temporary basis and may be located anywhere – drinks may be taken back to seats. Patrons with access needs receive a 50 per cent discount, companion free. The accessible toilet is a Portaloo in the car park, near the accessible entrance. For details of assisted performances (audio-described, sign-language interpreted and captioned) call the box office or visit the Society of London Theatres website (see p191). Assistance dogs welcome.*

Sadlers Wells

Rosebery Avenue, EC1R 4TN (0844 412 4300, www.sadlerswells.com). Angel tube. **Box office** In person 9am-8.30pm Mon-Sat. By phone 24hrs daily. **Tickets** £10-£60.

Purpose-built in 1998 on the site of a 17th-century theatre of the same name, this dazzling complex is home to impressive local and international performances. The modest Lilian Baylis Studio offers smaller-scale new works and works-in-progress, and the Peacock Theatre (on Portugal Street in Holborn) operates as a satellite venue.

Notes *No steps through entrance on Rosebery Avenue into foyer through automatic doors. Textured flooring to Box Office with lowered counters and induction loop. Lifts to all levels on the right of the foyer, or 42 steps to First Circle, 63 to Second Circle. Signage raised and repeated at wheelchair accessible height. Voice announcements, Braille signage and monitor in lifts. There are 15 spaces for wheelchair users in rows J–K of Stalls and in Stalls side gallery. Six spaces at First Circle, take the lift from the foyer. Companions can sit beside or nearby, subject to seat availability. Infrared system (avoid back of stalls) with 15 headsets, book in advance, deposit required. Bars at stalls, First Circle and Second Circle levels all have moveable seats and tables and accessible counters. Assistance dogs allowed, staff available to dog-sit. Five accessible toilets: by right-hand entrance to stalls, by lifts to First Circle and Second Circle (Male & Female), at basement (Male) and mezzanine (Female) levels. For details of assisted performances (audio-described, sign-language interpreted and captioned), call the box office or see the Society of London Theatres website (see p191).*

Soho Theatre

21 Dean Street, Soho, W1D 3NE (7478 0100, www.sohotheatre.com). Tottenham Court Road tube. **Box office** In person 10am-6pm Mon-Sat; 10am-7.30pm performance nights. By phone 10am-7pm Mon-Sat. **Tickets** £5-£20.

Its cool blue neon lights and front-of-house café help it blend it into the Soho landscape, but this theatre has made a name for itself since reopening in 2000. It attracts a young, hip crowd and helps to develop would-be writers with a free script-reading service and workshops.

Notes *Slight slope through entrance on Dean Street into foyer through automatic double doors opening outwards. Box office and information desk on left with lowered counters. Lift, with voice announcements and Braille signage, to all levels just beyond box office on left. Seating in the Studio is moveable. Seating is unreserved, but for special-access requirements seats can be reserved. The Lorenz Auditorium has four spaces for wheelchair users in front and back rows of main auditorium. Theatre can accommodate three wheelchairs and one scooter transferee. The Studio has slight slope on level 3 with four spaces for wheelchair users in front row. Infrared system with five headsets in auditorium, book in advance. Induction loop in studio. Audio guides on CD, and Touch Tours available on request. Bar on the ground floor is accessible to wheelchair users. Accessible toilets on ground level past the lift and opposite the main entrance. Further accessible toilets on levels 2 and 3. People with access requirements can buy tickets at concession rate. For details of assisted performances, call box office. Assistance dogs can be taken into the auditorium or left with staff. The theatre can accommodate two dogs per performance.*

Roundhouse. *See p205.*

Rolling down the river

William Forrester heads out on a step-free tour of the South Bank.

ROUTE DETAILS

Start & finish London Eye

Distance 2.5 miles/4km

Time 1.5 hours

Getting there & back Waterloo station (Northern, Bakerloo, Jubilee or Waterloo & City lines or rail) and short walk to/from the London Eye

Notes Unless stated, all venues are accessible to wheelchair users and have an accessible café and toilets. One unavoidable problem is cobbles, making for a rough ride near Southwark Cathedral and the Oxo Tower. Ironically, these cobbles often replace flat paving to give an area 'heritage appeal'.

Start under the **London Eye** (*see p79*), the fully accessible 443-foot (135-metre) high Ferris wheel near where Chicheley Street joins Belvedere Road. The ten-tonne capsules rotate slowly enough for non-disabled people to board while the wheel is in motion, but the wheel is stopped for disabled and elderly passengers. Turn left for the **Sea Life London Aquarium** (*see p84*) in

County Hall, which contains London's biggest collection of fish from all over the world, housed over three floors and in over 2 million litres of water. New for 2011 is the penguin exhibit, featuring eight Gentoo penguins in an artificial icy habitat.

From here, continue through the tunnel under Westminster Bridge for a view of the **Houses of Parliament** (*see p78*), completed in 1870 and designed by the architect Charles Barry. The previous parliament building on the same site was destroyed by fire in 1834. This building was itself constructed on foundations of earlier buildings dating back to the 13th century. The Clock Tower is widely known as Big Ben after the bell it contains. Turn back to continue the walk.

The two pyloned walkways either side of Hungerford Bridge (named after a market that once stood on the north side of the bridge) give great views and are accessible by lift. These bridges opened in 2002, replacing a rusting hulk originally constructed for the Festival of Britain in 1951. Past the bridge and just before the Festival

Pier you can deviate from the riverside. A ramp leads down to the cafés and restaurants beneath the **Royal Festival Hall**. Go in through the automatic double doors near Strada, catch the lift to level 5 for the views and return to level 2 for the high walkway. Turn right along the terrace and you will pass the **Queen Elizabeth Hall** (QEH) and Purcell Room foyers; take the ramp up to the right of QEH and pass the Hayward Gallery, staying on the left. These three buildings form the core of the **Southbank Centre**, much modified since the Royal Festival Hall was constructed for the Festival of Britain. The most recent changes to incorporate the shops, restaurants and open piazza you see today were completed in 2006, alongside a Festival Hall refurbishment that finished one year later.

After passing under Waterloo Bridge, go in through the manual doors of the **National Theatre**, whose lifts will transport you up for more views and down to the riverside again.

If sticking to the riverside, turn back on yourself slightly to arrive under Waterloo Bridge, where there's a second-hand book market and the riverside entrance to the British Film Institute's complex, **BFI Southbank** (*see p198*). (Just beyond, turn right and head straight for 150m if you want to visit the IMAX cinema.) Turn round again, and it's 300m or so past the NT and the Gourmet Pizza Company to the red-brick **Oxo Tower**.

It's hard to believe, but less than 30 years ago, much of this area was threatened with demolition and wholesale commercial redevelopment. The area you see now, from the National Theatre through to the Oxo Tower along the Thames Path was preserved or restored by the Coin Street Community Builders (CSCB), which

Tower Bridge. *See p214.*

The highly accessible South Bank.

City Hall. See p214.

sprang out of a local action group opposed to the redevelopment of the area.

CSCB ploughs the money generated from shop leases, often to upmarket companies such as Harvey Nichols in the Oxo Tower, back in to community projects. This is why development progress is slow, and even now the areas to the rear of some buildings feel oddly derelict. CSCB plans one day to construct a public swimming pool on some of the land that is still available.

There are lifts at the back of the Oxo Tower and a viewing area at level 8. Harvey Nichols' Oxo Tower Restaurant, Bar & Brasserie is next door. Pricey, but with spectacular views. The **gallery@oxo exhibition** space at riverside level is also worth a peep. Until late 2011, building work around Blackfriars station means you can't continue by the riverfront; instead, take a right down Marigold Alley (look for a Sea Containers House sign), then left along Upper Ground. Cross Blackfriars Road, turn right and follow the diversion signs along the east side of Blackfriars Road, left along Southwark Street and left into

Hopton Street. Head through the tunnel just before Bankside Gallery (no wheelchair toilet or café, but there's a Starbucks nearby) until you rejoin the Thames Path, to the rear of the **Founders Arms** pub. A ramp up to the left takes you to the pub's riverside terrace.

Beyond the pub is the enormous chimney of the former Bankside Power Station, now **Tate Modern**. Another building saved from the wrecking ball by local protest after its closure in 1981, it was designed by Sir Giles Gilbert Scott, who also gave London its red telephone boxes. It reopened as Tate Modern in 2000, after a conversion by the Swiss architects Jacques Herzog and Pierre de Meuron. The regularly changing main hall exhibits are specially commissioned to fit the giant turbine hall, and are always worth a look.

There are impressive views from level 7, over the Millennium footbridge to St Paul's Cathedral. Leave Tate Modern and continue. Just before **Shakespeare's Globe**, (see p85) take the ramp down off the riverside to the roadway (called Bankside; it's partially cobbled). In my experience, you cannot see or hear Globe performances well from a wheelchair in the Gentlemen's Rooms. The Yard is cheaper and has more atmosphere, but is 'standing' only. If attending a performance, ask for the wheelchair platform in the Yard. There is also an excellent exhibition and guided tour.

Continue on under Southwark Bridge, central London's quietest bridge, for the **Anchor Tavern**. Nearby is Vinopolis, an exploration of the world's wines (complete with tastings). On under Cannon Street railway arch into Clink Street. Here the Clink Prison Museum and the Golden Hinde replica are completely inaccessible to wheelchair users. Console yourself with views of the remains of the 12th-century Winchester Palace and the **Old Thameside Inn** by the ship instead.

The roadway beyond takes you to the west end of **Southwark Cathedral**, London's first Gothic church, built between 1220 and 1420. Enter through the south-west door and take the south side up into the south transept. Ask staff for the steep ramp into the choir area and for the cunningly concealed ramp into the retro-choir. A stone in the choir commemorates Shakespeare's brother Edmund, who was buried here in 1607. The Bard himself is glorified in a 19th-century stained-glass window. Double back to the lift on the north side of the nave, which takes you to the café, shop and exhibition area.

To continue, return to the roadway and turn right (if the cathedral is closed, follow round its north side into Montague Close). Some 50m beyond London Bridge, turn left (just before St Olaf's House) to rejoin the riverside at Queen's Walk. Beyond London Bridge City Pier, Hay's Galleria opens to the right.

HMS Belfast (*see p76*) is far from easy, but is possible in parts (disabled users get a discount on admission). Access to the ship is via a gangway with a wheelchair lift to lower you on board. Once there, you can

National Theatre. *See p209.*

Shakespeare's Globe Theatre. See p212.

explore much of the living quarters with its exhibitions, and take the lift to the boat deck above. Many of the below-deck areas are inaccessible for wheelchair users, though modifications have been made to provide a limited tour of the ship including the Quarterdeck, the Boat Deck and the Walrus Café.

I recommend ending the walk with a view of **Tower Bridge** *(see p87)* – still stunning, especially at night. Until the bridge opened in 1894, the only way to cross the river at this point on foot was by the now forgotten Tower Subway, a tunnel that ran from Tower Hill on the north side to Tooley Street on the south. Although contemporary reaction to the new bridge was decidedly mixed, by the early 20th century it had become a true London icon. Its bascules weigh 1,000 tonnes each, and are counterbalanced by giant weights in the basement of the towers. It takes five minutes to raise.

Beside you is the rotund **City Hall**, HQ of the Greater London Authority, aka 'The Sliced Egg', which was designed by promi-

nent British architect Norman Foster and opened in 2002. Apart from its shape, the building contains several innovative eco-friendly features, including roof-mounted solar panels and an air-conditioning system that draws ground water to cool the air. After the water has cooled the building, it is used to flush the lavatories.

If you are still keen to proceed, you can go a little further by heading under Tower Bridge Approach into Shad Thames. In a few hundred feet a passageway (Maggie Blake's Cause) takes you back into the Thames Path. Along here is the **Design Museum** *(see p95)*, which opened in 1989 and claims to be the world's first museum devoted to design. The building in which it is housed was once a banana warehouse.

A little further and you arrive at the elegant stainless steel bridge over St Saviour's Dock, the limit of our walk.

To return, head back to Hay's Galleria, pass through it to Tooley Street and turn right. Cross the road and catch the RV1 bus, which stops outside the London

Dungeon. It takes you back to the London Eye. Disabled car drivers should note that this walk can also be performed in reverse; there are two Blue Badge parking bays behind the Design Museum. They cannot be reserved, however.

The author is a prize-winning London Blue Badge Guide. A wheelchair user, he leads tours for individuals and groups around the capital, and can arrange individual packages to suit. He operates a telephone advice service for anyone planning to visit the UK in a wheelchair and can be reached on 01483 575401.

EATING & DRINKING

Anchor Bankside
34 Park Street, SE1 9EF (7407 1577). **Open** *11am-11pm Mon-Sat; noon-10.30pm Sun.* **Food served** *noon-10pm Mon-Sat; noon-9pm Sun.* Real ales, river views and fair food.

Founders Arms
52 Hopton Street,, SE1 9JH (7928 1899, www.foundersarms.co.uk). **Open** *10am-11pm Mon-Thur; 10am-midnight Fri; 9am-midnight Sat; 9am-11.00pm Sun.* **Food served** *10am-10pm Mon-Fri; 9am-10pm Sat, Sun.* Decent pub with better-than-average food and gorgeous views.

Gourmet Pizza Company
Gabriel's Wharf, 56 Upper Ground, SE1 9PP (7928 3188). **Food served** *11am-11:30pm Mon-Thur; 11.30am-midnight Fri, Sat; 11.30am-11pm Sun.* Overly ambitious pizzas, but a sunny terrace with great river views.

Old Thameside Inn
Pickfords Wharf, 1 Clink Street, SE1 9DG (7403 4243, http://bit.ly/nJacx8). **Open** *11am-11pm Mon-Sat; noon-10.30pm Sun.* **Food served** *10am-10pm daily.* Riverside views, real ales and a restaurant.

Oxo Tower Restaurant, Bar & Brasserie
8th floor, Oxo Tower Wharf, Barge House Street, SE1 9PH (7803 3888 www.harveynichols.com). **Food served** *Brasserie noon-3.15pm, 5.30-11pm Mon-Sat; noon-3.45pm, 6-10.15pm Sun.* **Restaurant** *noon-2.30pm,6-11pm Mon-Sat; noon-3pm, 6.30-10pm Sun.* Classy modern European cuisine.

Skylon
Royal Festival Hall, Belvedere Road, SE1 8XX (7654 7800, www.skylon-restaurant.co.uk). **Open** *Bar noon-1am daily.* **Food served** *Restaurant noon-2.30pm, 5.30-10.30pm Mon-Sat, noon-3.30pm, 5.30-10.30pm Sun.* Bar, brasserie and restaurant serving top-notch Modern European food. Inside the RFH, with views.

Southwark Cathedral Refectory
Montague Close, SE1 9DA (7407 5740, http://cathedral.southwark.anglican.org). **Open** *8.30am-6pm Mon-Sat; 8.30am-5pm Sun.* Self-service café (sandwiches, cakes, some hot dishes). Tables in the cobbled courtyard. Accessible toilet.

SIGHTS

Bankside Gallery
48 Hopton Street, SE1 9JH (7928 7521, www.banksidegallery.com). **Open** *11am-6pm daily.* **Admission** *Free.* No accessible toilet.

BFI Southbank
South Bank, SE1 8XT (7928 3232 box office, www.bfi.org.uk). **Open** *Box office 11.30am-8.30pm daily.* **Admission** *£9, £5.25-£6.25 reductions.*

City Hall
The Queen's Walk, SE1 2AA (7983 4000, london.gov.uk/city-hall). **Open** *2nd floor and below incl cafe 8.30am-6pm Mon-Thur; 8.30am-5.30pm Fri.*

Clink Prison Museum
1 Clink Street, SE1 9DG (7403 0900, www.clink.co.uk). **Open** *July-Sept 10am-9pm daily, Oct-June 10am-6pm Mon-Fri; 10am-7.30pm Sat, Sun.* **Admission** *£6; £5.50 reduction.* Not accessible to wheelchair users.

Design Museum
See p95.

Gallery@ Oxo
Oxo Tower Wharf, Bargehouse Street, SE1 9PH (7021 1600, www.coinstreet.org). **Open** *11am-6pm daily.* Small ground-floor gallery with regularly changing exhibitions. No accessible toilet.

Golden Hinde
St Mary Overie Dock, Cathedral Street, SE1 9DE (0870 011 8700, www.goldenhinde.co.uk). **Open** *10am-5.30pm daily.* **Admission** *£6; £4.50 reductions; £20 family; free under-4s.* No accessible toilet.

HMS Belfast
Morgan's Lane, SE1 2JH (7940 6300, http://hmsbelfast.iwm.org.uk). **Open** *Mar-Oct 10am-6pm daily. Nov-Feb 10am-5pm daily.* **Admission** *£12.95; £10.40 reductions; free under-16s (must be accompanied by an adult).*

Hayward Gallery
South Bank Centre, Belvedere Road, SE1 8XX (0844 875 0073, www.hayward.org.uk). **Open** *10am-6pm Mon-Thur, Sat, Sun; 10am-10pm Fri.* **Admission** *varies.*

IMAX Cinema
1 Charlie Chaplin Walk, Cathedral Street, SE1 8XR (7199 6000 www.bfi.org.uk/imax). **Open** *Phone bookings 10.30am-7.30pm daily.* **Tickets** *£8-£14; £5.25-£10.25 reductions.*

London Eye
See p79.

National Theatre
South Bank, SE1 9PX (Box office 7452 3000, www.nationaltheatre.org.uk). **Open** *Box office 9.30am-8pm Mon-Sat. Tickets £10-£44.*

Sea Life London Aquarium
See p84.

Shakespeare's Globe
21 New Globe Walk, SE1 9DT (7902 1500, www.shakespeares-globe.org). **Open** *Exhibition 10am-5pm daily.* **Globe Theatre Tour** *Oct-Apr 10am-5pm daily. May-Sept 9.30am-12.30pm Mon-Sat; 9.30-11.30am Sun.* **Rose Theatre Tour** *May-Sept 1-5pm Mon-Sat; noon-5pm Sun. Tours every 30min.* **Admission** *£10.50; £6.50-£8.50 reductions.* The theatre season runs from late April to early October.

Southbank Centre
South Bank, Belvedere Road, SE1 8XX (7960 4200, southbankcentre.co.uk). **Open** *Box office 10am-8pm daily.*

Southwark Cathedral
Montague Close, SE1 9DA (7367 6700, www.southwark.anglican.org). **Open** *9am-5pm daily (except religious holidays).* **Services** *phone for times.*

Tate Modern
Bankside, SE1 9TG (7887 8888, www.tate.org.uk). **Open** *10am-6pm Mon-Thur, Sun; 10am-10pm Fri, Sat. Tours 11am, noon, 2pm, 3pm daily.* **Admission** *Free; special-exhibition prices vary.*

Vinopolis
1 Bank End, SE1 9BU (7940 8300, www.vinopolis.co.uk). **Open** *noon-10pm Thur-Sat; noon-6pm Sun.* **Admission** *£21-£40.*

Directory

Resources A-Z

How things work in London, and who to contact if they don't.

Addresses

London postcodes are less helpful than they could be for locating addresses. The first element starts with a compass point – N, E, SE, SW, W and NW, plus the smaller EC (East Central) and WC (West Central). However, the number that follows relates not to geography (unless it's a 1, which indicates central) but to alphabetical order. So N2 is way out in the boondocks (East Finchley), while W2 covers the very central Bayswater.

Age restrictions

Buying/drinking alcohol 18.
Driving 17.
Sex 16.
Smoking 18.

Attitude & etiquette

Don't mistake reserve for rudeness: strangers striking up a conversation are likely to be foreign or drunk. The weather is a safe topic for a first conversation. Avoid personal questions or excessive personal contact beyond a handshake.

If you want to rile a Londoner in the Underground, try blocking an escalator in rush hour (stand on the right, walk on the left).

Business

As the financial centre of Europe, London is well equipped to meet the needs of business travellers. The financial action is increasingly centred on Canary Wharf. Advertising and entertainment companies have a strong presence in the West End.

Conventions & conferences

Visit London *7234 5800, www.visitlondon.com.* Enquiries.
Queen Elizabeth II Conference Centre *Broad Sanctuary, Westminster, SW1P 3EE (7222 5000, www.qeiicc.co.uk).* Westminster tube. **Open** *8am-6pm Mon-Fri.* **Conference facilities** *24hrs daily.* Excellent conference facilities.

Couriers & shippers

DHL *0844 248 0999, www.dhl.co.uk.*
FedEx *0845 607 0809, www.fedex.com.*
UPS *0845 787 7877, www.ups.com.*

Office services

British Monomarks *27 Old Gloucester Street, WC1N 3XX (7419 5000, www.britishmonomarks.co.uk). Holborn tube.* **Open** *9am-5.30pm Mon-Fri.*

Children

Education

Advisory Centre for Education (ACE) *0808 800 5793, 7704 9822 exclusion advice line, www.ace-ed.org.uk.* **Open** 10am-5pm Mon-Fri.

Phone the centre for advice about your child's schooling; the phone line is for parents whose children have been excluded from school, have been bullied, or have special educational needs. School admission appeals advice is also available.

British Association for Early Childhood Education *136 Cavell Street, E1 2JA (7539 5400, www.early-education.org.uk).* **Open** Phone enquiries 9am-5pm Mon-Fri.

A charitable organisation that provides information on infant education from birth to eight years.

ISC Information Service London & South-East *7766 7070, www.iscis.uk.net.* **Open** Phone enquiries 9am-5pm Mon-Fri.

The Independent Schools Council Information Service works to help parents find out about independent schools.

Kidsmart *www.kidsmart.org.uk.*

Kidsmart is an internet safety awareness programme run by Childnet International, funded by the DfES and Cable & Wireless. Its printed guide is available to all primary schools.

Parenting UK *Unit 431, Highgate Studios, 53-79 Highgate Road, NW5 1TL (7284 8370, www.parenting uk.org).* **Open** Phone enquiries 9.30am-5pm Mon-Fri.

Information about parenting classes and support for parents. It was set up for people who work with parents, but parents can call as well.

Pre-School Learning Alliance *Fitzpatrick Building, 188 York Way, N7 9AD (7697 2500, www.pre-school.org.uk).* **Open** Phone enquiries 9am-5pm Mon-Fri.

A leading educational charity specialising in the early years. It runs courses and workshops in pre-schools around the country for parents of under 5s.

Fun & games

Gymboree Play & Music *www.gymboree-uk.com.*

A parent-and-child play organisation for children aged 16 months to four-and-a-half years.

National Association of Toy & Leisure Libraries (NATLL) *1A Harmood Street, NW1 8DN (7428 2286 helpline, www.natll.org.uk).* **Open** Helpline 9am-5pm Mon, Tue, Thur.

For information on more than 1,000 toy libraries around the UK.

PGL *Alton Court, Penyard Lane, Ross-on-Wye, Herefordshire HR9 5GL (0844 371 0101, www.pgl.co.uk).*

Sport and activity camps for children aged seven to 16 in the UK and Europe.

TumbleTots *0121 585 7003, www.tumbletots.com.* **Open** Phone enquiries 9am-5.30pm Mon-Fri.

Phone to find out about TumbleTots play centres in your area.

Wickedly Wonderful *Russett Cottage, Itchenor, West Sussex PO20 7DD (07941 231168, www.wickedlywonderful.com).*

A holiday company that runs weekly buses from London down to the beach during the summer holidays.

Health

Asthma UK *0800 121 6244, www.asthma.org.uk.* **Open** Helpline 9am-5pm Mon-Fri.

Advice and help if you or your child has asthma.

Contact-a-Family *0808 808 3555,
www.cafamily.org.uk.* **Open** Helpline
9.30am-5pm Mon-Fri.
Support for parents of children with
disabilities. This organisation is for
those who feel isolated while caring for
their disabled children.

Family & Parenting Institute
*430 Highgate Studios, 53-79 Highgate
Road, NW5 1TL (7424 3460,
www.familyandparenting.org).* **Open**
Phone enquiries 9.30am-5.30pm
Mon-Fri; 24hr answerphone other times.
Resource centre that produces factsheets
covering all aspects of parenting.

Family Natural Health Centre
*106 Lordship Lane, SE22 8HF
(www.fnhc.co.uk, 8693 5515).* **Open**
9.30am-9.30pm Mon-Thur; 9.30am-6pm
Fri, Sat; 11am-5pm Sun.
A wide range of alternative therapies,
from acupuncture to osteopathy, are
practised here. French classes, sing and
sign classes, children's yoga and art
therapy are also offered.

Greatcare *www.greatcare.co.uk.*
A useful resource for those looking for
childcare. Greatcare has over 44,000
registered users, including nannies, au
pairs, babysitters, mothers' helps and
maternity nurses.

NHS Direct Helpline
0845 4647, www.nhsdirect.nhs.uk.
Open Helpline 24hrs daily.
Confidential information and health
advice; an invaluable resource.

WellChild Helpline *0845 458 8171,
www.wellchild.org.uk.*
This national charity offers practical
and emotional support to sick children
and their families.

Help & support

Bestbear *0870 720 1277,
www.bestbear.co.uk.* **Open** 9am-6pm
Mon-Fri; 24hr answerphone other times.
Information about childcare agencies.
now also provides a reference checking
service.

Childcare Link
0800 234 6346, www.childcarelink.gov.uk.
Open Phone enquiries 9am-5pm
Mon-Fri.
Provides a list of childcare organisations
in your area.

ChildLine *0800 1111,
www.childline.org.uk.*
Confidential 24-hour helpline for young
people in the UK. The counsellors are
trained to listen and help with all kinds
of issues, from bullying and abuse to
drugs and STDs.

Daycare Trust *2nd Floor, Novas
Contemporary Urban Centre, 73-81
Southwark Bridge Road, SE1 0NQ
(7940 7510, 0845 872 6251 helpline,
www.daycaretrust.org.uk).* **Open**
10am-1pm, 2-5pm Mon, Tue, Thur, Fri;
2-5pm Wed.
A national charity that works to promote
affordable childcare. If you are a parent
or carer who is paying for childcare, the
www.payingforchildcare.org.uk site
provides easy-to-read introductions to
each of the main types of benefits, grants
and subsidies available to help ease the
financial burden of paying for childcare.

4Children *7512 2112, 7512 2100
information line, www.4children.org.uk.*
Open Phone enquiries 9am-5pm
Mon-Fri.
The national children's charity for
children and young people aged up to
19. It works with government, local
authorities, primary care trusts,
children's service providers, and
children and parents to ensure joined-up
support for all children and young
people in their local community.

Kids *6 Aztec Row, Berners Road, N1
0PW (7359 3635, www.kids.org.uk).*
Open Phone enquiries 9.30am-5.30pm
Mon-Fri.
An organisation that seeks to enhance
the lives of disabled children, through
play, leisure, education, family support,
information, advice and training, with a
view to empowering them in society.

London Au Pair & Nanny Agency
www.londonnanny.co.uk.
Matches up families with child carers.
London Mums
www.londonmums.org.uk.
A group of new mums based in London
who support each other by sharing
views and tips online and organising
activities for mums (and dads) and
babies, such as trips to view exhibitions
at the National Gallery, movies at the
local cinema and nature walks.
Nannytax *PO Box 988, Brighton,*
East Sussex BN1 3NT (0845 226
2203, www.nannytax.co.uk). **Open**
Phone enquiries 9am-5pm Mon-Fri.
For £270 a year, Nannytax registers
your nanny with the Inland Revenue,
organises National Insurance payments
and offers advice.
Night Nannies *7731 6168,*
www.nightnannies.com.
Night Nannies provides a list of
qualified carers who may be able to offer
respite from sleepless nights.
Parent Company *6 Jacob's Well*
Mews, W1U 3DY (0845 094 4220,
www.theparentcompany.co.uk). **Open**
Bookings 9am-3pm Mon-Fri.
The company runs first aid training
courses for parents and carers of babies
and children. The courses are delivered
by paediatric nurses, either in the home
or workplace.
Parentline Plus *0808 800 2222*
helpline, www.parentlineplus.org.uk.
Open *Helpline 24hrs daily.*
Organises nationwide courses on how to
cope with being a parent. For more
details, call the free helpline.
Parents for Inclusion *0800 652*
3145, www.parentsforinclusion.org.
Open Helpline 10am-noon, 1-3pm
Mon, Wed.
Organises workshops for parents of
disabled children as well as providing
training for working teachers who
want to develop more inclusive policies
in their schools.

Parent Support Group
72 Blackheath Road, SE10 8DA
(8469 0205 helpline, www.psg.org.uk).
Open Helpline 10am-8pm Mon-Thur;
24hr answerphone other times.
As well as the helpline, staff run one-to-
one support sessions and offer courses
on parenting skills to the parents and
carers of 'difficult' adolescents.
Post-Adoption Centre *5 Torriano*
Mews, Torriano Avenue, NW5 2RZ
(7284 0555, 7284 5879 advice line,
www.postadoptioncentre.org.uk). **Open**
Advice Line 10am-1pm Mon-Wed, Fri;
10am-1pm, 5.30-7.30pm Thur.
Registered charity providing advice,
support and information for anyone
affected by adoption, including
adoptive/foster parents and their
children, adopted adults, birth relatives
and professionals who work with them.
Simply Childcare
www.simplychildcare.com.
If you're looking to employ a nanny,
check this site.
Sitters *0800 389 0038,*
www.sitters.co.uk. **Open** Phone
enquiries 9am-5pm Mon-Fri.
A babysitting agency with locally
based nurses, teachers and nannies
on its books.

Consumer
Consumer Direct *0845 4040 506,*
www.consumerdirect.gov.uk.
Funded by the government's Office of Fair
Trading. A good place to start for con-
sumer advice on all goods and services.

Councils
Barnet *8359 2000, www.barnet.gov.uk.*
Brent *8937 1200, www.brent.gov.uk.*
Camden *7974 4444,*
www.camden.gov.uk.
Corporation of London
7606 3030, www.cityoflondon.gov.uk.
Ealing *8825 5000, www.ealing.gov.uk.*
Greenwich *8854 8888,*
www.greenwich.gov.uk.

Hackney *8356 3000,*
www.hackney.gov.uk.
Hammersmith & Fulham
8748 3020, www.lbhf.gov.uk.
Haringey *8489 0000,*
www.haringey.gov.uk.
Hounslow *8583 2000,*
www.hounslow.gov.uk.
Islington *7527 2000,*
www.islington.gov.uk.
Kensington & Chelsea
7361 3000, www.rbkc.gov.uk.
Lambeth *7926 1000,*
www.lambeth.gov.uk.
Lewisham 8314 6000,
www.lewisham.gov.uk.
Merton *8274 4901,*
www.merton.gov.uk.
Newham *8430 2000,*
www.newham.gov.uk.
Richmond upon Thames *0845 612*
2660, www.richmond.gov.uk.
Southwark *7525 5000,*
www.southwark.gov.uk.
Tower Hamlets *7364 5020,*
www.towerhamlets.gov.uk.
Waltham Forest *8496 3000,*
www.walthamforest.gov.uk.
Wandsworth *8871 6000,*
www.wandsworth.gov.uk.
Westminster *7641 6000,*
www.westminster.gov.uk.

Customs

Vistors entering the UK from outside the EU must adhere to duty-free import limits:
• 200 cigarettes or 100 cigarillos or 50 cigars or 250g of tobacco.
• 2 litres still table wine plus either 1 litre spirits or strong liqueurs (above 22% abv) or 2 litres fortified wine (under 22% abv), sparkling wine or other liqueurs.
• 60cc/ml perfume.
• 250cc/ml toilet water.
• Other goods to the value of no more than £300.
The import of meat, poultry, fruit, plants, flowers and protected animals is restricted or forbidden; there are no restrictions on the import or export of currency.

People over the age of 17 arriving from an EU country are able to import unlimited goods for their own personal use, if bought tax-paid (therefore not duty-free). For full details on restrictions, see www.hmrc.gov.uk.

Disabled

As a city that evolved long before the needs of disabled people were considered, London is difficult for wheelchair users, though access and facilities are slowly improving. The capital's bus fleet is now low-floor for easier wheelchair access; there are no steps for any of the city's trams; and all DLR stations have either lifts or ramp access. However, steps and escalators to the tube and overland trains mean they are often of only limited use to wheelchair users.

For an alphabetical list of stations with step-free access, *see p256*. Our tube map (*see p254*) gives the location of all stations on the network with public toilet facilities. The **Tube Access Guide** booklet is free; call 0843 222 1234 for more details. For London Overground, call 0845 601 4867.

Most major attractions and hotels offer good accessibility, though provisions for visitors with visual or hearing impairments are patchier. The information in this book should be considered a reliable guide, but it's always a good idea to call ahead and check facilities in advance. **Access in London** is a good companion to this book for disabled travellers, with a new edition due in 2011. It's available for a £10 donation (sterling cheque, cash US dollars or via PayPal to gordon.couch@virgin.net) from Access Project (39 Bradley Gardens, W13 8HE, www.accessproject-phsp.org).

Useful numbers and websites
Access in London
www.accessinlondon.org The website to go with the book (*above*).

Action on Hearing Loss
www.actiononhearingloss.org.uk The
new name for the Royal National
Institute for the Deaf, which offers help
and advice for deaf and hard of hearing
people in the UK.
Artsline *www.artsline.org.uk*.
Information on disabled access to arts
and culture.
Bikes R Us Mobile Service
23 Oakwood Avenue, N14 6QH
(8882 8288). Mobile wheelchair
repair service.
Can Be Done *11 Woodcock Hill,*
Harrow, Middx HA3 0XP (8907 2400,
www.canbedone.co.uk). Kenton tube/rail.
Open 9.30am-5pm Mon-Fri. Disabled-
adapted holidays and tours in London,
around the UK and worldwide.
DIAL UK *www.dialuk.info* National
network run by disabled people, gives
local info and advice.
Direct Enquiries
www.directenquiries.com National Access
Register that lists businesses throughout
the UK, with information about their
accessibility.
Directgov *www.direct.gov.uk* Range of
UK government information, including
travel and holidays for disabled people.
Direct Mobility *8370 7888,*
www.directmobility.co.uk. Long and short
term hire of wheelchairs, scooters and
mobility aids.
Disabled Living Foundation
www.dlf.org.uk Help and advice for
disabled people, and the people who care
for them.
Disability Now
www.disabilitynow.org.uk
Campaigning newspaper for disabled
people with lots of useful information.
DisabledGo *www.disabledgo.com* One
of the key collaborators on this book;
site is packed with access information.
Disabled Motoring UK
www.disabledmotoring.org Known as
Mobilise until 2011, this is the
campaigning group for disabled drivers.

Enabled London
www.enabledlondon.com
Access consultancy with an interesting
selection of maps of step-free routes.
London Wheelchair Rental
0845 094 8455, www.london-
wheelchair-rental.com Hires out
wheelchairs from £45/week, including
delivery to hotels.
Mencap *www.mencap.org.uk* National
learning and disability charity with a
very useful online holiday resource list.
Options Holidays
optionsholidays.co.uk Not-for-profit
organisation that runs escorted holidays
for adults with learning difficulties.
RADAR *12 City Forum, 250 City*
Road, Islington, EC1V 8AF (7250
3222, 7250 4119 textphone,
www.radar.org.uk). Old Street tube/rail.
Open 9am-5pm Mon-Fri.
The Royal Association for Disability
Rights publishes books and the
bimonthly magazine *New Bulletin*
(£35/yr). It also operates the National
Key Scheme, which offers disabled
people access to locked public toilets.
RNIB *3123 9999, www.rnib.org.uk* The
Royal National Institute of Blind People
offers help and advice to people with
visual impairments.
Tourism for All *0845 124 9971,*
www.tourismforall.org.uk. **Open**
Helpline 9am-5pm Mon-Fri.
Information for older people and people
with disabilities in relation to accessible
accommodation and more. One of the
key sources of information for this book.
Wheelchair Travel & Access Mini
Buses *1 Johnston Green, Guildford,*
Surrey GU2 9XS (01483 233640,
www.wheelchair-travel.co.uk). **Open**
9am-5pm Mon-Fri; 9am-noon Sat.
Hires out converted vehicles (driver
optional), plus cars with hand controls
and wheelchair-adapted vehicles.
Youreable *www.youreable.com* Online
discussion forum for disabled people,
run by the Disabled Living Foundation.

Drugs

Illegal drug use remains higher in London than the UK as a whole, though it's becoming less visible. Despite fierce debate, cannabis has been reclassified from Class C to Class B (where it rejoins amphetamines), but possession of a small amount might attract no more than a warning for a first offence. More serious Class B and A drugs (ecstasy, LSD, heroin, cocaine) carry stiffer penalties, with a maximum of seven years in prison for possession.

Electricity

The UK uses the European 220-240V, 50-cycle AC voltage. British plugs use three pins, so travellers with two-pin European appliances should bring an adaptor, as should anyone using US appliances, which run off 110-120V, 60-cycle. Mobile devices such as laptops and phone charges, are usually designed to run at both voltages, but check before plugging in.

Embassies & consulates

American Embassy *24 Grosvenor Square, Mayfair, W1A 2LQ (7499 9000, http://london.usembassy.gov). Bond Street or Marble Arch tube.* **Open** 8.30am-5.30pm Mon-Fri.
Australian High Commission *Australia House, Strand, WC2B 4LA (7379 4334, www.uk.embassy.gov.au). Holborn or Temple tube.* **Open** 9am-5pm Mon-Fri.
Canadian High Commission *38 Grosvenor Street, W1K 4AA (7258 6600, www.canada.org.uk). Bond Street or Oxford Circus tube.* **Open** 8am-4pm Mon-Fri.
Embassy of Ireland *17 Grosvenor Place, Belgravia, SW1X 7HR (7235 2171, 7225 7700 passports & visas, www.embassyofireland.co.uk). Hyde Park Corner tube.* **Open** 9.30am-5pm Mon-Fri.
New Zealand High Commission *New Zealand House, 80 Haymarket, SW1Y 4TQ (7930 8422,*

www.nzembassy.com). Piccadilly Circus tube. **Open** 9am-5pm Mon-Fri.

Emergencies

In the event of a serious accident, fire or other incident, call **999** – free from any phone, including payphones – and ask for an ambulance, the fire service or police. For hospital Accident & Emergency departments, *see p225*; for helplines, *see p226*; for police stations, *see pp231-232*.

Gay & lesbian

Time Out Gay & Lesbian London (£12.99) is the ultimate handbook to the capital. The phonelines below offer help and information; for HIV and AIDS, *see p226*.

London Friend *7837 3337, www.londonfriend.org.uk.* **Open** 7.30-9.30pm Tue, Wed, Fri.
London Lesbian & Gay Switchboard *7837 7324, www.llgs.org.uk.* **Open** 10am-11pm daily.

Health

British citizens or those working in the UK can go to any general practitioner (GP). People ordinarily resident in the UK, including overseas students, are also permitted to register with a National Health Service (NHS) doctor. If you fall outside these categories, you will have to pay to see a GP. Your hotel concierge should be able to recommend one.

A pharmacist may dispense medicines on receipt of a prescription from a GP. NHS prescriptions cost £7.20; under-16s and over-60s are exempt from charges. Contraception is free for all. If you're not eligible to see an NHS doctor, you'll be charged cost price for any medicines prescribed.

Free emergency medical treatment under the NHS is available to the following:
• EU nationals and those of Iceland, Norway and Liechtenstein; all may also be entitled to state-provided treatment for

non-emergency conditions with an EHIC (European Health Insurance Card).

• Nationals of New Zealand, Russia, most former USSR states and the former Yugoslavia.
• Residents (irrespective of nationality) of Anguilla, Australia, Barbados, the British Virgin Islands, the Falkland Islands, Iceland, the Isle of Man, Montserrat, Poland, Romania, St Helena and the Turks & Caicos Islands
• Anyone who has been in the UK for the previous 12 months, or who has come to the UK to take up permanent residence
• Students and trainees whose courses require more than 12 weeks in employment in the first year.
• Refugees and others who have sought refuge in the UK.
• People with HIV/AIDS at a special STD treatment clinic.

There are no NHS charges for services including:
• Treatment in A&E wards.
• Emergency ambulance transport to a hospital.
• Diagnosis and treatment of certain communicable diseases.
• Family planning services.
• Compulsory psychiatric treatment.

Accident & emergency

Below are most of the central London hospitals that have 24-hour Accident & Emergency (A&E) departments.

Charing Cross Hospital *Fulham Palace Road, W6 8RF (8846 1234, www.imperial.nhs.uk). Barons Court or Hammersmith tube.*
Chelsea & Westminster Hospital *369 Fulham Road, SW10 9NH (8746 8000, www.chelwest.nhs.uk). South Kensington tube.*
Royal Free Hospital *Pond Street, NW3 2QG (7794 0500, www.royalfree.nhs.uk). Belsize Park tube or Hampstead Heath rail.*
Royal London Hospital *Whitechapel Road, E1 1BB (7377 7000,*

www.bartsandthelondon.nhs.uk). Whitechapel tube.
St Mary's Hospital *Praed Street, W2 1NY (7886 6666). Paddington tube/rail.*
St Thomas' Hospital *Lambeth Palace Road, SE1 7EH (7188 7188, www.guysandstthomas.nhs.uk). Westminster tube or Waterloo tube/rail.*
University College Hospital *235 Euston Road, NW1 2BU (0845 155 5000, www.uclh.nhs.uk). Euston Square or Warren Street tube.*

Complementary medicine

British Homeopathic Association *0870 444 3950, www.trusthomeopathy.org.* **Open** Enquiries 9am-5pm Mon-Fri.

Contraception & abortion

Family planning advice, contraceptive supplies and fitting, and abortions are free to British citizens on the NHS, and to EU residents and foreign nationals living in Britain. Phone 0845 310 1334 or go online, at www.fpa.org.uk, for details of your local Family Planning Association. The 'morning after' pill (around £25), effective up to 72 hours after intercourse, is available over the counter at pharmacies. Frequent use is discouraged.

British Pregnancy Advisory Service *0845 730 4030, www.bpas.org.* **Open** Helpline 8am-9pm Mon-Fri; 8.30am-6pm Sat; 9.30am-2.30pm Sun. Callers are referred to their nearest clinic for treatment.
Brook Advisory Centre *7284 6040, 0808 802 1234 helpline, www.brook.org.uk.* **Open** Helpline 9am-7pm Mon-Fri. Information on sexual health, contraception and abortion, plus free pregnancy tests for under-25s.
Marie Stopes House Family Planning Clinic/Well Woman Centre *108 Whitfield Street, Fitzrovia, W1T 5BE (0845 300 8090, www.mariestopes.org.uk). Warren Street tube.* **Open** Clinic 8.30am-5pm Mon,

Wed, Fri; 9.30am-6pm Tue, Thur; 9am-4pm Sat. Helpline 24hrs daily.
Contraceptive advice, emergency contraception, pregnancy testing, an abortion service, cervical and health screening or gynaecological services. Fees may apply.

Dentists

Dental care is free for resident students, under-18s and people on benefits. All others must pay. To find an NHS dentist, contact the local Health Authority or a Citizens' Advice Bureau (*see right*).
Dental Emergency Care Service *Guy's Hospital, St Thomas Street, SE1 9RT (7188 0511). London Bridge tube/rail. Open 9am-5pm Mon-Fri.*
Queues start forming at 8am; arrive by 10am if you're to be seen at all.

Hospitals

For a list of hospitals with Accident & Emergency departments, *see p225*; for other hospitals, consult the Yellow Pages directory.

Pharmacies

Also called 'chemists' in the UK. Branches of Boots and larger supermarkets have a pharmacy, and there are independents on the high street. Staff can advise on over-the-counter medicines. Most pharmacies keep shop hours (9am-6pm Mon-Sat).

STDs, HIV & AIDS

NHS Genito-Urinary Clinics (such as the Centre for Sexual Health) are affiliated to major hospitals. They provide free, confidential treatment of STDs and other problems, such as thrush and cystitis, offer counselling about HIV and other STDs, and can conduct blood tests.
The 24-hour Sexual Healthline *0800 567 123, www.playingsafely.co.uk* is free and confidential. See online for your nearest clinic.
Mortimer Market Centre for Sexual Health *Mortimer Market WC1E 6JB (3317 5100). Goodge Street* or *Warren Street tube. Open 9am-6pm Mon, Thur; 9am-7pm Tue; 1-6pm Wed; 8.30am-3pm Fri.*
Terrence Higgins Trust Lighthouse *314-320 Gray's Inn Road, WC1X 8DP (0845 122 1200, www.tht.org.uk). King's Cross tube/rail. Open Helpline 10am-10pm Mon-Fri; noon-6pm Sat, Sun.*
Advice for those with HIV/AIDS, their relatives, partners and friends. Also has free leaflets about AIDS and safer sex.

Helplines

Helplines for sexual health issues are under STDs, HIV & AIDS (*see above*).
Alcoholics Anonymous *0845 769 7555, www.alcoholics-anonymous.org.uk.*
Open 10am-10pm daily.
Citizens' Advice Bureaux *www.citizensadvice.org.uk.*
The council-run CABs offer free legal, financial and personal advice. Check the phone book or see the website for your nearest office.
Missing People *0500 700 700, www.missingpeople.org.uk.*
Open 24hrs daily. Information on anyone reported missing.
NHS Direct *0845 4647, www.nhsdirect.nhs.uk.*
Open 24hrs daily.
A free, first-stop service for medical advice on all subjects.
Rape & Sexual Abuse Support Centre *0808 802 9999, www.rapecrisis.org.uk.* **Open** noon-2.30pm, 7-9.30pm daily. Information and support.
Samaritans *0845 790 9090, www.samaritans.org.uk.* **Open** 24hrs daily. General helpline.
Victim Support *0845 303 0900, www.victimsupport.org.uk.* **Open** 9am-9pm Mon-Fri; 9am-7pm Sat, Sun.
Emotional and practical support to victims of crime.

Identification

You're unlikely to be asked for ID in London when buying alcohol or tobacco, although many shops and some bars check anyone who looks 21 or under. Passports and photographic driving licences are acceptable forms of ID.

Internet

Many hotels now have high-speed internet access, whether via a cable or as wireless. Many cafés have wireless access; see below for four central establishments. You'll also find internet terminals in public libraries (*see right*).

Benugo Bar & Kitchen
BFI Southbank, Belvedere Road, SE1 8XT (7401 9000, www.benugo.com). Waterloo tube/rail. **Open** 11am-11pm Mon-Sat; 11am-10.30pm Sun.
5th View Waterstone's
203-206 Piccadilly, W1J 9HA (7851 2433, www.5thview.co.uk). Piccadilly Circus tube. **Open** 9am-9pm Mon-Sat; noon-5pm Sun.
Hummus Brothers
88 Wardour Street, Soho, W1F 0TH (7734 1311, www.hbros.co.uk). Oxford Circus tube. **Open** noon-10pm Mon-Wed, Sun; noon-11pm Thur-Sat.
Peyton & Byrne
Wellcome Collection, 183 Euston Road, NW1 2BE (7611 2138, www.peytonandbyrne.com). Euston tube/rail. **Open** 10am-6pm Mon-Wed, Fri, Sat; 10am-10pm Thur; 11am-6pm Sun.

Insurance

Insuring personal belongings can be difficult to arrange once you have arrived, so do so before you leave home. Medical insurance is usually included in travel insurance packages. Unless your country has an arrangement with the UK (*see p224*), it's important to ensure you have adequate health cover.

Left luggage

Airports

Gatwick Airport *01293 502014 South Terminal, 01293 569900 North Terminal.*
Heathrow Airport *8745 5301 T1, 8759 3344 T3, 8897 6874, T4, 8759 3344 T5.*
London City Airport *7646 0162.*
Stansted Airport *01279 663213.*

Rail & bus stations

Security concerns mean that most London stations have left-luggage desks rather than lockers. Call 0845 748 4950 for details.

Charing Cross *7930 5444.*
Open 7am-11pm daily.
Euston *7387 8699.*
Open 7am-11pm daily.
King's Cross *7837 4334.*
Open 7am-11pm daily.
Paddington *7313 1514.*
Open 9am-5.30pm Mon-Fri.
Victoria *7963 0957.*
Open 9am-5.30pm Mon-Fri.

Legal help

Those in difficulties can visit a Citizens' Advice Bureau (*see opposite*) or contact the groups below. Try the **Legal Services Commission** (*0845 345 4345, www.legalservices.gov.uk*) for information. If you're arrested, your first call should be to your embassy (*see p224*).
Law Centres Federation *7839 2998, www.lawcentres.org.uk.*
Open 10am-5.30pm Mon-Fri. Free legal help for people who can't afford a lawyer; this office connects you with the nearest law centre.

Libraries

Unless you're a resident, you won't be able to join a lending library. At the British Library, only exhibition areas are open to non-members, but the libraries below can be used for reference by all.

Barbican Library *Barbican Centre,
Silk Street, EC2Y 8DS (7638 0569,
www.cityoflondon.gov.uk/barbicanlibrary).
Barbican tube.* **Open** 9.30am-5.30pm
Mon, Wed; 9.30am-7.30pm Tue, Thur;
9.30am-2pm Fri; 9.30am-4pm Sat.
Holborn Library *32-38 Theobald's
Road, WC1X 8PA (7974 6345).
Chancery Lane tube.* **Open** 10am-7pm
Mon-Fri; 10am-5pm Sat.
Kensington Central Library
*12 Philimore Walk, Kensington,
W8 7RX (7361 3010, www.rbkc.gov.uk/
libraries). High Street Kensington tube.*
Open 9.30am-8pm Mon, Tue, Thur;
9.30am-5pm Wed, Fri, Sat.
Marylebone Library *109-117
Marylebone Road, NW1 5PS (7641
1300, www.westminster.gov.uk/libraries).
Baker Street tube or Marylebone
tube/rail.* **Open** 9.30am-8pm Mon, Tue,
Thur, Fri; 10am-8pm Wed; 9.30am-5pm
Sat; 1.30-5pm Sun.
Victoria Library *160 Buckingham
Palace Road, SW1W 9UD (7641 1300,
www.westminster.gov.uk/libraries).
Victoria tube/rail.* **Open** 9.30am-8pm
Mon; 9.30am-7pm Tue, Thur, Fri; 10am-
7pm Wed; 9.30am-5pm Sat.
Westminster Reference Library
*35 St Martin's Street, Westminster,
WC2H 7HP (7641 1300,
www.westminster.gov.uk/libraries).
Leicester Square tube.* **Open** 10am-8pm
Mon-Fri; 10am-5pm Sat.
Women's Library *25 Old Castle
Street, E1 7NT (7320 2222,
www.thewomenslibrary.ac.uk). Aldgate
tube or Aldgate East tube.* **Open**
Reading room 9.30am-5pm Tue, Wed,
Fri; 9.30am-8pm Thur.

Lost property

Always inform police if you lose anything,
if only to validate insurance claims; *see
p231* for police station locations. Dial 999 in
emergencies; use 101 or 0300 123 1212 for
non-emergencies. Report lost passports
both to police and your embassy (*see p224*).

Airports

For items left on a plane, contact your air-
line. Otherwise, phone the following:

Gatwick Airport *0844 335 1802.*
Heathrow Airport *8745 7727.*
London City Airport *7646 0000.*
Luton Airport *01582 395219.*
Stansted Airport *01279 663293.*

Public transport

If you've lost property in an overground
station or on a train, call 0870 000 5151,
and give the operator the details.
Transport for London Lost
Property Office *200 Baker Street,
NW1 5RZ (7918 2000, www.tfl.gov.uk).
Baker Street tube.* **Open** 8.30am-4pm
Mon-Fri.
Allow three working days from the time
of loss. If you lose something on a bus, call
0843 222 1234 and ask for the numbers of
the depots at either end of the route. For
tube losses, pick up a lost property form
from any station.

Taxis

The Transport for London office (*see
above*) deals with property found in registered black cabs. Allow seven days from
the time of loss. For items lost in a minicab, contact the relevant company.

Media

Magazines

Time Out remains London's only quality
listings magazine, and the most reliable
source of news and reviews. Available in
central London every Tuesday, it gives
full listings for the week from Thursday.
If you want to know what's going on and
whether it's any good, look here.

Nationally, *Loaded*, *FHM* and *Maxim*
are big men's titles, while women often
buy *Glamour* and *Grazia* alongside *Vogue*,
Marie Claire and *Elle*. The appetite for
gossip rags such as *Heat*, *Closer* and *OK*
has abated only slightly.

The Spectator, Prospect, the *Economist* and the *New Statesman* are at the serious, political end of the market, with the satirical *Private Eye* bringing some levity to the subject. The *London Review of Books* ponders life and letters in considerable depth. The laudable *Big Issue* is sold across the capital by registered homeless vendors.

Newspapers

London's main daily paper is the *Evening Standard*, published Monday to Friday. It became a freesheet in 2009, after a major revamp under a new owner failed to bring in enough sales. In the mornings, in tube station dispensers and discarded in the carriages, you'll still find *Metro*, a free *Standard* spin-off that led a deluge of low-quality free dailies.

Quality national dailies include, from right to left of the political spectrum, the *Daily Telegraph* (best for sport), *The Times*, the *Independent* (which launched a cheap daily digest, *i*, in 2010) and the *Guardian* (best for the arts). All go into overdrive on Saturdays and all have bulging Sunday equivalents bar the *Guardian*, which instead has a sister Sunday paper, the *Observer*. The pink *Financial Times* (daily except Sunday) is the best for business.

In the middle market, the leader is the right-wing *Daily Mail* (and *Mail on Sunday*); the *Daily Express* (and *Sunday Express*) competes.

The tabloid leader is the *Sun*, with the *Daily Star* and the *Mirror* its main low-brow contenders. The best-selling Sunday tabloid, the *News of the World*, was closed by the phone hacking scandal of 2011.

Radio

The stations below broadcast on standard wavebands as well as digital (DAB), where they are joined by some interesting new channels (mostly from the BBC). Most stations also transmit online, either via iTunes or www.radioplayer.co.uk.

Absolute *105.8 FM*. Laddish rock.
BBC Radio 1 *98.8 FM*. Youth-oriented pop, indie and dance.
BBC Radio 2 *89.1 FM*. Bland during the day; better after dark.
BBC Radio 3 *91.3 FM*. Classical music dominates, but there's also discussion, world music and arts.
BBC Radio 4 *93.5 FM, 198 LW*. The BBC's main speech station is led by news agenda-setter Today (6-9am Mon-Fri, 7-9am Sat).
BBC Radio 5 Live *693, 909 AM*. Rolling news and sport. Avoid the morning phone-ins.
BBC London *94.9 FM*. Local news and views.
BBC World Service *648 AM*. Some repeats, some new shows, transmitted globally.
Capital FM *95.8 FM*. Pop and chat.
Classic FM *100.9 FM*. Easy-listening classical.
Heart FM *106.2 FM*. Capital for grown-ups.
Kiss *100 FM*. Dance music.
LBC *97.3 FM*. Phone-ins, London news and talk.
Magic *105.4 FM*. Familiar pop.
Smooth *102.2 FM*. Aural wallpaper.
Resonance *104.4 FM*. Arts radio – an inventively oddball mix.
Xfm *104.9 FM*. Alternativish rock.

Television

With a multiplicity of formats, there are plenty of pay-TV options. However, the relatively high quality of free TV keeps subscriptions from attaining US levels.

The five main free-to-air networks are as follows:
BBC1 The Corporation's mass-market station. Relies too much on soaps, game shows and lifestyle TV, but does have quality offerings. As with all BBC stations, there are no commercials.
BBC2 A reasonably intelligent cultural cross-section, but now upstaged by

BBC4 (*see below*).

ITV1 Monotonous weekday mass-appeal shows. ITV2 does much the same on digital.

Channel 4 Extremely successful US imports (the likes of *Ugly Betty* and *ER*), more or less unwatchable home-grown entertainments and the occasional great documentary.

Five From high culture to lowbrow filth. A strange, unholy mix.

Satellite, digital and cable channels include:

BBC3 Often appalling home-grown comedy and sensationalist documentaries aimed at teens.

BBC4 Highbrow stuff, including fine documentaries and dramas.

BBC News Rolling news.

BBC Parliament Live debates.

CBBC, CBeebies Children's programmes, the latter is younger.

Discovery Channel Science and nature documentaries.

E4, **More4**, **Film4** Channel 4's entertainment and movie channels.

Fiver US comedy and drama, plus Australian soaps.

ITV2, **ITV3**, **ITV4** US shows on 2, British reruns on 3 and 4.

Sky News Rolling news.

Sky One Sky's version of ITV.

Sky Sports Live cricket and Premier League football on four channels (and sometimes on a 3D channel, too).

Money

Britain's currency is the pound sterling (£). One pound equals 100 pence (p). Coins are copper (1p, 2p), silver (round: 5p, 10p; seven-sided: 20p, 50p), yellowy-gold (£1) or silver in the centre with a yellowy-gold edge (£2). Paper notes are blue (£5), orange (£10), purple (£20) or red (£50). You can exchange foreign currency at banks, bureaux de change and post offices; there's no commission charge at the last of these. Many large stores also accept euros (€).

Western Union *0800 833833, www.westernunion.co.uk.*
The old standby. Chequepoint (*see below*) also offers this service.

Banks & ATMs

ATMs can be found inside and outside banks, in some shops and in larger stations. Machines in many commercial premises levy a charge for each withdrawal, usually £1.50. If you're visiting from outside the UK, your card should work via one of the debit networks, but check charges in advance. ATMs also allow you to make withdrawals on your credit card if you know your PIN; you'll be charged interest plus, usually, a currency exchange fee. Generally, getting cash with a card is the cheapest form of currency exchange but there are hidden charges, so do your research.

Credit cards, especially Visa and MasterCard, are accepted in most shops (except the smallest corner shops) and restaurants (except caffs). However, American Express and Diners Club tend to be accepted only at more expensive outlets. You will usually have to have PIN number to make a purchase. For more, see www.chipandpin.co.uk.

No commission is charged for cashing sterling travellers' cheques if you go to one of the banks affiliated with the issuing company. You do have to pay to cash travellers' cheques in foreign currencies, and to change cash. You will always need to produce ID to cash travellers' cheques.

Bureaux de change

You'll be charged for cashing travellers' cheques or buying and selling foreign currency at bureaux de change. The commission varies. Major stations have bureaux, and there are many in tourist areas and on major shopping streets. Most open 8am-10pm.

Chequepoint *550 Oxford Street, W1C 1LY (7724 6127,*

*www.chequepoint.com). Marble Arch
tube.* **Open** 24hrs daily. Other locations
throughout the city.
Garden Bureau *30A Jubilee Market
Hall, WC2E 8BE (7240 9921). Covent
Garden tube.* **Open** 9.30am-6pm daily.
Thomas Exchange *13 Maddox
Street, W1S 2QG (7493 1300,
www.thomasexchange.co.uk). Oxford
Circus tube.* **Open** 9am-5.30pm Mon-Fri.

Lost/stolen credit cards

Report lost or stolen credit cards both to
the police and the 24-hour phone lines
listed below. Inform your bank by phone
and in writing.

American Express *01273 696933,
www.americanexpress.com.*
Diners Club *0870 190 0011,
www.dinersclub.co.uk.*
MasterCard *0800 964767,
www.mastercard.com.*
Visa *7795 5777, www.visa.com.*

Tax

With the exception of food, books, news-
papers and a few other items, purchases
in the UK are subject to Value Added Tax
(VAT), aka sales tax, of 20%. VAT is
included in all prices quoted by main-
stream shops, although it may not be
included in hotel rates.

Foreign visitors may be able to claim
back the VAT paid on most goods that are
taken out of the EC (European Community)
as part of a scheme generally called 'Tax
Free Shopping'. To be able to claim a
refund, you must be a non-EC visitor to the
UK, or a UK resident emigrating from, or
resident outside, the EC. When you buy the
goods, the retailer will ask to see your
passport, and will then ask you to fill in a
simple refund form. You need to have one
of these forms to make your claim; till
receipts alone will not do. If you're leaving
the UK direct for outside the EC, you must
show your goods and refund form to UK
customs at the airport/port from which

you're leaving. If you're leaving the EC via
another EC country, you must show your
goods and refund form to customs staff of
that country.

After customs have certified your form,
get your refund by posting the form to the
retailer from which you bought the goods,
posting the form to a commercial refund
company or handing your form at a
refund booth to get immediate payment.
Customs are not responsible for making
the refund: when you buy the goods, ask
the retailer how the refund is paid.

Opening hours

Government offices close on bank (public)
holidays (*see p236*), but big shops often
remain open, with only Christmas Day
sacrosanct. Most attractions remain open
on the other public holidays.

Banks 9am-4.30pm (some close at
3.30pm, some 5.30pm) Mon-Fri; some
also Sat mornings.
Businesses 9am-5pm Mon-Fri.
Post offices 9am-5.30pm Mon-Fri;
9am-noon Sat.
Pubs & bars 11am-11pm Mon-Sat;
noon-10.30pm Sun.
Shops 10am-6pm Mon-Sat, some to
8pm. Many also open on Sun, usually
11am-5pm or noon-6pm.

Police

London's police are used to helping
visitors. If you've been robbed, assaulted
or involved in a crime, go to your nearest
police station. (We've listed a handful in
central London; look under 'Police' in
Directory Enquiries or call 118 118, 118
500 or 118 888 for more.)

If you have a complaint, ensure that you
take the offending officer's identifying
number (it should be displayed on his or
her epaulette). You can then register a
complaint with the **Independent Police
Complaints Commission** (90 High
Holborn, WC1V 6BH, 0845 300 2002,
www.ipcc.gov.uk). In non-emergencies,

call the new 101 service (calls cost 15p from landlines and mobile phones); for emergencies, dial 999, *see p224.*

Belgravia Police Station *202-206 Buckingham Palace Road, SW1W 9SX (0300 123 1212). Victoria tube/rail.*
Camden Police Station *60 Albany Street, NW1 4EE (0300 123 1212). Great Portland Street tube.*
Charing Cross Police Station *Agar Street, WC2N 4JP (0300 123 1212). Charing Cross tube/rail.*
Chelsea Police Station *2 Lucan Place, SW3 3PB (0300 123 1212). South Kensington tube.*
Islington Police Station *2 Tolpuddle Street, N1 0YY (0300 123 1212). Angel tube.*
Kensington Police Station *72 Earl's Court Road, W8 6EQ (0300 123 1212). Earl's Court tube.*
Marylebone Police Station *1-9 Seymour Street, W1H 7BA (0300 123 1212). Marble Arch tube.*
West End Central Police Station *27 Savile Row, W1S 2EX (0300 123 1212). Piccadilly Circus tube.*

Postal services

The UK has a fairly reliable postal service. If you have a query, contact Customer Services on 08457 740740. For business enquiries, call 08457 950950.

Post offices are usually open 9am-5.30pm during the week and 9am-noon on Saturdays, although some post offices shut for lunch and smaller offices may close for one or more afternoons each week. Some central post offices are listed below; for others, call the **Royal Mail** on 0845 722 3344 or check online at www.royalmail.com.

You can buy individual stamps at post offices, and books of four or 12 first- or second-class stamps at newsagents and supermarkets that display the appropriate red sign. A first-class stamp for a regular letter costs 46p; second-class stamps are 36p. It costs from 68p to send a postcard

abroad. For details of other rates, see www.royalmail.com.

See also p218 **Business: Couriers & shippers**.

Post offices

Post offices are usually open 9am-6pm Mon-Fri and 9am-noon Sat, with the exception of Trafalgar Square Post Office (24-28 William IV Street, WC2N 4DL, 0845 722 3344), which opens 8.30am-6.30pm Mon-Fri and 9am-5.30pm Sat. Listed below are the other main central London offices. For general enquiries, call 0845 722 3344 or consult www.postoffice.co.uk.

Albemarle Street *nos.43-44, W1S 4DS. Green Park tube.*
Baker Street *no.111, W1U 6SG. Baker Street tube.*
Great Portland Street *nos.54-56, W1W 7NE. Oxford Circus tube.*
High Holborn *no.181, WC1V 7RL. Holborn tube.*

Poste restante

To receive mail while you're away, have it sent to Trafalgar Square Post Office (*see above*), where it will be kept for a month. Your name and 'Poste Restante' must be marked on the letter. You'll need photo ID in order to collect your mail.

Religion

Times may vary; phone to check.

Anglican & Baptist

Bloomsbury Central Baptist Church *235 Shaftesbury Avenue, Covent Garden, WC2H 8EP (7240 0544, www.bloomsbury.org.uk). Tottenham Court Road tube.* **Services & meetings** 11am, 5.30pm Sun.
St Paul's Cathedral *For details, see p82.* **Services** 7.30am, 8am, 12.30pm, 5pm Mon-Sat; 8am, 10.15am, 11.30am, 3.15pm, 6pm Sun.
Westminster Abbey *For details, see p88.* **Services** 7.30am, 8am, 12.30pm,

5pm Mon-Fri; 8am, 9am, 12.30pm, 3pm Sat; 8am, 10am, 11.15am, 3pm, 5.45pm, 6.30pm Sun.

Buddhist

Buddhapadipa Thai Temple *14 Calonne Road, SW19 5HJ (8946 1357, www.buddhapadipa.org). Wimbledon tube/rail then 93 bus.* **Open** Temple 9-6pm Sat, Sun. Meditation retreat 7-9pm Tue, Thur; 4-6pm Sat, Sun. London Buddhist Centre *51 Roman Road, Bethnal Green, E2 0HU (0845 458 4716, www.lbc.org.uk). Bethnal Green tube.* **Open** 10am-5pm Mon-Fri.

Catholic

Brompton Oratory *Thurlow Place, Brompton Road, SW7 2RP (7808 0900, www.bromptonoratory.com).* **Services** 7am, 8am (Latin mass), 10am, 12.30am, 6pm Mon-Fri; 7am, 8am, 10am, 6pm Sat; 7am, 8am, 9am (tridentine), 10am, 11am (sung Latin), 12.30pm, 4.30pm, 7pm Sun. Westminster Cathedral *For more information, see p90.* **Services** 7am, 8am, 10.30am, 12.30pm, 1.05pm, 5.30pm Mon-Fri; 8am, 9am, 10.30am, 12.30pm, 6pm Sat; 8am, 9am, 10.30am, noon, 5.30pm, 7pm Sun.

Islamic

East London Mosque *82-92 Whitechapel Road, E1 1JQ (7650 3000, www.eastlondonmosque.org.uk). Aldgate East tube.* **Services** Friday prayer 1.30pm (1.15pm in winter). Islamic Cultural Centre & London Central Mosque *146 Park Road, NW8 7RG (7725 2213, www.iccuk.org). Baker Street tube or bus 13, 113, 274.* **Services** times vary; check website for details.

Jewish

Liberal Jewish Synagogue *28 St John's Wood Road, NW8 7HA (7286 5181, www.ljs.org). St John's Wood tube.* **Services** 6.45pm Fri; 11am Sat.

West Central Liberal Synagogue *21 Maple Street, W1T 4BE (7636 7627, www.wcls.org.uk). Warren Street tube.* **Services** 3pm Sat.

Methodist & Quaker

Methodist Central Hall Central Hall *Storey's Gate, SW1H 9NH (7222 8010, www.c-h-w.co.uk). St James's Park tube.* **Services** 12.45pm Wed; 11am, 6.30pm Sun. Religious Society of Friends (Quakers) *173-177 Euston Road, NW1 2BJ (7663 1000, www.quaker.org.uk). Euston tube/rail.* **Meetings** 7pm Mon; 6.30pm Thur; 11am Sun.

Safety & security

There are no real 'no-go' areas in London; despite the civil strife of 2011, you're more likely to get hurt in a car accident than as a result of criminal activity, but thieves haunt busy shopping areas and transport nodes, as they do in all cities.

Use common sense and follow some basic rules. Keep wallets and purses out of sight, and handbags securely closed. Never leave bags or coats unattended, beside, under or on the back of a chair – even if they aren't stolen, they're likely to trigger a bomb alert. Don't put bags on the floor near the door of a public toilet. Don't take short cuts through dark alleys and car parks. Keep your passport, cash and credit cards in separate places. Don't carry a wallet in your back pocket. And always be aware of your surroundings.

Smoking

Since July 2007 smoking has been banned in all enclosed public spaces, including pubs, bars, clubs, restaurants, hotel foyers and shops, as well as on public transport. Smokers now face a penalty fee of £50 or a maximum fee of £200 if they are prosecuted for smoking in a smoke-free area. Many bars and clubs offer smoking gardens or terraces.

Telephones

Dialling & codes

London's dialling code is 020; standard landlines have eight digits after that. You don't need to dial the 020 from within the area, so we have not given it in this book.

If you're calling from outside the UK, dial your international access code, then the UK code, 44, then the full London number, omitting the first 0 from the code. For example, to make a call to 020 7813 3000 from the US, dial 011 44 20 7813 3000. To dial abroad from the UK, first dial 00, then the relevant country code from the list below. For more international dialling codes, check the phone book or see www.kropla.com/dialcode.htm.

Australia 61
Canada 1
New Zealand 64
Republic of Ireland 353
South Africa 27
USA 1

Mobile phones

Mobile phones in the UK operate on the 900 MHz and 1800 MHz GSM frequencies common throughout most of Europe. If you're travelling to the UK from Europe, your phone should be compatible; if you're travelling from the US, you'll need a tri-band handset. Either way, check your phone is set for international roaming, and that your service provider at home has a reciprocal arrangement with a UK provider.

The simplest option may be to buy a 'pay-as-you-go' phone (about £50-£200); there's no monthly fee, you top up talk time using a card. Check before buying whether it can make and receive international calls. Phones4u (www.phones4u.co.uk) and the oddly named outlet Carphone Warehouse (www.carphonewarehouse.com), which both have stores throughout the city, offer options. For phone rental, *see also p260.*

Operator services

Call 100 for the operator: if you have difficulty in dialling; for an alarm call; to make a credit card call; for information about the cost of a call; and for help with international person-to-person calls. Dial 155 for the international operator if you need to reverse the charges (call collect) or if you can't dial direct. Warning: this service can be very expensive.

Directory enquiries

This service is now provided by various six-digit 118 numbers. They're pretty pricey to call: dial (free) 0800 953 0720 for a rundown of options and prices. The best known is 118 118, which charges 49p per call, then 14p per minute thereafter; 118 888 charges 49p per call, then 9p per minute; 118 180 charges 25p per call, then 30p per minute. Online, the www. ukphonebook.com offers five free credits a day to UK residents; overseas users get the same credits if they keep a positive balance in their account.

Yellow Pages *www.yell.com* This 24-hour service lists the phone numbers of thousands of businesses in the UK. Dial 118 247 (81p connection charge plus 30p/min) and identify the type of business you require, and in which area of London.

Public phones

Public payphones take coins or credit cards (sometimes both). The minimum cost is 60p (including a 40p connection charge), which buys a 110-second local call. Some payphones, such as the countertop ones found in pubs, require more. International calling cards, offering bargain minutes via a freephone number, are widely available.

Telephone directories

There are several telephone directories for London, divided by area, which contain private and commercial numbers. Available at post offices and libraries, these hefty tomes are also issued free to all residents, as is the invaluable Yellow Pages directory (also online at www.yell.com), which lists businesses and services.

Time

London operates on Greenwich Mean Time (GMT), five hours ahead of the US's Eastern Standard time. In spring (25 March 2012) the UK puts its clocks forward by one hour to British Summer Time. In autumn (28 October 2012), the clocks go back to GMT.

Tipping

In Britain it's accepted that you tip in taxis, minicabs, restaurants (some waiting staff rely on tips), hotels, hairdressers and some bars (not pubs). Around 10% is normal, but some restaurants add as much as 15%. Always check whether service has been included in your bill: some restaurants include an automatic service charge, but also sneakily leave space for a gratuity on your credit card slip.

Toilets

Pubs and restaurants generally reserve the use of their toilets for customers. However, all mainline rail stations and a few tube stations – Piccadilly Circus, for one – have public toilets (you may be charged a small fee). Department stores usually have loos that you can use free of charge, and museums (most of which no longer charge an entry fee) generally have good facilities. At night, options are worse. The coin-operated toilet booths around the city may be your only option.

An online list of public toilets is maintained by pub site **Last Rounds**, at bit.ly/psP83W. A location-based list of public toilets across London, complete with accessibility information, can also be found at www.toiletmap.co.uk (*see p71*). In Westminster, text the word TOILET to 80097 to receive details of the nearest public toilet. The service is called SatLav.

Tourist information

Britain & London Visitor Centre
1 Regent Street, Piccadilly Circus, SW1Y 4XT (7808 3800, www.visitbritain.com). Piccadilly Circus tube. **Open** 9.30am-6.30pm Mon; 9am-6.30pm Tue-Fri; 9am-5pm Sat; 10am-4pm Sun.
City of London Information Centre
St Paul's Churchyard, EC4M 8BX (7332 1456, www.visitlondon.com). St Paul's tube. **Open** 9.30am-5.30pm Mon-Sat; 10am-4pm Sun.
Greenwich Tourist Information Centre *Pepys House, 2 Cutty Sark Gardens, SE10 9LW (0870 608 2000, www.greenwichwhs.org.uk). Cutty Sark DLR.* **Open** 10am-5pm daily.
London Information Centre
Leicester Square, WC2H 7BP (7292 2333, www.londontown.com). Leicester Square tube. **Open** 10am-6pm daily. Helpline 8am-10pm Mon-Fri; 9am-8pm Sat, Sun.
Richmond Tourist Information Centre *Old Town Hall, Whittaker Avenue, TW9 1TP (8734 3363, www.visitrichmond.co.uk). Richmond tube/rail.* **Open** 10am-5pm Mon-Sat.

Visas & immigration

EU citizens do not require a visa to visit the United Kingdom; citizens of the USA, Canada, Australia, South Africa and New Zealand can also enter with only a passport for tourist visits of up to six months as long as they can show they can support themselves during their visit and plan to return. Go online to www.ukvisas.gov.uk to check your visa status well before you travel, or contact the British embassy, consulate or high commission in your own country. You can arrange visas online at www.fco.gov.uk.

Home Office Immigration & Nationality Bureau *Lunar House, 40 Wellesley Road, CR9 1AT (0870 606 7766 enquiries, 0870 241 0645 applications, www.homeoffice.gov.uk).*

Weights & measures

It has taken a considerable amount of time, and some heavy-handed intervention from Europe, but the UK is moving towards full metrication. Distances are still measured in miles, but all goods are officially sold in metric quantities, with no legal requirement for the imperial equivalent to be given. We've used the still more common imperial measurements in this guide.

Below are some useful conversions, first into the metric equivalents from the imperial measurements, then from the metric units back to imperial:

1 inch (in) = 2.54 centimetres (cm)
1 yard (yd) = 0.91 metres (m)
1 mile = 1.6 kilometres (km)
1 ounce (oz) = 28.35 grams (g)
1 pound (lb) = 0.45 kilograms (kg)
1 UK pint = 0.57 litres (l)
1 US pint = 0.8 UK pints or 0.46 litres

1 centimetre (cm) = 0.39 inches (in)
1 metre (m) = 1.094 yards (yd)
1 kilometre (km) = 0.62 miles
1 gram (g) = 0.035 ounces (oz)
1 kilogram (kg) = 2.2 pounds (lb)
1 litre (l) = 1.76 UK pints or 2.2 US pints

When to go
Climate

The British climate is famously unpredictable, but Weathercall on 0906 857 5751 (60p/min) can offer some guidance. The best websites for weather news and features include www.metoffice.gov.uk, www.weather.com and www.bbc.co.uk/london/weather, which all offer good detailed long-term forecasts and are easily searchable.

Spring extends from March to May, though frosts can last into April. March winds and April showers may be a month early or late, but May is often very pleasant.

Summer (June, July and August) can be very unpredictable, with searing heat one day followed by sultry greyness and violent thunderstorms the next. There are usually pleasant sunny days, though they vary greatly in number from year to year. High temperatures, humidity and pollution can create problems for those with hay fever or breathing difficulties, and temperatures in the tube can be uncomfortably hot. Do as the locals do, and carry a bottle of water.

Autumn starts in September, when the weather can still have a summery feel. Real autumn comes with October, when the leaves start to fall; on sunny days, the red and gold leaves can be breathtaking. When the November cold, grey and wet set in, though, you'll be reminded that London is situated on a northerly latitude.

Winter can have some delightful crisp, cold days, but don't bank on them. The usual scenario is for a disappointingly grey, wet Christmas, followed by a cold snap in January and February, when London may even see a sprinkling of snow, and public transport chaos.

Public holidays

On public holidays (bank holidays), many shops remain open, but public transport services generally run to a Sunday timetable. On Christmas Day, almost everything, including public transport, closes down. All dates below are for 2012.

Good Friday Fri 6 Apr
Easter Monday Mon 9 Apr
May Day Holiday Mon 7 May
Spring and Diamond Jubilee Bank Holidays Mon-Tue 4-5 June
Summer Bank Holiday Mon 27 Aug
Christmas Day Tue 25 Dec
Boxing Day Wed 26 Dec
New Year's Day Tue 1 Jan 2013

Women

London is home to dozens of women's groups and networks; www.gn.apc.org and www.wrc.org.uk provide information and many links. It also has Europe's largest women's studies archive, the Women's Library (see p228).

Index

Index

Maps

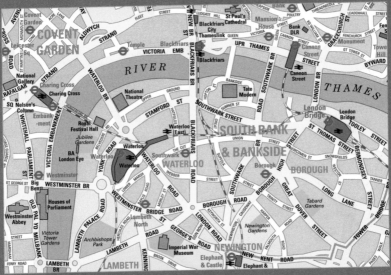

London Overview

© Copyright Time Out Group 2011

Central London
by Area

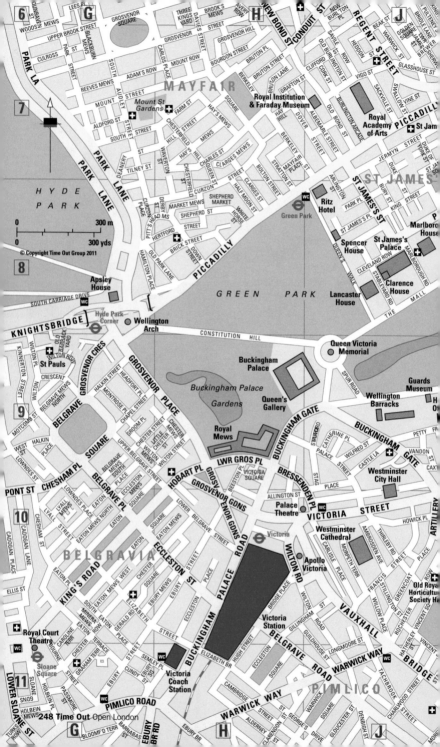

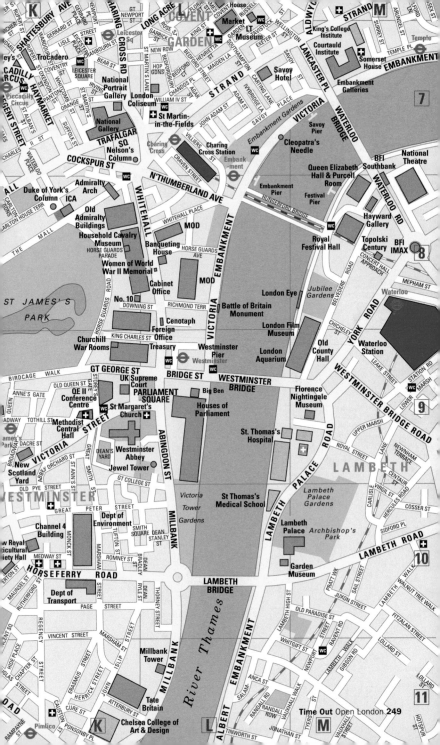

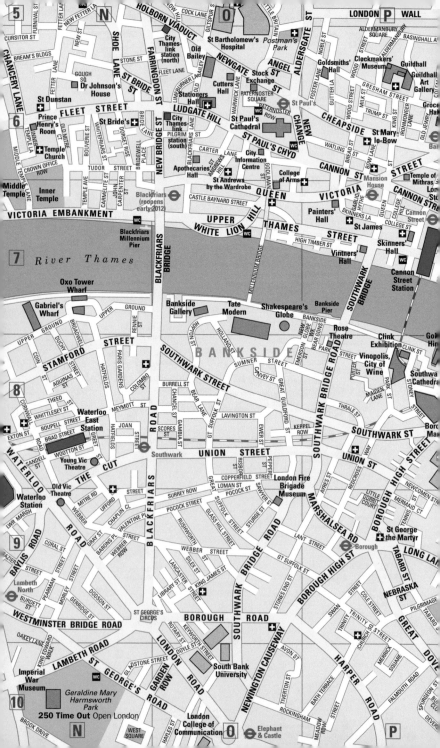

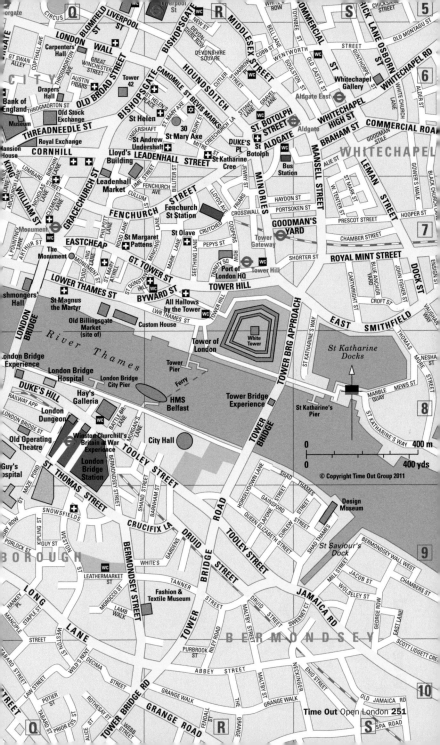

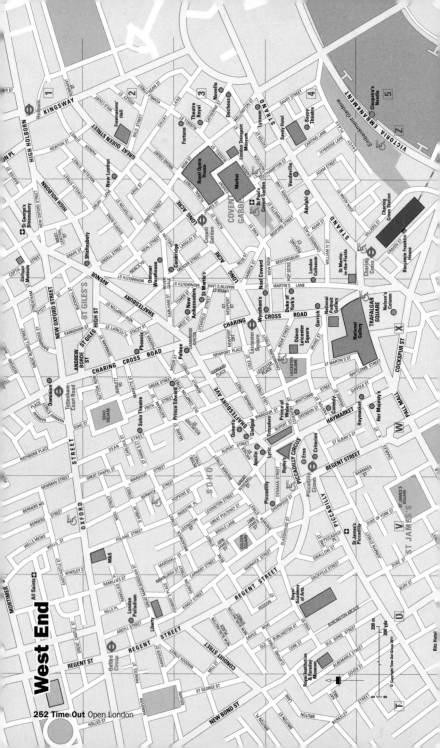

West End

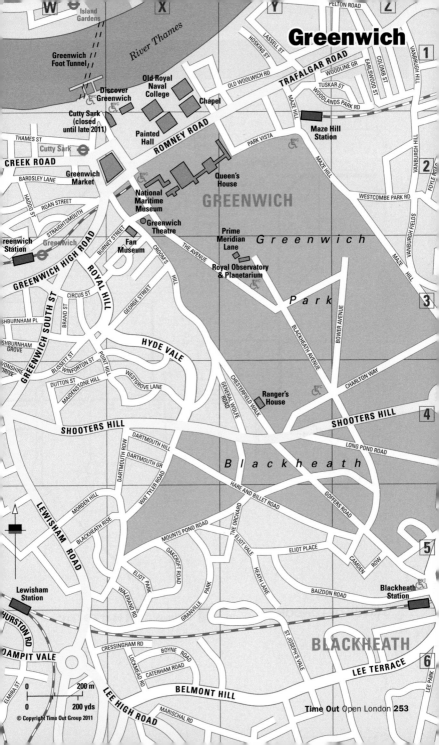

Greenwich

© Copyright Time Out Group 2011

Tube map

Website

tfl.gov.uk

24 hour travel information
0843 222 1234*

*You pay no more than
from a BT landline. The
Charges from mobiles

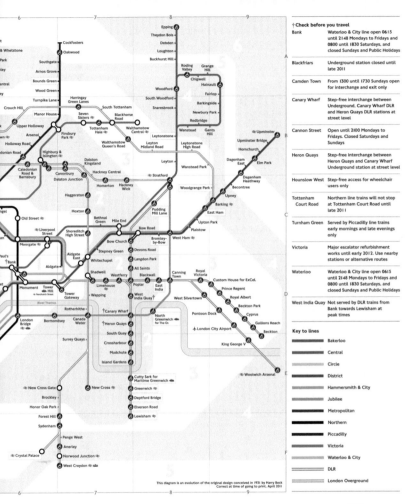

Travel information at stations
Help points

minute if calling
be a connection charge.
landline providers may vary.

Transport for London

UNDERGROUND

Index to stations

Explanation of symbols

P	Stations with car parks
☺	Stations with bicycle parking
✦✦	Male/female/baby changing/accessible toilets outside ticket gateline
✦✦&	Male/female/baby changing/accessible toilets inside ticket gateline
†	Toilet not managed by London Underground. You may be charged for these facilities. Ask staff for information
&	Stop-free access between platform and the street
☺	Stations with London Travel Information Centre
+	Check before you travel. See key overleaf